SPEED
SAFETY
AND COMFORT

SPEED
SAFETY
AND COMFORT

THE ORIGINS
OF
DELTA
AIR LINES

JAMES JOHN HOOGERWERF

LOUISIANA STATE UNIVERSITY PRESS BATON ROUGE

Published by Louisiana State University Press
lsupress.org

Manufactured in the United States of America
First printing

DESIGNER: Michelle A. Neustrom
TYPEFACE: Calluna
PRINTER AND BINDER: Sheridan Books, Inc.

COVER PHOTOGRAPH: Delta Air Service personnel with Travel Air 6000.
Morning Monroe Post, October 1929. Photograph courtesy of
Delta Airlines Corporate Archives.

LIBRARY OF CONGRESS CATALOGING-IN-PUBLICATION DATA

Names: Hoogerwerf, James John, author.
Title: Speed, safety, and comfort : the origins of Delta Air Lines / James John Hoogerwerf.
Description: Baton Rouge : Louisiana State University Press, [2023] |
 Includes bibliographical references and index.
Identifiers: LCCN 2023015981 (print) | LCCN 2023015982 (ebook) | ISBN 978-0-8071-8007-5
 (cloth) | ISBN 978-0-8071-8124-9 (pdf) | ISBN 978-0-8071-8123-2 (epub)
Subjects: LCSH: Delta Air Lines—History. | Airlines—United States—History. | Aerial
 spraying and dusting in agriculture—Southern States.
Classification: LCC HE9803.D44 H66 2024 (print) | LCC HE9803.D44 (ebook) |
 DDC 387.706/573—dc23/eng/20230705
LC record available at https://lccn.loc.gov/2023015981
LC ebook record available at https://lccn.loc.gov/2023015982

═ **CONTENTS** ═

Photographs follow page 64.

≡ ACKNOWLEDGMENTS ≡

This project would have been impossible without the help, support, and encouragement of the many people I encountered during my years of study. Regretfully, there is little I can do to adequately express my appreciation to each individually. Rest assured, though, I am most grateful for your interest and willingness to share insights, stories, documents, photographs, names, places, reviews, and suggestions. Because of you, this study is more consequential than otherwise would have been possible.

I credit my motivation and dedication to my father and mother. Dad was born in the Netherlands and became a naturalized citizen (hence the Dutch name). He was an executive for Ford Motor Company, and as a child, I remember a picture of young Henry Ford tinkering with a watch hanging on the wall of our home. Many years later I saw a parallel between the humble beginnings of Ford Motor Company and Delta Air Lines. It is fitting, therefore, to first of all thank my parents for a warm and supportive home—and for my curiosity.

It was my good fortune to be selected for flight training in the U.S. Air Force and live the life of a Delta Air Lines pilot. One cloudless day, as a junior second officer aboard a Douglas DC-8 jetliner cruising comfortably over the Mississippi River delta region, my senior captain commented, "There's Monroe, where Delta got its start." I thought, how did that happen? Little did I know that answering this question would lead to my early retirement from flying, earning a PhD at Auburn University, and writing this book. During layovers and in private travel, I met with people and visited libraries and archives across the country and in South America. In Atlanta I accessed the Delta Air Lines Corporate Archives and spent many hours under the guidance of archivist Marie Force. Her dedication to Delta's heritage is evidenced throughout these pages. I am very grateful for her help and insight.

My quest began in earnest at the doorstep to Delta's world headquarters, a complex of simulators and offices situated on the grounds of the old Candler Field, Atlanta's original airport. The old railroad depot in Hapeville, Georgia, housed the Hapeville Historical Society, where I met with a retiree group to discuss the early years of aviation in Atlanta. I am indebted to Ed Milton, who wrote a history of Hapeville; Dick Bennett, who was connected with Pitcairn Aviation; Bishop Simpson, who began his aviation career with Blevin's Aircraft Corporation; and Capt. T. P. "Pre" Ball, the retired director of operations of Delta Air Lines. Their perspectives piqued my interest and motivated me on a course of discovery spanning twenty-eight years. My brother Jerry has shared my literary journey, as well as a life in aviation, and many adventures.

I am indebted to the head of the Special Collections and Archives at Wright State University, Dawne Dewey, and the staff there for their help in accessing the Harold R. Harris Papers, which were so critical to this study. My good friends Herbert H. Moll and Javier Watanabe in Lima, Peru, enthusiastically offered their insights on Peruvian aviation. Moll shared his research on the history of Peruvian airmail, while Watanabe took me on a drive to the old Limatambo airport—the runways are now long, wide boulevards, and the terminal is an office building.

When I retired, I was privileged to be admitted as a PhD candidate in the History of Technology program at Auburn University. David Burke and I began our studies together. He has been a supportive classmate and one of my best friends ever since. We were protégés of Dr. W. David Lewis, our major professor. Lewis approved my plan of study, focusing on Delta's early years. At Auburn, I valued the collegial interaction, encouragement, friendship, and support of Donna Bohannan, Larry Gerber, Marie Francois, Jim Hansen, Tiffany Sippial, David Lucsko, Chris Haveman, Gary Frost, Alan Meyer, and other faculty and students. Following the untimely passing of Lewis, Dr. William F. Trimble assumed the role of my major professor. A large measure of my academic accomplishment is attributable to Professors Lewis and Trimble, and I am grateful for their tutelage, advice, and friendship.

I thank my wife, Arlene, and my family for supporting the frequent absences that characterize the lifestyle of an airline pilot's family. Every month my schedule changed. I could be anywhere—on the other side of the continent or across an ocean. This was not good on occasion, for example, when the sink leaked or the car did not start for carpool duty. Graduate school offered some improvement, but with its own drawbacks. Although "present" at home, my head could be stuck in a book or my mind deep in thought. On the positive side, we vacationed frequently as a family to interesting places (sometimes with me as the pilot). I hope this compensated somewhat for missing children's activities. Arlene, Brian, and Karen, this book is in a large part made possible by your devotion and support. Thank you and love forever.

Through the years, progress on the manuscript came by fits and starts. Life's demands inconveniently interfered just when there were new insights, questions, or facts to explore. Occasionally, a well-intentioned questioner asked when it would be finished. Through the highs and lows, I never had an answer until recently. That is thanks to the Louisiana State University Press and Rand Dotson, editor. His encouragement and support along with the insights offered by the outside reader are a testament to the noteworthiness of this study to aviation history. I am very grateful for their guidance.

Finally, this book would not have come to fruition without the support, encouragement, and help of many unmentioned friends and contributors—I apologize for not having space to recognize each of you individually.

To all, I offer a humble thank you and blue skies!

SPEED
SAFETY
AND COMFORT

INTRODUCTION

An Airbus A321neo, one of Delta Air Lines' newest and most fuel-efficient jets, pushes back from its gate at the Hartsfield-Jackson International Airport in Atlanta, Georgia. One hundred and ninety-four passengers are settled inside the pressurized and temperature-controlled cabin. Soon they will be whisked away, propelled by two powerful turbofan engines at a speed of 525 miles per hour (mph) to a distant destination. Almost ten decades previously, one row of the main cabin's six people might have departed from a much-different airfield on the same site while seated on wicker chairs aboard one of the most modern aircraft of the time, a Delta Air Service single-engine Travel Air S-6000-B.

To the west, at Scott Field in Tallulah, Louisiana, a turbine-powered Thrush 510P is loaded for an agricultural-application flight. Following a hot turn, the Pratt & Whitney PT6A-34AG engine will take it flying low over the ground, quickly and efficiently spraying 510 pounds of pesticide on nearby fields. One hundred years earlier, the Thrush's forbearers pioneered crop dusting at the same airfield, spreading calcium arsenate powder in experiments to save cotton fields from the ravenous boll weevil.

The airliner and the crop duster have distinctive missions but share a common origin. Both began when the boll weevil crossed the Rio Grande from Mexico and found a home in the border cotton fields of Texas. Unwelcomed but comfortably ensconced, it thrived. Generations later, provisioned by endless fields of cotton, these insects had advanced across the southern states, leaving behind a trail of destruction. Each bug lays its eggs in the cotton bolls, which, thus damaged and spoiled, fall to the ground. Methods were devised to mitigate the damage, and therein lies the story behind the Thrush 510P and the Airbus A321neo. Denuded cotton fields, impoverished farmers, and cultural upheaval drew a blanket of uncertainty and apprehension over the South. From the lowest social stratum to the highest, all were affected in the land of King Cotton. The boll weevil's legacy underscores its relevance to the profound changes exemplified by the Thrush and Airbus.

Today, about 1,350 aerial-application businesses operate across the United States, treating approximately 71 million acres of cropland annually.[1] Daily, 4,000 Delta Air Lines flights serve 275 destinations on six continents, many from Hartsfield-Jackson Atlanta International Airport, "the world's largest airline hub and most travelled airport."[2] These achievements had their start with a quarter-inch bug that can barely fly.

The iconic book on Delta is *Delta: The History of an Airline,* by Auburn University professors W. David Lewis and Wesley Phillips Newton. Lewis and Newton were contracted to write the story of the airline, from its beginnings through deregulation of the industry in 1978, to commemorate the fiftieth anniversary of the commencement of passenger service. It is an excellent book but lacks details of the airline's origins. This is not a fault of the authors or their research. Many of the sources used in the current volume were unavailable to them.[3]

When the boll weevil crossed into the United States, a series of events unfolded. It is not uncommon to find references to this pest as the company's origin. For example, on its website corporate Delta attributes its founding to Huff Daland Dusters, the world's first crop-dusting company, which began operations in 1925; it became an airline in 1928.[4] These years are valid demarcations but not indicative of Delta's real beginnings. Highlighting them thus denies the relevance or credit due the preceding people, places, and times.

A new study on Delta Air Lines was necessary. To understand Delta's origin, visualize a staircase. The boll weevil is at the bottom; at the top is the corporate airline. The people, places, and time on each step of the climb contribute to its progression. The most logical point of Delta's origin is with the boll weevil on the U.S.-Mexico border in 1892. By World War II, it was an established regional airline. This book tells the story of Delta in-between.

The roots of Delta Air Lines are in the soil, widely spread and tangled. They reach from Texas to the border of Canada and as far away as Latin America. When the boll weevil arrived in the Mississippi Delta, planters feared their

African American laborers would leave the land. Southern elites, intent on preserving their privilege and power, searched for an answer to the problem. The Percy family of Mississippi, among others in high positions, advocated for a solution. The federal government stepped in and established the Southern Field Crop Insect Investigations Laboratory, also known as the Delta Laboratory, at Tallulah, Louisiana. Methods to understand and control the boll weevil were studied under Director Bert Raymond Coad, leading to the discovery of calcium arsenate. This poison proved to be an effective pesticide but presented a challenge. It had to be dispensed at night, when dew was on the plants, by labor-intensive ground-based machinery. The outlook improved when the advantages of an airplane's speed and mobility were introduced for application. The discovery of calcium arsenate and the achievement of powered flight were transforming to cotton agriculture. These two elements developed separately but concurrently.

The first use of an airplane to spread insecticide from the air occurred on a grove of catalpa trees in Ohio. The astonishing success of this method suggested its feasibility for dusting cotton. During the summers of 1922 and 1923, military training planes and pilots converged on Tallulah. Experiments with airplanes proved their practicality. Tests from the air were successful, and the crop-dusting business was born. On a recommendation from Coad, Huff Daland Company of Ogdensburg, New York, a manufacturer of military aircraft, designed the first plane specifically for spreading dust from the air.

Huff Daland Dusters, predecessor to Delta Air Service, pioneered crop dusting in the United States. Beginning operations in Macon, Georgia, its executive team consisted of George Birkbeck Post as general manager; Harold Ross Harris, operations manager; and Collett Everman Woolman, chief entomologist and salesman. The enterprise remained in Georgia only briefly due to insufficient business before relocating to Monroe, Louisiana, induced by Travis Oliver, president of Central Savings Bank and Trust, and other air-minded citizens.

Huff Daland Company (parent of the subsidiary duster business) outgrew its facilities in Ogdensburg and moved manufacturing to Bristol, Pennsylvania, where, with the help of New York financier Richard Farnsworth Hoyt, it reorganized as the Keystone Aircraft Corporation. Hoyt promoted aviation, particularly Pan American Airways but also Pan American–Grace Airways (Panagra). His involvement in these enterprises redirected Delta's trajectory from a crop-dusting firm to a passenger-carrying airline. As a consequence, the history of Delta is entwined with those of Pan American and Pan American–Grace Airways.

The political and economic climate under Peruvian president Augusto B. Leguía encouraged North American investment in his country. When pests threatened cotton in Peru, Huff Daland Dusters sent expeditions to South America. Contrary to Delta mythology, this Huff Daland's dusting opportunity originated from south of the equator, not the other way around. Pedro Beltrán, a prominent Peruvian planter, traveled to the United States and sought help from the dusters in Monroe. Woolman transited the recently completed Panama Canal on his journey to Lima and negotiated government concessions and commitments for services. Harris followed with an operating expedition of pilots, planes, and poison to fulfill Woolman's contracts.

Hoyt, with his Wall Street investor's perspective, had a grander vision than the dusting business in South America. Working with Juan Terry Trippe, he wanted to establish an airline. While in Peru, Harris talked to pilots with the Army Air Corps Pan American Good Will Flight. Taking notes, he studied the potential for airmail and air routes in Latin America. Harris understood the challenges of building a sound commercial air-travel venture. On arrival in New York, he briefed Hoyt and Trippe.

Meanwhile, Woolman returned to Peru with a dual mandate: supervise the dusting business and negotiate government airmail and passenger concessions. The permits acquired in Huff Daland Dusters' name were transferred first to Peruvian Airways, then to Pan American. Subsequently, Pan American partnered with the W. R. Grace Company in a joint enterprise, Pan American–Grace Airways.

When the domestic air-transportation system was consolidating, Huff Daland's operating team—Harris, Woolman, and the company's comptroller, Irwin E. Auerbach—decided to buy out the dusting business. Initially rebuffed, Hoyt, who controlled all financing, later decided to sell on favorable terms. Woolman was in Peru at this time, so it was up to Harris and Auerbach to negotiate a deal. While talks were ongoing, Trippe appointed Harris to manage the newly established Peruvian Airways. Harris was on board a ship to Peru and Woolman still away when Auerbach attempted to sell the company for his own benefit. In resolving the situation, Delta Air Service, Inc., succeeded Huff Daland Dusters. From this point forward, Delta's and Woolman's futures were intrinsically entwined.

Delta Air Service proved to be a short-lived venture. It curtailed operations in 1930 after Postmaster General Walter Folger Brown awarded the southern transcontinental mail contract to American Airways. The company reorganized as Delta Air Corporation and survived by expanding its dusting operation and providing aircraft services in Monroe. At this time, Coad, the entomological researcher and influential advocate for crop dusting at the Delta Laboratory, pleaded guilty to charges of defrauding the government. Released on probation a year later, he returned to Monroe, where the episode was forgotten.

In 1934 Pres. Franklin D. Roosevelt rebid all the mail contracts following the "spoils conference" fiasco. Having won the contract along an extended route from Charleston, South Carolina, to Fort Worth, Texas, Delta restored its pioneering passenger "Trans Southern Route" service.

The last step "up the staircase" brought Delta's beginning to a logical endpoint at the outbreak of World War II. Key factors contributed to its prospects in the 1930s. With the award of Contract Air Mail Route 24 in 1934, Delta had the wherewithal to succeed financially as an airline. It developed a viable route structure, modernized its fleet, and accessed the capital markets. A sound management team and stable workforce was assembled, and in 1941 Delta shifted its headquarters to Atlanta, Georgia.

The boll weevil's arrival in 1892 had set Delta on its developmental course. As war clouds loomed in 1941, secured by the firmness of its southern roots, Delta Air Lines faced the future.

THE SOUTH, COTTON, AND
THE BOLL WEEVIL

The Mississippi Delta begins in the lobby of the Peabody Hotel
in Memphis and ends in Catfish Row in Vicksburg.

—DAVID L. COHN, *God Shakes Creation*

James C. Cobb described the Yazoo-Mississippi Delta region as a throwback to an earlier time. There, the soil and climate were ideal for King Cotton, the land was flat, and African Americans, following the Civil War, still labored under a white planter class, no longer as slaves but as sharecroppers. More than a place, Cobb observed, the Delta was a feeling. One does not go to the Delta; rather, one travels "'into the Delta' the implication being that of passage back in time, to a setting—that if such a thing were possible—seemed even more southern than the rest of the state." Cobb examines southern "interaction with, rather than its isolation from the larger global and national setting," discovering the Delta as being "a part of the world rather than a world apart."[1] This perspective led to an understanding of those factors that first influenced the merger of agriculture and aeronautics to control the boll weevil from the air and then fostered the development of the Delta's namesake airline—Delta Air Lines. The Delta, for purposes of this discussion, includes regions of both Mississippi and Louisiana.

The Mississippi River drops only 290 feet in elevation as it wends its way 1,100 bending miles from Cairo, Illinois, to the Gulf of Mexico. The gentle slope would seem to tame the river's power, but it is just the opposite. "The Mississippi is never at rest. It roils. It follows no set course. Its waters and currents are not uniform. Rather, it moves south in layers and whorls, like an uncoiling rope." The flow is so random and unpredictable that the study of its turbulent stream gave rise to the chaos theory of the 1970s as an explanation of its complexity.[2] Among other factors, its hydraulics are governed by the tremendous volume of water. With its tributaries, the Mississippi drains 41 percent of the contiguous United States.[3] Precipitation that falls as far west as Montana disgorges into the Gulf of Mexico, as does that from parts as far east as New York and Pennsylvania, all via the Missouri, Ohio, and Mississippi Rivers.[4] Both beneficial and destructive, the Mississippi both accelerated and delayed the Delta's development.

Historically, seasonal high water crested over the river's banks and replenished the land with a layer of fresh topsoil and nutrients. The lush, dense vegetation that flourished from this enrichment promised high yields for cotton, but at a price. The Mississippi and its tributaries first had to be tamed, the swamps drained, the protective levees raised, and the land cleared. After the Civil War, a special breed of southerner—men of means with foresight and a world outlook—challenged the Delta. Epitomizing this planter class, the Percy family of Mississippi "helped to create the Deep South—not just as slave holding frontiersmen, but as agents of change in the Post-War years." With vision and resourcefulness, Delta planters marshaled the human and mechanical energy necessary to build the levees, remove the native trees and undergrowth, prepare the land, and plant the fields with cotton.[5]

In the aftermath of the Civil War, landlords lost the investment value of their slaves. Whether those who managed to hold on transformed themselves into a new entrepreneurial or industrial class is the subject of scholarly debate. Cobb agrees with C. Van Woodward's "general blueprint" that "survival or success as a planter describes the experience of many prominent late nineteenth-century Delta planters whose interests and holdings actually made them some combination of planter and merchant, or lawyer."[6] This described the Percy family, who "as planters, lawyers, physicians, militia officers, corporation lawyers, and bank directors complemented their energetic civic work."[7] LeRoy Percy (1860–1929), as the attorney representing the Yazoo-Mississippi Levee District and U.S. senator from Mississippi (1910–13) during a time when senators were chosen by state legislators before the Seventeenth Amendment to the Constitution, made valuable political relationships. He hobnobbed socially with the nation's elites and even hunted with President Theodore Roosevelt and Stuyvesant Fish, president of the Illinois Central Railroad, in the Sunflower River area of the Delta in 1902.[8]

Before railroads, efficient transportation west of the Appalachians was confined to inland waterways. Mark Twain eloquently depicted the steamboat as the workhorse of Midwest expansion. With "about 1,250,000 square miles," he visualized the Mississippi river basin as the "Body of the Nation."[9] But water transportation limited interior development, whereas railroads, when they came, opened vast new areas for cultivation. Between 1880 and 1890, land values in Delta counties increased by as much as 50 percent. A mature Twain, returning to the river after an absence of twenty-one years, found few passenger boats still in service on which to book passage. The railroads had transformed "an essentially untamed wilderness frontier to a modern plantation kingdom." Planters such as the Percy family, with connections to banks, railroads, world markets, and Wall Street, looked outward. As ties to national and foreign economies solidified, elites were socioeconomically and politically separated from everyone else in the region.[10] Nevertheless, wealthy landholders continued to view themselves symbolically as planters. "The Delta owner of extensive lands lived, not on a farm, but on a plantation. He was known not as a farmer, but as a planter," which linked him with "the antebellum past, reminiscent of the dream, if not always the reality, of what had been. It conjured up the lordship of the living and a touch of the romantic" and "suggested aristocracy and inherited wealth, the habit of command, and a 'cavalier dash that mocked the dull virtue of caution and scorned the pedestrian uses of compound interest piling up in the bank.'"[11] Nevertheless, an antebellum legacy draped this fanciful imagery like Spanish moss. Delta planters' thoughts were first and foremost for keeping as field hands the Black labor force they had relied on in creating their agricultural empire.[12]

When the value of slaves was lost, entrepreneurial incentives were redirected toward investment in land. The potential return from the productivity and value of land, not slaves, created wealth. Labor lords became landlords.[13] Former slaves were lured to Louisiana and Mississippi with promises of "enormous wages" and "images of opportunity and even lushness."[14] Gavin Wright explains this southern condition was the result of market forces. After the Civil War, output per acre of land became paramount. Labor was now a variable cost that had to be covered by the value of crops. This fostered a new relationship between landowners and freedmen. Black and poor-white sharecroppers lived and worked on the land for a share of the crop, which, in a vicious cycle at the end of the season, went to pay off accounts at plantation stores owned by planters.[15] Sharecropping balanced "freedman's desire for autonomy and the employer's interest in extracting work effort and having labor when it was needed." Keeping its workforce in place remained a nagging concern for land holders, especially since indebtedness with the company store did not necessarily keep African Americans or whites from leaving.[16]

The situation became more acute when the boll weevil first arrived and then advanced across the South, averaging 40 to 160 miles per year.[17] The bugs crossed the Rio Grande from Mexico in 1892, first appearing near Brownsville, Texas. They expanded unimpeded by natural barriers and provisioned by endless fields of cotton. "Growers were totally defenseless, and havoc continued to engulf one county after another."[18] As the pests approached the Percy estate, LeRoy "feared their arrival would trigger a panic that would be more harmful than the insects themselves. 'One great danger to be guarded against,' he warned, 'is the stampeding of the Negro labor. This would bring about all of the loss that the weevil might ultimately cause and could be fully as difficult to remedy.'"[19] The boll weevil threatened the relationship between planters and their exploited Black labor force and had to be destroyed.

"Boll weevil" (*Anthonomus grandis* Boheman) is the common name for one of the groups of snout beetles that infect cotton plants. The female punctures the buds and fluffy cotton bolls to lay her eggs inside. When the eggs hatch, larvae feed on the buds and bolls, which then fall to the ground. Any remaining damaged bolls are stunted or dwarfed. The life cycle of the boll weevil is about three weeks, allowing four or five generations in one season. Federal programs to study agricultural pests began in the 1870s, with the cotton-leaf worm and boll worm the focus of early research. The boll weevil rose in priority when the magnitude of the threat was realized.[20] In 1901, Congress funded the first boll weevil investigation under the direction of Walter David Hunter, who remained in charge of the project until his death in 1925. States, not relying solely on the federal government, took independent action, but this did not impede the weevil's natural dispersal. Georgia's quarantine laws, adopted in 1903, prohibited importation of living boll weevils and required fumigation of cotton seed from Texas and Louisiana. The Louisiana legislature established the Crop Pest Commission in 1904, with broad authority to establish and regulate state policy on agricultural pests and diseases.[21]

Weevils fly, though not far, seeking shelter for winter hibernation. Wind affects the distance and direction traveled. Timbered regions with an abundance of Spanish moss offer the best protection from cool temperatures. Field hibernation is important only in the more southern areas.[22] A federal research laboratory first established in Victoria, Texas, relocated to Dallas in 1905. Then in 1907 the pest crossed the Mississippi River, threatening the large plantations to the east, and in 1909 the government moved the laboratory to Tallulah, Louisiana, where heavy infestations were anticipated due to the Delta's unique climate, ecology, fertile soil, and extended growing season.[23] Perhaps another reason was because LeRoy Percy, with his extensive holdings at risk, supported the move.[24]

Founded in 1857, Tallulah is the seat of largely agricultural Madison Parish. Known informally as the "Delta Laboratory," the Southern Field Crop Insect Investigations Laboratory operated under the Bureau of Entomology, U.S. Department of Agriculture (USDA).[25] Until methods of control or eradication were found, the bureau sought to determine the weevil's seasonal spread and estimate its winter survival rate. To gauge conditions, inspections were taken at widely separated sites, usually in early June. Agents surveyed a specific number of plants to determine a ratio of weevils to cotton plants. Changing weather was another factor that could affect damage from subsequent generations. The laboratory periodically updated its assessment during the season.[26] Invariably, forecasting weevil damage was not conclusive, only advisory.

Life-cycle studies first suggested cultural methods of control. Early planting and use of fertilizer quickened plant maturity, which could moderate damage if the cotton was harvested before the weevils reproduced. Immediately destroying cotton stalks removed them as a hibernation habitat for the pests.[27] Initially, chemical methods of control had little success. William Newell, a Georgia state entomologist, tested a powdered form of lead arsenate, but the results from his experiments were inconclusive. More heartening, experiments with calcium arsenate in 1916 proved successful: "The most striking results were obtained in a plot in a field of heavily infested cotton that . . . the owner had abandoned as an absolute loss."[28] Calcium arsenate is an inorganic compound, "probably the first insecticide resulting from deliberately planned manufacture."[29] It is highly toxic, but apparently dispensing dust on the ground or in low-flying aircraft was not considered a health risk before World War II.[30]

William C. Piver, a University of North Carolina graduate and young entrepreneur in the insecticide industry, reasoned that if arsenic could be combined with a more common and less expensive substance such as lime, it would be cheaper to manufacture than other chemicals in use, including Paris Green (which contains a copper compound) and lead arsenate. Orders lagged for Piver's product until the Delta Laboratory began experiments using it. "In 1918, on the basis of Government tests, a Federal Entomologist [likely Coad] telegraphed Piver for 40 tons of the calcium arsenate—the largest single order he had ever received and a third larger than his yearly production."[31] With further refinement, calcium arsenate proved to be the most effective pest control, not only of cotton but for other crops as well, and it became "one of the most widely used materials throughout the Nation." Research to improve its physical and chemical properties, along with the rapidity to which it was put to use, is mostly a result of the work done at the Delta Laboratory under Coad's supervision.[32]

So involved was Coad with the laboratory that his name is synonymous with the boll weevil. But his background remains mostly a mystery. Coad was born on July 4, 1893, in Murphysboro, Illinois, where he graduated from high school. The University of Illinois Office of Admissions and Records confirms he attended the university during the summer months in 1910, taking two courses in the College of Science. The university has no record of his graduating, and he does not appear in the yearbook, *Illio*.[33] When Coad died in 1966, his obituary noted that he was survived by his wife, two sons, two daughters, and seven grandchildren.[34] Additional information on family or on other formal education is lacking. Where he was between the years 1910 and 1913 and why he ended up in the Delta is not known. He was often identified by others as "Doctor" Coad, but there is no evidence of an earned or honorary doctorate degree, even though he authored or coauthored many government bulletins on the boll weevil (and never titled "Dr." in any of these). Thus, the appellation of "Doc" was probably first used informally as a familiar term of respect that then became an honorific. It appears Coad served an apprenticeship under the supervision of Walter Hunter (one of Coad's sons is named Hunter), with whom he coauthored several USDA farmers bulletins. The number of bulletins Coad authored himself, the quality of his work, his leadership of the laboratory, and the esteem with which he was held by others as a scientist all attest to his expertise, whether formally or informally acquired.

Coad is often seen in photographs with a pipe. He was described as a short, "solemn man (until you get to know him)," having "little patience with ceremony," and known as a "good whiskey drinker."[35] An avid sportsman, Coad was elected president of the Bear Lake Hunt Club.[36] Its elevated single-level clubhouse with a wraparound porch, located approximately nine miles north of Tallulah, likely served as a center of social activity as well as a base camp. On a hunt in 1907, Teddy Roosevelt described the setting in his inimical prose: "Our new camp was beautifully situated on the bold, steep bank of Bear Lake—a tranquil stretch of water, part of an old river-bed, a couple of hundred yards broad, with winding length several miles. Giant cypress grew at the edge of the water, the singular cypress knees rising in every direction round about, while at the bottoms of the trunks themselves were often cavernous hollows opening beneath the surface of the water, some of them serving as dens for alligators." Roosevelt successfully tracked and killed a bear that year.[37]

Coad began work at the Delta Laboratory on April 1, 1913, studying the Thurberia weevil (*Anthonomus grandis thurberiae*), a close relative of the boll weevil, in the native cotton of Arizona.[38] In 1915 he succeeded G. D. Smith as the director of the Tallulah laboratory and supervised the development of calcium arsenate into an effective agent.

During the first few years it was used, calcium arsenate was a crude product. First, the chemists at the Tallulah Laboratory stabilized its physical and chemical properties; the dust formulation they developed was considered the best ever, from the standpoint of the quantities necessary for good plant coverage. Then, the Tallulah chemists produced calcium arsenate with varying percentages of water-soluble arsenic as well as containing no free lime, yet none of these variants replaced regular calcium arsenate. Meanwhile, field experiments occurred in Tallulah and in many places throughout the Cotton Belt to determine the correct poundage of the chemical to use and the intervals between applications that would give the best return.[39]

Once modified, a method to apply the poison to the plants was needed.

The Delta Laboratory experimented with various types of machinery to disperse the dust. "With the cooperation and aid of the Bureau of Public Roads, engineers stationed at Tallulah developed a rotary-type hand gun that could be used to dust 8 acres of cotton every 4 or 5 days; a 2-nozzle traction machine for 75–150 acres; power operated machines for 200–300 acres; and tractor operated machines for still larger acreages."[40] Coad patented innovations "in the name of the public, which will prevent any manufacturer from naming anybody else."[41] For example, the manufacturer of the Root Saddle Gun claimed the device operated from horses or mules and was "constructed in accordance with the specifications of the Delta Laboratory United States Department of Agriculture, Tallulah, La. They have endorsed its use."[42] As poisons and machinery evolved, Coad not only recommended utilizing the right equipment but also stressed the importance of dusting in a timely manner.[43]

Depending on location, the combined operating cost of poison and machinery varied between five to fifteen dollars per acre. This was excessive for small farmers, who produced 75 percent of the South's cotton. Acknowledging the expense, Coad considered a four-dollar rate could be achieved by scaling production and from reduced freight costs. The price of machinery varied from fifteen dollars for a hand gun to six hundred dollars for a two-mule wagon. Coad hoped "that within the near future a dusting machine would be perfected that could be sold at a price that will fit the pocketbooks of the little farmers."[44] In contrast to the material and equipment expense of small farmers and tenants, planters required a large and expensive labor pool to apply the poison on their estates. In addition to the cost of its use, applying calcium arsenate was inconvenient since it would only stick to plants with dew present on the cotton stalks, which only occurred overnight. As he considered these factors in 1921, Coad did not foresee aerial applications as a solution.

As Coad pondered the science of weevil control at the laboratory, farmers in Texas learned to deal with the boll weevil without chemicals and systematically increased their yield per acre by 35 percent over preweevil days, which challenged the idea of the boll weevil's destructiveness.[45] Both approaches had merit, but a combination—intense cultivation with judicious application of calcium arsenate—seemed a successful strategy for widespread control. Moderating losses was an antidote to planter's fear of the exodus of Black labor. In Mississippi, LeRoy Percy applied calcium arsenate to some of his fields and, according to his son William, achieved "a practically normal yield of high-grade cotton."[46]

Another approach eliminated cotton altogether as a cash crop. In Coffee County, Alabama, John Pitman, county agricultural agent, traveled to Texas in 1913 to see firsthand what to expect when the boll weevil arrived. With what he learned, Pitman encouraged Alabama farmers to diversify to corn, potatoes, peanuts, and other crops to "take better care of their land." When the weevil struck in 1915, Coffee County ginned only 10,000 bales of cotton—each bale weighing 500 pounds—instead of the expected 30,000 bales. To counter the economic effect, Enterprise banker H. M. Sessions convinced C. W. Baston, a local farmer, to plant 125 acres in peanuts. At the end of the 1916 season, Baston earned eight thousand dollars. Meanwhile, Enterprise's gins produced only 1,500 bales of cotton, down from 15,000 in 1914 and 5,000 in 1915. Thus encouraged, many farmers followed Baston's example. To commemorate the community's unexpected victory and economic windfall, Enterprise erected a monument in the town center in honor of the boll weevil. In changing farmer's attitudes toward cotton and substituting peanuts as the cash crop, the weevil brought prosperity to the region. The promise of diversification raised people's hopes, but unfortunately, this did not last.[47]

The boll weevil reached the limit of its natural dispersal in 1922, with the estimated cost of the damage exceeding $200,000,000. Hunter and Coad recommended a combination of direct and indirect control methods to combat the pest. They suggested cultural preferences first, followed by poisoning utilizing specialized terrestrial, one- or two-mule-drawn traction machines. Interestingly, at this stage of mechanization (considering the development of aerial applications to come), engine-powered ground equipment was found to be "too complicated for satisfactory operation except by expert labor." Dusting had to occur with calm winds and moisture on the plants, meaning lots of overnight and early morning work for field hands. If that were not hindrance enough, a heavy rain event would require another round of dusting within twenty-four hours, yet the resulting muddy fields might make this impossible.[48]

In 1898 the Georgia legislature established the Georgia State Board of Entomology, as a separate agency of the Georgia Department of Agriculture. When the boll weevil arrived in that state, it devastated the cotton industry.

From a high of 2,800,000 bales ginned in 1914, Georgia's output decreased dramatically after 1915; only 600,000 bales were produced in 1923. The board innovated using lead arsenate in a powdered formulation to dust cotton. Moreover, taking another approach, it tried developing a weevil-resistant variety of cotton. Eventually, the state decided to distribute calcium arsenate to farmers at cost.[49] Georgia's aggressive response likely factored in attracting the world's first aerial crop-dusting company, Huff Daland Dusters, Inc., to locate its operating base in Macon in 1925.

Delta Air Lines has roots not only in the land of the South but also in its people, many of whom became employees. Doris Elizabeth Davidson worked for fifty-six years as a pilot-crew scheduler. She grew up as a sharecropper's daughter in rural Campbell County (now part of Fulton County), Georgia, southwest of Atlanta. In the 1930s, although her family was poor, she noted: "We had plenty to eat. We were never hungry [and] had enough to wear." Everyone was poor, she said, so her circumstances were not unusual. Their house—when she swept the floor, the dust fell through the cracks—and the land they worked were provided by the landlord for a share of the cotton they produced. Davidson's family raised turnip greens "on the bottoms, down by the [Chattahoochee] river," which was prone to flooding, and sold the crop in the city. At night, a single kerosene lamp gave light: "We didn't have electricity until 1938." Davidson picked cotton, trapped rabbits for fifteen cents, and helped with household chores. When the boll weevil made its appearance, her father bought poison at the country store and spread it with a hand gun. Despite their modest means, her "mother and daddy" valued education and made allowances for her to attend school. She graduated valedictorian of her class and attended business school. Davidson was hired by Delta Air Lines in 1946.[50]

As Davidson's story attests, Delta has roots spread widely across the South. In fact, they reach from the border with Mexico north to Canada.

DUSTING
FROM THE AIR

The poisoner steers close to the bush, shoots his calcium arsenate,
and mixes death with Miss Weevils morning tipple.

—HARRIS DICKSON, "Borgias of the Air,"
Saturday Evening Post

T he Mississippi Delta's unique geography and history factored in the
evolution of Delta Air Lines. In the early twentieth century, the region's prominent citizens were informed and outward looking. They
were engaged economically and politically on local, national, and global
stages. Cotton remained the dominant cash crop, but following the turn of the
century, the boll weevil threatened the status quo between planters and their
field laborers. The Delta Laboratory in Tallulah addressed the weevil problem
scientifically. Although the bug was not eliminated, it could be controlled by
using indirect agricultural methods, supplemented by the application of calcium arsenate with ground-based machinery. The airplane, first used to apply pesticides in the North against tree insects, proved to be a more effective
means to dispense the poison swiftly and efficiently on southern plantations.

In the spring of 1921, Charles Robert Neillie, the city entomologist for
Cleveland, Ohio, had a problem. His spray equipment would not reach the
tops of large, closely spaced trees in a park. It occurred to him that an airplane,
or even an airship, might easily do the job. He contacted state agricultural
authorities regarding his idea, and the Ohio Agricultural Experiment Station
assigned John Samuel Houser, a forest entomologist, to help him. Together

they enlisted the assistance of the Army Air Service's aviation research-and-development center at McCook Field in Dayton.[1]

The War and Agriculture Departments already cooperated in diverse agricultural activities. Military aircraft scouted for forest fires in California and Oregon and helped enforce crop-control laws to prevent the spread of pink boll worms in Texas. The departments even shared a common tragedy. On August 7, 1919, Lt. William H. Tillisch and his observer, E. L. Diven of the Agriculture Department, perished in a Curtiss JN-4H two-seat advanced-trainer biplane while surveying for "outlaw" cotton in the cotton-free zone at Eagle Pass along the border with Mexico. Despite this unfortunate loss, inspectors preferred aerial surveying; it was better than enduring long patrols on horseback.[2]

Neillie and Houser encountered mixed reactions to the idea of dispensing insecticide from the air. They were often greeted with skepticism or "much good-natured chaffing." Fortunately, officials at McCook were supportive. Maj. Thurman H. Bane, director of the air station, and Maj. Harold S. Martin, chief engineer, agreed to give Neillie and Houser "priority over everything in the Field for one entire day."[3] Etienne Dormoy, "a tough, intelligent little Frenchman," designed a hopper that "consisted of an irregularly shaped flat metal box with a capacity for holding a little more than 100 pounds of dry arsenate of lead powder."[4] The device attached on the outside of a JN-6, adjacent to the observer's position. This was not very aerodynamic but nevertheless served the purpose. To operate the mechanism, a crewman opened a sliding gate at the bottom of the hopper and turned a crank to meter the powder into the aircraft's slipstream.[5]

An outbreak of catalpa sphinx (*Ceratomia catalpae Bdv*) in a grove of catalpa trees belonging to Harry A. Carver presented Neillie, Houser, and the air service an opportunity to put their plan to a practical test. Located about twenty miles from Dayton near Troy, Ohio, the grove was situated on level ground and measured about 800 feet long and 325 feet wide. Mature trees were 25–30 feet in height. An adjacent field allowed a low-flying airplane to pass unobstructed along the tree line. Operating out of McCook on August 3, 1921, Lt. John A. Macready, with Dormoy handling the dispenser, made six runs, releasing some 175 pounds of poison in about fifty-four seconds. The experiment exceeded expectations. "The plane flew at a speed of eighty miles an hour at an altitude of from 20 to 35 feet and in a line 53 yards to the windward and parallel to the grove. The dense cloud of poison dust thrown out behind the moving plane was grasped by the wind and floated through and over the grove, covering the foliage in its passage." A postapplication assessment determined that fewer than 1 percent of the insects remained alive.[6]

In "light of up-to-date experience," Julius Augustus Truesdell authored an article that appeared in the *New York Times*. He suggested that Congress fund experiments with army aircraft to spread calcium arsenate from the air on cotton fields infested by boll weevils.[7] A month later, Truesdale testified at a hearing of the House Committee on Agriculture on the topic. Introducing himself as "a farmer from Bluemont, Va.," he modestly declared his intention: "I am not here representing anybody in particular—no associations, no chambers of commerce even, but just simply with an idea, and that is the use of the airplane to spray cotton and control the boll weevil." The Troy experiment, Truesdell opined, "suggested to me—I suppose it has to a great many people—the use of the airplane to spray cotton." He envisioned a public rather than private enterprise. "It is not expected that this thing can be done by individuals." Truesdell thought state and federal agencies should cooperate and consolidate their operations into districts. Each would have a central headquarters to manage resources, including some aircraft in reserve for unexpected blights. He presciently described the economic benefit and efficiency of an airplane's speed, agility, and mobility to offset the high cost of aerial applications.[8]

Truesdell did not claim to be the first to suggest dusting cotton from the air, although his is the earliest discovered statement of the idea. Coad agreed that "it presented a proposition that ought to be considered."[9] Following Truesdell at the hearing, Leland O. Howard, chief of the Bureau of Entomology, Department of Agriculture, testified suggesting that either the Post Office Department or the War Department arrange "an experiment with the use of the airplane—I think it can be done—this coming season."[10] In fact, tests were conducted that August. Thus, the impetus for aerial dusting sprang from Truesdell's *New York Times* article and his and Howard's congressional testimony.

The airmen who flew the Troy experiment, Lieutenant Macready and Dormoy, did not have any difficulties with the operation other than perhaps the drag from the hopper. The flight was straightforward: "What had been a big thing to them [the entomologists] had been a short, easy flying job for us."[11] But unanswered questions remained about dusting low-growing cotton. Could airplanes deliver the poison at "night, when the dew has gathered on the plant and the insect in taking a drink, gets the poison into his 'pantry'?" To answer this and other questions, the army at first hesitated but then said it was feasible. "'We have men trained for just this sort of flying,' said one officer who took up the subject. 'We have observation planes, bombing planes, pursuit planes, all planned for night work, and the service is full of men who are equal to all that is called for in this proposition.'"[12] Centrally located in the heart of the Cotton Belt in the flat Mississippi Delta, the Delta Laboratory was ideally situated to undertake the experiment.

The War Department dispatched personnel and aircraft from Maxwell Field in Montgomery, Alabama, to Tallulah. Initial tests were not against the boll weevil as contemplated, but on the cotton leaf worm (*Alabama argillacea, Hubn.*). A July outbreak of the worm proved a fortuitous coincidence. The weevil affects cotton bolls internally, so the damage is more difficult to assess than from the externally feeding leaf worm.[13] Coad at first thought airplane dusting should be considered, but later equivocated, saying it "might sound foolish." His reservation vanished in August when he testified before Congress: "It proved fairly practical, and not only that, it cost less to use an airplane than the ordinary ground machine."[14] Encouraged, Coad optimistically predicted "a great future for airplanes in insect control."[15]

Conspicuously absent in Coad's research is any mention of C. E. Woolman's collaboration. *USDA Department Bulletin 1204, Dusting Cotton by Airplanes,* fully summarizes the experiments. Its three authors and their affiliations highlight the cooperative nature of the undertaking: Coad, Bureau of Entomology; E. Johnson, agricultural engineer, Bureau of Public Roads; and 1st Lt. Guy L. McNeil, 22nd Observation Squadron, U.S. Army Air Service. The authors acknowledge the help of several assistants in this work: "In conducting the experiments described in this bulletin the writers were assisted by a number of men from the Delta Laboratory force at Tallulah, La. They are particularly indebted to the following: A. J. Chapman, R. H Flake, S. B. Hendricks, R. L. Hodges, I. T. Jones, H. Kirkpatrick, P. D. Sanders, C. M. Smith, and M. T. Young."[16] Woolman is not listed. If, as the story goes, he helped Coad in the fight against the boll weevil and partnered in the development of aerial techniques, his role should have been acknowledged. An inspection of Woolman's field diaries from July 1916 through June 1919 and loose pages of his field diary from January to November 1922 do not mention working or meeting with Coad, although Woolman frequently visited Tallulah.[17]

Maj. Gen. Mason Patrick, in charge of the air service, thought commercial aviation could benefit the army. He supported nonmilitary research and would have done more if Congress had approved funding. Two Hispano-powered Curtiss JN-6Hs, piloted by 1st Lt. Guy McNeil and 1st Lt. Charles T. Skow, were assigned to Tallulah. A meadow on Shirley Plantation, just outside town, served as a landing field. The 22nd Squadron pilots, along with three airmen, were temporarily assigned to the Department of Agriculture.[18] Support equipment included acetylene lights (which suggests night operations) and wind gauges. Skow participated from August 13 to August 26, when he was replaced by Lt. C. L. Simon.[19] Two fundamental questions guided their flying. First, could they maneuver their airplane to overfly entire cotton fields? Second, would the distributed dust reach all parts of the plant, adhere to the leaves, and kill the insects?[20]

The Maxwell aircraft were not configured for dusting. The Troy hopper was still in Ohio and being used to eliminate the cankerworm on the "beautiful estate of John. L. Serverance" near Cleveland and on a grove of catalpa trees near Casstown. Meanwhile in Tallulah, attempts were made to release calcium arsenate from the airplane by hand, either over the side or through a hole in the bottom of the fuselage. These methods proved unsatisfactory. The Troy hopper eventually arrived in Louisiana, but by then two improved, internally mounted devices had been fabricated.[21] The new models fit inside the aircraft but took up half of the observer's compartment. The operator was forced to use the mechanism while standing within the reduced confines. One model, termed the "hand cranked" type, discharged the material when its crank was turned. The other had a funnel facing forward into the airstream so that air pressure ejected the dust by opening a damper. No attempt was made during the tests to improve these mechanisms to discharge the material evenly.[22]

Shirley and Hermione Plantations, like many others near Tallulah, were heavily infested with leaf worms and presented different challenges for the fliers. Shirley's fields were small and randomly dotted with cabins. The Hermione cabins lined the perimeter of the fields, permitting long, straight-line flights. The difficulty was in maintaining a track. Initially, maps used ground features to identify targeted fields, but these proved inadequate. Mosaic maps made from reconnaissance photos taken by the air service arrived later. These helped pilots preplan the best possible flight paths for each field.[23]

With preparations completed, the moment of truth was at hand. Amazingly, the "first flights furnished an absolute surprise." As it exited the plane, the calcium arsenate was "immediately broken up into a circular cloud which was quickly blown down among the plants." The combination of the aircraft's wash and propeller blast overcame the "light breezes, or other slight air movements existing on the ground." Subsequent flights under a variety of conditions were carefully documented.[24]

Scientists discovered adhesion of the chemical to plants from aerial distribution was superior to that of ground equipment, but the reason was not immediately understood. George B. Post, a Huff Daland Company pilot, provided the explanation. "Reasons for this surprising adhesion were at first hand rather hard to find, but later tests have fully substantiated the correctness of the original observations, and it is now felt that the combined effect of the powerful air blast, and an appreciable amount of static electricity, formed during the violent ejection of the dust through the hopper orifice, are responsible for the usual results obtained."[25] This discovery alleviated the need for night operations when dew was on the plants, greatly enhancing the efficiency of aerial applications.

The military planes used in these tests were not suitable for conditions in the Delta due to their diminished performance resulting from high midday temperatures. Thermals made flying low to the ground unsafe, and the high ambient temperature quickly overheated engines. Planes could only operate safely during early morning and late afternoon. Despite these limitations, the crews developed fundamental techniques of aerial dusting. Pilots studied and treated each field individually, taking into consideration the wind direction and speed. To dust, a pilot entered the field by diving to the proper altitude; skimmed swiftly over the tops of the plants, releasing the pesticide; then zoomed upward at the end, turning around to make another run. By flying back and forth, he covered the entire field from one side to the other. With experience, they learned to maneuver their aircraft to deliver dust into almost any field, but due to faults in the feeders, repeat passes were necessary to ensure uniform coverage. Nevertheless, air applications were estimated to use two pounds of calcium arsenate per acre, whereas ground machines required five pounds. Coad, Johnson, and McNeil anticipated even greater efficiency with an aircraft capable of carrying a larger payload and a more reliable dispensing system operated solely by the pilot.[26]

As the 1922 summer's activities wound down, the assessment was encouraging. Pilots demonstrated that aircraft could operate successfully under a variety of conditions during daytime, dispensing dust from the air accurately and efficiently at low altitude. The question remained whether aerial applications could be successful against the boll weevil, but the outlook was promising. "It was suddenly noted that cotton squares not infested with the weevils were becoming fairly common, and by the end of the experimental period both [Shirley and Hermione] plantations were blooming rather freely wherever the [leaf worm] poisoning had been done." Whether the boll weevil could be controlled by aerial applications remained uncertain, but Coad, Johnson, and McNeil felt that "all records bearing on this question appear to furnish decidedly favorable indications of success."[27]

With this encouraging information, the Agriculture Department appealed to Congress for a $5,000,000 appropriation to buy calcium arsenate to distribute to farmers at cost and spread it by using army aircraft. The subsidy would particularly help small planters, who otherwise found the cost of the poison burdensome. But legislators did not authorize the funding, so the army could only send three aircraft to Louisiana in 1923.[28] Lieutenant McNeil returned to Tallulah, where he served as commander, Air Service Detachment, Delta Laboratory from April through August.[29] Accompanying him were Lt. John B. Patrick, MSgt. William M. McConnel, and Pvts. W. D. Bridges and J. W. Holley.[30] The airplanes for this second round of testing were de Havilland 4B (DH-4B) models, powered by 400-horsepower (hp) Liberty engines and capable of carrying between 500 and 700 pounds of poison. The more powerful engines permitted greater lift and allowed for swifter climbs to avoid obstacles compared to those on the Curtiss aircraft, although the larger type might prove a handicap under certain conditions, especially over small fields.[31] The Agriculture Department arranged for aerial photographs of selected fields to compare with the surveys in official reports.[32]

Experiments the previous year had validated the maneuverability of aircraft to reach all parts of fields and scatter dust effectively. The 1923 tests had two objectives: first, to demonstrate aircraft could be economically and efficiently utilized to combat the boll weevil on a community-wide basis, and, second, to improve delivery systems. Better results were anticipated with the DH-4B and a new dispenser designed by A. L. Morse from the Engineering Division at McCook Field. Usually, 350 pounds of poison was dispensed on each flight.[33] The improved design prevented the hopper from clogging, and a wider feed gate matched to the width of the fuselage spread the dust more uniformly as it was ejected into the slipstream.[34]

Based on these experiments, Coad went before Congress in May 1924 to request money to develop a more suitable airplane than the military types. "You have to have a plane for different purposes the same as motor vehicles," he said. Coad revealed that commercial organizations were prepared to begin aerial dusting in Greenville, South Carolina, and San Antonio, Texas; probably Huff Daland Company.[35] In fact, in September that company flew the "first commercial airplane crop dusting for insect control in the United States" at Heathman, Mississippi, between Leland and Indianola. The Robertshaw Company contracted to treat a 1,000 acres at thirty-five cents per acre.[36]

Huff Daland Company cooperated with Tallulah officials to develop a purpose-built dusting plane. The company probably had representatives in Louisiana as early as 1923. Post traveled widely to investigate commercial uses for aircraft and saw the need for a suitable dusting airplane as an opportunity. He outlined the specifications of a suitable design.[37] It had to carry a good load, be highly maneuverable, and be powerful enough to operate safely at low altitudes in confined areas. Several models and variations were tested in conjunction with the Delta Laboratory. From his observations of these trials, Post documented the economic advantages of airplane dusting:

- Less calcium arsenate was required to cover a given field.
- It was applied during daytime and did not require dew, eliminating the need for night applications.
- The calcium arsenate could be dispensed immediately after a heavy rain with no delay due to muddy fields.
- A single aircraft would cover 200–1,000 acres per hour, as opposed to 30 acres an hour by other means.

- Each airplane was so efficient that it replaced fifty to seventy-five horse carts.
- The airplane was so highly mobile that only a small number were needed to operate throughout the Cotton Belt.
- With a crop-duster airplane, farmers could respond immediately to an unexpected discovery of an infestation.[38]

For more than a year, Huff Daland Company collaborated with government agents in the tests at Tallulah. These determined that two methods of flying and two aircraft types were required depending on the size of clearings. A lighter, more maneuverable model was appropriate for small parcels; a larger one was better for "clearings of from 300 to 500 acres, with open stretches of level country a mile, or more, in length." Huff Daland Company had a design for each class of flying. The Model 5 serviced small fields; the Model 31, larger fields. "Dusting demonstrations [were] held at Athens and Cordele, Georgia, on August 26th and 28th respectively in cooperation with the Georgia State College of Agriculture." The planes were used in a commercial application to "obtain data under actual operating conditions" in the Mississippi Delta under the supervision of the Delta Laboratory. Coad observed of the company's models, "they come as near meeting all of the features which have been found desirable for dusting purposes as it is possible to do so."[39]

In July 1924 Coad sent a letter to Huff Daland Company officials in Ogdensburg lending scientific support for the economic viability of establishing a dusting company. He confirmed the airplane's effectiveness against the boll weevil and assuaged any lingering doubts of corporate officials about investing hundreds of thousands of dollars on a new venture. Coad wrote, "I would say that while airplane dusting is certainly in the developmental stage, the main features of whether or not it is successful and profitable have decidedly passed the experimental stage."[40] Dusting from the air was a viable option to Prof. J. W. Fox, manager of the Delta and Pine Land Plantation at Scotts, Mississippi, who predicted that aerial dusting companies would be organized to contract with individual planters "at a certain price per acre."[41]

Much as Truesdell anticipated, Post developed a proposal for a decentralized commercial dusting enterprise, with small units operating relatively independently throughout a cotton-growing district. A centrally located repair depot would maintain the equipment and store aircraft over the winter. Post envisioned nine dusting units actively flying and three in reserve, treating approximately 65,000 acres per year. The cost for farmers would be at a lower overall cost than other methods.[42]

Aviation's first aerial applications company, Huff Daland Dusters, Inc., essentially followed Post's plan.

3

A CORPORATE PIONEER
IN THE DELTA

[Richard Farnsworth] Hoyt was one of the of the earliest
aviation financiers. In spite of his many and complicated financial
transactions—a corollary of his principal business as a partner
of Hayden, Stone—many fliers felt that he had a sportsman's
interest in aviation, and had furthered its development.

—ELSBETH FREUDENTHAL,
The Aviation Business

F ollowing World War I, the ready availability of large numbers of surplus
military aircraft discouraged venture capitalists from designing and
building new models and retarded the advancement of the aviation industry in the United States. Nevertheless, some research and development did
occur. Thomas Henri Huff and Elliot Daland, both engineers, submitted the
winning entry of a U.S. Army bid for an improved training-aircraft design. In
1920 they opened a private aviation-manufacturing enterprise in Ogdensburg,
New York, on the southern shore of the Saint Lawrence River, across from the
Canadian towns of Prescott and Brookville, Ontario. Huff was president and
Daland vice president of Huff Daland Company. As a predecessor company to
Delta Air Lines, it had a far-reaching and long-lasting influence on American
commercial aviation.

Huff was born in Glassboro, New Jersey, on June 22, 1892. He attended the
University of Pennsylvania and Massachusetts Institute of Technology, where
he taught aeronautical engineering from 1915 to 1916. From 1917 to 1919, he

was chief engineer at the Standard Aero Corporation, Elizabeth, New Jersey, where Daland was likewise employed from 1918 to 1919. Daland was born in Brookline, Massachusetts, on January 3, 1886, and educated in private schools. He graduated from Harvard in 1909 with a B.A. degree. His advanced education included studies in applied science in 1910 and later, in 1918, aeronautical engineering at the Massachusetts Institute of Technology.[1]

Huff and Causten Brown, the company's secretary-treasurer, met with Robert J. Donahue, president of the National Bank of Ogdensburg, who brought to their attention Joseph Leyare's vacant factory. Leyare had produced high-speed watercraft and had some experience in aircraft construction from work with Glenn Curtiss during World War I. The plant and a pool of craftsmen were immediately available; woodworking was an essential skill in the manufacture of boats as well as aircraft of that era. Huff and Daland partnered with Leyare in "the construction of airplanes, hydroplanes and hydroairplanes."[2] As an inducement, the local chamber of commerce raised $3,000 to rent the plant for a year "and place it in readiness for occupancy." Initially known as the Ogdensburg Aeroway Corporation, the Huff Daland Airplane Company was incorporated in Delaware in the spring of 1920, with capital stock of $150,000 but reportedly no local financing.[3] "The men connected with the project are thoroughly acquainted with their business," according to an Ogdensburg news article, "splendid gentlemen and are backing the enterprise with all their energy to make it a great, big humming success."[4] Thus a present-day quintessentially southern company, Delta Air Lines, has roots that reach from the border with Mexico to the doorstep of Canada.

One of Delta's earliest and longest-serving employees, Catherine Fitz-Gerald, was born in Ogdensburg on September 21, 1897, and hired as a stenographer.[5] Locally raised and educated at Saint Mary's Academy and the Ogdensburg Business School, she spent two years working for Huff Daland Company until it relocated to Bristol, Pennsylvania, in 1925.[6] In time, she joined Huff Daland Dusters in Monroe, Louisiana, and eventually moved with Delta to Atlanta, where she retired in 1966 after forty-two years.

Another early employee, George B. Post, recognized the potential of aviation. The nephew of Col. William H. Post and related to Mrs. Edward Crabb, both prominent Thousand Islands–area residents, on June 30, 1920, Post pioneered a flight from New York City to Ogdensburg, sharing the controls with

Lt. Virgil McKennea. Sources identify the aircraft as a "Model F" flying boat—assuredly a Curtiss Model F Flying Boat, as Huff Daland had not yet produced any aircraft. Over the summer, area residents were delighted with rides at Casino Island, near Alexandria, and at the Ogdensburg fair. Envisioning the possibility of an air route to New York City, local publicity enhanced the already favorable opinion of Huff Daland Company before production of its air machines had even begun.[7]

Post logged several hundred hours of flying time in many different types of aircraft before joining Huff Daland. Born on January 9, 1897, in New York City, he attended Cornell University for three years, studying mechanical engineering, and briefly did experimental work at Standard Aero Corporation at the same time as Huff and Daland. Post attended U.S. Navy primary flight training at Bayshore, Long Island, in 1918 and continued with advanced training at Pensacola, Florida. He held Naval Aviator Certificate No. 1198.[8]

In the fall of 1920—late but nonetheless timely in meeting the army's contest deadline—Huff Daland completed the prototype of its winning design and shipped it to McCook Field in Dayton for evaluation. Designed as a trainer, the HD 4 was powered by a 140-hp A.B.C. Wasp engine and had, as its distinguishing design feature, the upper-wing attachment incorporated directly into the airframe. "The fuselage is of special interest in that the lorogens [longerons] are carried directly to the upper wing, eliminating the use of the center section struts and wires. These gave rigidity to the structure, an additional factor of safety for the pilot and student. A special feature of the design is the entire absence of any wires. It is of the rigid trussed type with the struts of special Huff Daland design."[9]

In January 1921 the local newspaper approvingly noted that the factory employed about fifty workers and was busy building seven airplanes, "one of them for a Boston party who expects to use it in passenger and freight service."[10] The company's intent to provide commercial machines was evident from its earliest days.

A year later, in January 1922, Huff Daland won a competition for a new type of training plane to be used by both the army and navy. The design, named the Petrel, exemplified the company's philosophy of simplicity in design to facilitate production and repair. In a test flight conducted by Post, with a sales associate along as a passenger, the "'Petrel' broke all records for speed and climb for a machine with a 90-horse power Curtiss motor." Evaluation tests continued with favorable results at McCook Field, where Lt. Harold Ross Harris served as one of the army's test pilots.[11]

A pioneering aviator, Harris distinguished himself in a long career in both military and commercial air service. Born in Chicago in 1895 but raised in Los Angeles, California, his daughter, Alta Mae Stevens, described him as "a large genial man" with a "hearty laugh" and "an outsized appetite for work, for play, for food, as well as for competition."[12] Harris graduated from the California Institute of Technology and served in Italy as an army pilot, conducting Caproni bomber operations in Foggia during World War I. "After World War I, from 1918 to 1925, Harris served as Test Pilot and Chief of Flight Test research for the U. S. Army Air Service at McCook Field. Harris, then a lieutenant, became the first [military] pilot in this country to parachute in an emergency when he bailed out of his disintegrating experimental pursuit plane near Dayton, Ohio. Also, during this time Harris competed in many Aviation meets, and in 1926 held thirteen world flying records."[13]

In 1922 Huff Daland expanded into additional facilities along the waterfront on Riverside Avenue. Its plants hummed with activity to meet demand from a rush government order for pontoons to be delivered by early spring the following year. This production was in addition to aircraft orders that kept the factories operating night and day. In late 1923 a new opportunity materialized for an agricultural aircraft: "T. Porter and Thomas Huff have been in Pensacola, Florida, and Tallulah, Miss. [sic, Louisiana], in connection with securing a contract for constructing machines to be used for spraying cotton fields with boll weevil exterminators."[14] Post tested the Petrel's suitability for dusting in Tallulah. When he departed on a flight to Brooks Field at San Antonio, Texas, about 200 miles along his route, he encountered engine trouble. Although he escaped without injury from a forced landing, the severely damaged aircraft had to be shipped back to Ogdensburg for extensive repairs.[15]

It is a testament to Huff's and Daland's decisiveness and their company's manufacturing capabilities that a design was quickly adapted—it is believed from the Petrel—for crop-dusting purposes in 1924. The Puffer, as it was affectionately nicknamed, was a rugged ship with a sturdy landing gear. It had a large-capacity hopper with a top-access door for fast loading. The bin, situated near the center of gravity, contributed to the aircraft's in-flight stability and maneuverability. A 200-hp Wright Whirlwind engine permitted cruise speeds of 80–90 mph, quick takeoffs, a slow approach speed, and enough reserve power to climb steeply over 100-foot trees that might surround a field. Rounding out its features were good visibility for the pilot and enough fuel, carried in upper-wing tanks, for four to five hours' endurance.[16] These characteristics along with balloon tires, a later modification, met the design specifications resulting from experiments using obsolescent aircraft on loan from the military under Coad's direction at the Delta Laboratory.[17] Huff Daland designed two crop-dusting airplanes: a smaller version, the Model 5, and a larger one, the Model 31.

Lieutenant Harris, at McCook Field, and Sgt. William McConnell, with the Agriculture Department, test flew the smaller prototype on July 28 and 30, 1924. The plane then departed for Tallulah on August 4, piloted by Sergeant McConnell and carrying Harris and Daland, who spent some time with Coad and others evaluating the experimental activities underway at the laboratory.[18]

In February 1925 Harris tested a large duster aircraft—probably the Model 31—under difficult conditions over the windy, ice-covered Saint Lawrence River. Weather forced the cancelation of flight operations on the appointed day, but a few days later, more-favorable conditions prevailed. Flight Commander Hobbs, with the Canadian Department of Aviation; Commander Zarr, chief of training, representing the Argentine air forces; Elmer Johnson, chief engineer at the Delta Laboratory; and other interested representatives observed the event.[19]

The need for a larger aircraft was evident from demonstrations conducted on peach orchards in Georgia in November 1924 and again in March 1925, which were conducted by smaller types. Oliver Snapp of the U.S. Peach Insect Laboratory at Fort Valley, Georgia, observed that a bigger bin was necessary for commercial operations. The new Model 31 duster was that larger airplane required, carrying more payload.[20] Both the large and small Huff Daland models had their advantages and disadvantages, depending on the size and shape of fields and obstructions.

Huff Daland Dusters was incorporated in Delaware on March 2, 1925, capitalized at $250,000 and with Post named as director and general manager. Its business objectives were broadly stated, to include "the carrying and transportation of passengers, goods, wares, and merchandise, for all kinds of commercial purposes, including agriculture and forestry, such as dusting, seeding, planting, and fertilizing, forestry patrol and survey, for aerial survey and photography, for any and all kinds of uses, for exhibiting or advertising purposes, at any place within or without the United States."[21]

By 1925, Huff Daland Company had outgrown its facilities, with no room to expand in Ogdensburg. After identifying the former Harriman Merchant Ship Building plant on thirty acres fronting the Delaware River in Bristol, Pennsylvania, as available, the move to that site was completed in September 1925. Three training planes, the third built under a contract for the Argentine government, were shipped from New York as soon as they were finished, even before being test flown. During its five years in Ogdensburg, Huff Daland had improved manufacturing processes and advanced airplane performance and design. An important innovation was the elimination of wire bracing thanks to strengthened struts and wing structures. In addition to its military designs, the company explored commercial uses of aircraft. Crop-dusting, air-ambulance, and photo-mapping models were contemplated or developed during the company's time in New York.

In 1926, by now an established aircraft design and manufacturing company, Huff Daland attracted the attention of Richard Farnsworth Hoyt, an ambitious Wall Street financier.[22] The significance of Hoyt's role in the evolution of Delta Air Lines has not been fully understood and deserves comment. Notwithstanding his high profile in business, society, and sport, he is noteworthy for promoting American aviation. A fixture in New York banking and finance, Hoyt "was regarded as Wall Street's aviation oracle, a gatekeeper of its inside paradise, the man to see about any proposition that had to do with aviation."[23] In his capacity as a partner in the Hayden, Stone, & Company investment-banking firm, with offices in New York and Boston, Hoyt had a hand in creating some of the aviation industry's giants, among them Pan American Airways and the Curtiss-Wright Corporation. Not only did he help broker deals, but he also held positions on several boards of directors. From his financial and executive perches, Hoyt wielded power, influence, and vision.[24] When Huff Daland relocated to Bristol, it piqued his aviation interest.

Hoyt was born on July 3, 1888, in Revere, Massachusetts. He attended the private Volkmann School and matriculated at Harvard, where he graduated magna cum laude in 1910. Afterward he started as a clerk at the New York investment firm Hayden, Stone, & Company. During World War 1, he worked with Col. Jesse G. Vincent at McCook Field, where the army concentrated its engine- and aircraft-development programs. With the knowledge of aviation acquired during the war and as a testament to his capability, he rose rapidly in the investment firm, becoming a partner in 1919. As chairman of the board of Wright Aeronautical Corporation, Hoyt helped facilitate the merger of Curtiss Aeroplane and Motor Company with Wright Aeronautical in 1929 to form the giant Curtiss-Wright Corporation, serving as the chairman of its board.[25]

Yet Hoyt's interest in aviation involved more than banking and finance. He took a personal interest in the field, too, becoming a pilot. In 1925 he served on the committee that arranged the New York Air Races that were held at Mitchel Field on Long Island. Hoyt also served as chairman of the Committee on Aeronautics of the Merchants Association, which advocated the need for a New York City airport. "The western side of Manhattan, across the Hudson River, is in many ways the logical point for a landing field," he observed. "Our committee is inclined to believe that a point somewhere on the Jersey Meadows is by far the most desirable location."[26] An alternate site was Governors Island, but the army refused to release it for development. Hoyt argued, with prescient foresight, that "commercial airports should be provided at public expense" so as to prevent any single company from "controlling service to the city."[27]

Hoyt supported the ill-fated attempt of the *American Legion,* piloted by Lt. Cmdr. Noel Davis and Lt. Stanton Wooster, to cross the Atlantic in early 1927. Following those men's unfortunate deaths on a test flight, Hoyt nevertheless praised Charles Lindbergh and the team of Clarence Chamberlin and Charles Levine (the first transatlantic passenger) who successfully completed the journey a few months later.[28]

Huff Daland thrived at its new location on the Delaware River and built on its success to became one of the largest aircraft manufacturers in the country. With the increased tempo of production and rising development costs for newer models, the company needed investment capital.[29] At a special meeting of stockholders held at 25 Broad Street in New York City, new stock was proffered and fully subscribed. Not surprisingly, this was Hoyt's business address.[30] The company was reorganized at this time as the Keystone Aircraft Corporation. Huff announced his retirement around the same time, and in November

1926 Edgar N. Gott, formerly of the Fokker and Boeing aircraft companies, was elected president and chairman of the board of directors of Keystone.[31] Gott also joined the Hayden, Stone group, signifying his close association with Hoyt.[32] Notwithstanding the name change, Keystone retained the original company's objective of encouraging the commercial use of airplanes. Both it and its subsidiary Huff Daland Dusters came under Hoyt's financial umbrella.

Huff Daland Dusters was headquartered in Macon, Georgia, with Post as general manager and Harris operations manager. Dan E. Tobin served as chief pilot, and Roger William Riis was its advertising manager. Farmers contracted with the company at the rate of $7 per acre. Following Post's earlier plan, a total of eighteen aircraft, twelve pilots, and twenty mechanics were to be staged in nine locations, two dusters each at each site. One of the planes would remain in reserve while the other dusted. A pilot and the mechanics would live nearby. Sites, including Macon, were selected from more than forty surveyed. Harris hired the pilots, the first being James "Joe" Greer.[33] Among the others he chose were Tobin, N. L. Cote, Eugene Stevens, George Ott, Arthur Gray, Elliot Dunn, Earl Potts, and, as chief of maintenance, Douglas Culver.[34] Charles A. Lindbergh, a potential candidate, turned down $2,400 for a year dusting cotton in Georgia—to him, "the pay seemed too low."[35]

Without Harris knowing, a position opened for him through an arrangement made between Huff Daland Dusters and the head of the Army Air Service in Washington. General Patrick granted Harris a leave of absence from the army for a year, conditioned on Harris's agreement to join the firm. Huff approached Harris in Dayton with the proposition, which he accepted. Harris left his position as chief of the Flight Test Branch, Engineering Division, Army Air Service in February 1925.

Sometime in 1925—the exact date is uncertain—Harris appeared as a witness before the Morrow board on national aviation policy. In his testimony Harris used as an example of the benefits of commercial aviation the development of crop-dusting pioneered by the Agriculture Department and American industry. The privately financed Huff Daland Dusters Company, Harris said, was "the first fundamentally sound commercial aeronautical venture in this country . . . [and] has met with a most amazingly cordial reception from the planters for which it has operated." The enterprise was successful, he testified, because it was an "economic service," not because it was an "airplane service."

To ensure standardization and safety, he advocated for governmental inspection of aircraft and licensing of operators.[36] The Morrow Board's recommendations were incorporated into the 1926 Air Commerce Act.

Some background is in order to understand the reasons why Huff Daland Dusters chose Macon for its headquarters and why it stayed there so briefly before moving to Monroe in the Mississippi Delta. Harris recollected: "I must have known at the time but can't remember now. Someone decided that the Duster headquarters should be in Macon, Georgia, so I moved to Macon from Dayton, Ohio."[37]

Perhaps one reason was that Georgia took an active approach to directly assist farmers and welcomed the new enterprise. Authorities reasonably assumed that having an aerial-applications company in the state would boost productivity and warranted official support. In 1924 the Georgia Department of Agriculture focused its attention on cotton as the most important factor in an estimated $27,000,000 gain in the total value of the state's crops. It praised the State College of Agriculture in Athens and other agencies for helping farmers with the timely application of calcium arsenate.[38] The department's assessment is justified when comparing the production results of 1923 to 1924. In 1923, 3,844,000 acres of cotton were planted, with an average yield of 82 pounds per acre; in 1924, there were 745,000 fewer acres planted, but the yield rose to 157 pounds per acre—a 91-percent increase.[39] A large measure of this success is attributable to the conventional application of calcium arsenate, as only a limited use of experimental aerial applications had occurred that might have influenced the results, namely, the flight demonstrations at Athens on August 26 and at Cordele on August 28, organized by the board of trustees of the State College of Agriculture.[40]

In November 1924 Oliver Snapp, in charge of the peach insect laboratory at Fort Valley, and Huff Daland Company conducted joint experiments to determine the suitability of aircraft in dusting peach orchards. Encouraged by the State College of Agriculture and the support of the U.S. Agriculture Department, as well as backing by Georgia's Department of Agriculture, Board of Entomology, and Board of Health, these flights continued into 1925.[41] With such institutional support and favorable publicity, there was good reason for Huff Daland Dusters to choose Macon as its operational base. Another inducement came from the city's chamber of commerce, which built a hangar for the company's use at Camp Wheeler Airfield.[42] Peach trees were dusted at Montezuma, Georgia, in March.[43] "Growers in this section are enthusiastic over the demonstration," one local newspaper reported. "Mr. [Dr. T. H.] McHatton, of the State College, Athens, and Mr. Demaree of the federal government, working in the pecan industry, were here to witness the demonstration as more than a hundred growers looked on." Harris claimed "complete satisfaction," and Snapp, "considered the world's leading peach authority," commended Huff Daland for the demonstration.[44] Lynn McKenzie reported on the success of the dusting: "I have never shipped more beautiful peaches in all my life, and I might say that I received more per package than any other grower in Montezuma."[45] Notwithstanding this testimonial, peach dusting from the air proved inconclusive. "Weather conditions were unfavorable for the development of both curculio and brown rot," Snapp reported. "The fruit from the orchards dusted from airplanes compared very favorably with that from orchards dusted from ground mule-drawn machine."[46]

By early June, a total of 250,000 peach trees had been treated, but the bulk of dusting work would come from cotton, once the boll weevil became active. The newly organized Huff Daland Dusters planned to treat 60,000–65,000 acres from nine locations in Georgia, Mississippi, North Carolina, Alabama, and Louisiana. The Laurinburg, North Carolina, unit was ready to begin dusting in Scotland County in July. Another unit was ready to go in Newellton, Tensas Parish, Louisiana. Everything appeared to be in readiness for a busy season; all that was necessary was for the boll weevil to make its appearance.[47]

Abruptly, on July 8, 1925, the *Macon Daily Telegraph* reported Huff Daland Dusters would cease operations in Georgia, stating insufficient business as the reason: "Officials of the company stated yesterday that less than 1,000 acres of cotton had been dusted in Georgia near Vidalia this year, which was not sufficient business to warrant continuing their operations in the state." Expecting to dust 25,000 acres in Louisiana (with 12,000 of that already completed) and 15,000 in North Carolina, the company chose to focus its resources elsewhere.[48]

The decision ultimately was due to unforeseen business developments. The company anticipated operating in only one or two states initially but found the demand stretched its resources too widely. A new plan established two maintenance bases and relocated employees to areas where the company could operate more efficiently. Louis H. Kohler, the Huff Daland's auditor, was to head the Louisiana base. Harris, who was now managing director, later gave two reasons for why the company left Georgia: "(A) the cotton farms were small and (B) the cotton was not long (1 1/4" each strand) staple and consequently didn't have as good a price on the market as the staple cotton grown in the Mississippi Delta."[49]

It appears the company began operations in Macon with the intention of dusting Georgia peach orchards, followed by the prospect of treating pecan trees. While this business was significant, the real money came from dusting cotton, which would begin later in the season. Boll weevil infestations were not uniform year over year, and 1925 appeared to be one of its light years. A total of 3,662,000 acres of cotton were planted in 1925, with a yield of 155 pounds per acre. While 18-percent more acreage was planted compared to 1924, the yield per acre dropped only 1 percent—virtually unchanged.[50] Probably, the need never arose for Georgia farmers to rely on expensive aerial dusting.

Historian James Giesen's explanation is more plausible. Before the boll weevil came to Georgia, it was already too expensive to grow cotton on the state's marginal farmland. Even with higher prices and increased production, he notes, "the costs of land, seed, fertilizer, ginning all increased as well, making it as hard to earn a profit when cotton was selling at thirty cents a pound as when the price was near eight cents."[51] Farmers were left with little money or credit to pay for aerial dusting.

In mid-1925, the dusters temporarily moved to Tallulah. Meanwhile, Monroe's air-minded civic and business leaders, who wanted to make the city an aerial center, emerged as some of the South's earliest and most consistent aviation proponents.[52] They induced Huff Daland Dusters to relocate to the city, constructed Smoot and Selman airports, and promoted airmail. They later supported Delta's transition from a crop-dusting company to an airline and helped finance the fledgling Delta Air Service. Without the vision of Monroe's leaders, Delta might have evolved into an airline elsewhere—or not at all.

Travis Oliver, president of the Central Savings Bank and Trust, one of Monroe's earliest and most influential aviation promoters, served on the Aviation Committee of the city's chamber of commerce. He encouraged Harris to make the move from Georgia to Louisiana; the company's presence would put the city on the nation's aviation map. City of Monroe and Ouachita Parish politicians, along with local businessmen, jointly agreed to provide a suitable landing field and hangar. The principal supporters were Oliver, Arnold Bernstein, Monroe's mayor; and Theodore F. Terzia, president of the Ouachita Parish Police Jury. Huff Daland Dusters began operating from a small airstrip, known as Smoot Field, built along the Winnsboro highway about two miles south of Monroe. As a customary military honor, Harris suggested naming the airstrip after H. Victor Smoot, World War I aviator and duster pilot, who had died recently from injuries in a crash during a heavy rainstorm while surveying high-tension power lines for the Louisiana Power Company.[53]

Harris also sat on the Monroe Chamber of Commerce Aviation Committee with Oliver as well as Prentiss M. "Print" Atkins; the last two significantly contributed to Delta's future. When Huff Daland Dusters relocated to the Mississippi Delta, it was a pioneer, albeit a corporate one, much like the Percy family of an earlier time. It, too, opened new territory based on treating cotton with pesticide, only applying it from the air. In time, its horizon extended far beyond the Delta and all the way to South America.

THE EAGLE AND THE CONDOR

> Such was the extent of Leguía's Yankeephilia that he ordered
> a portrait of President James Madison hung in the presidential
> palace and actually declared July fourth a national
> holiday in honor of the United States.
>
> —PETER FLINDELL KLARÉN,
> *Peru, Society, and Nationhood in the Andes*

Key events leading to the formation of Delta Air Lines occurred in South America. While there is justification to the argument that Huff Daland Dusters shifted operations during the winter months to the Andean country of Peru to more fully utilize its agricultural equipment south of the equator, where the seasons are reversed, a full explanation is more discerning. The company actually used the North American agricultural offseason to refurbish and repair equipment. In addition, winter dusting opportunities existed much closer to Monroe in Mexico and California than in South America. Even with the ease of transiting the Panama Canal (opened in 1914), operations in the Southern Hemisphere would not have been practical without tariff and tax incentives by the Peruvian government and contractual guarantees of cotton growers. The opportunity for profit balanced against the risk was acceptable at a time when the price of cotton on world markets was declining and competitors challenged Huff Daland Dusters' presence in the Mississippi Delta. Specifically, on October 6, 1925, the articles of incorporation of the White Flying Dusters, located in Tallulah (but not associated with the laboratory), were filed. Article VIII states: "The object and purpose of said corporation is for the operation of flying machines for commercial purposes and especially for the purpose of dusting agricultural crops and orchards with insect poison in the State of Louisiana and elsewhere."[1] The nature of the dusting business allowed operators quickly to set up shop anywhere, undercutting Huff Daland's lead in the industry.

Given the challenges, what compelling factors drew Huff Daland Dusters to South America? The incentive originated with Peru's president, Augusto B. Leguía, who welcomed foreign corporations to come and modernize his country. Some Peruvian history helps contextualize Leguía's vision and Huff Daland Dusters', Woolman's, and Harris's roles in the events that followed. To begin, historian Arthur V. Metcalfe provides a description of Leguía—the man was diminutive in stature but large in presence.

> Don Augusto, as he was sometimes called, was small and slight of appearance. A dapper little man, he dressed beautifully: slim feet in buttoned patent leather boots, skinny form well draped in a morning coat from London, a high silk hat which offset the too long sharp nose. Seen without the hat the nose gave the key to his being. The features were fox like: the chin was sharp, the mouth long, the bushy brows concealed eyes that glittered but did not warm. On the hands was black hair. Although the man was old the body was rhythmically agile and graceful.[2]

In Peruvian historiography, the period from 1895 to 1919 is generally known as the Aristocratic Republic, characterized by seeming political stability. The Civilista and Democrata Parties joined to overthrow the repressive regime of Andres Caceres and then governed through an elite oligarchy, "an informal group, known as the 'Twenty-Four Friends,' [that] met regularly at the exclusive Club National to discuss the management of national affairs." Bound by "family and kinship" and "culturally and intellectually" oriented toward Europe, particularly France, these elitists "hardly knew the rest of the country." Leguía, one of the club's members, after a term as treasury minister served as president for four years (1908-12). Subsequent discord within the dominant Civilistas and Leguía's attempt to rig the 1911 congressional elections weakened his party and ended his presidency. Leguía sat out the next seven years while waiting for circumstances to change. He lived in exile in London and New York, where he used his time contacting business and financial leaders who would help in reconstructing Peru's battered post–World War I economy.[3]

The economic disruptions of the Great War hit Peruvian workers hard. A falling standard of living provoked unrest, and a major strike in 1919 toppled Pres. José Pardo's government. Leguía returned from exile and once again became president, although now in opposition to his former Civilista Party. He advocated a populist national agenda, La Patria Nueva (New Fatherland), designed to marginalize political opponents and consolidate his power by appealing to a broader middle-class electorate.[4]

The eleven years of Leguía's rule, from 1919 to 1930, "was dubbed the 'Oncenio' by Peruvians who took the term from the Spanish word for 'eleven' or 'once.'" Following World War I, the United States replaced Britain as the country's primary investor, and American capital fueled the expansion of mining, agriculture, and urban development. The "cornerstone of Leguía's economic policy was . . . promotion of the export-import model of growth."[5] Cultivated land no longer produced consumable crops but was planted with exportable cash crops, primarily sugar and cotton. "Agriculture contributed greatly to the prosperity of the Peruvian economy throughout the Oncenio, with sugar and cotton heading the list of most valuable exports."[6] Leguía's other projects included road building and 600 miles of railroad construction.[7]

Foreign ideological influences promoted free-market capitalism and individual entrepreneurship within the country. The economic effects well suited Peru's elite, including Leguía, a successful businessman who, for a time, was the general manager of the Peruvian-Ecuadorian-Bolivian branches of the New York Life Insurance Company. He spoke fluent English and was "at home with the American business mentality." As president he "strongly believed that Peru's path to development lay in its ability to attract capital, technology, markets, and business know-how from advanced countries of the West."[8]

Ruling elites modernized Lima to conform to their European vision. Along with economic and class changes, they transformed the city's landscape socially and architecturally. During the Oncenio, the streets were paved and widened, middle- and upper-class houses constructed, parks created, and the city center brightened up with new buildings, shops, and hotels. "It became a showplace . . . to attract foreign investors and entrepreneurs on whom the administration was counting for an economic boost."[9] Indeed, the caption of a photograph showing an intersection with a traffic light, taken by Huff Daland Dusters' Harold Harris, reads, "the modern traffic system in Lima."[10]

Not only was early twentieth-century Lima's cityscape being reconstructed physically, but elites, influenced by positivist ideology and European culture, changed the cultural landscape as well, primarily through sports and recreation. Leguía's favorite recreation was "the regular Sunday afternoon horse races . . . at the Santa Beatriz Hippodrome," where "all Lima knew he would always be on hand."[11] In modernizing the capital, venues for public entertainment were designated and, with the advent of electric lighting, nighttime hours regulated. The "ruling class, happily ensconced in comfortable splendor in Lima, was thoroughly Eurocentric and Frenchified;" to Limeños, "Lima represented 'civilization.'"[12]

Coupled with the international outreach of Peruvian leaders came a new "air mindedness" that encouraged North American and European aviation interests in the Andean country. In the 1920s businessmen thought all of "Latin America appeared to be one of the single largest potential markets for aviation exploitation."[13] For example, in 1922 Capt. Walter Simon, an American who served as the assistant director of aeronautics for Peru, hoped "to bring about the establishment of air communications between Lima and Panama, which will mean the saving of much time and bring [t]his country nearer northern business markets."[14]

Having an American administrator in a Peruvian department was not unusual for Leguía. He "often argued that to elevate Peru to the level of the Western nations, the Peruvian would first have to acquire the skills and mentalities of the Westerner. On one occasion he stated: 'My hope is to put an American in charge of every branch of our government.'"[15] Leguía purposely turned to the United States for economic and technical assistance.

Aeronautical enterprises recognized the potential and made inroads into the market. Jimmy Doolittle, representing the Curtiss Aeroplane Export Company, sailed to South America in early 1926 (and again in 1928) to demonstrate the fast, maneuverable Curtiss P-1 Hawk fighter, powered by the 400-hp Curtiss D-12 engine.[16] Doolittle's liner made ports of call in Peru, but he did not demonstrate or sell any of the Curtiss machines; Peruvian authorities had already committed to buying military aircraft from rival Keystone Corporation. Subsequently, in the face of strong German competition, Doolittle sold nine Curtiss airplanes to Chile.[17]

Faucett Airlines, a prominent aeronautical company of local origins, started when Curtiss dispatched one of its mechanics, Elmer "Slim" Faucett, to Peru in 1920 as a service representative. He earned Peru's first civil pilot's license at the Aviation School at Bellavista.[18] Enterprising and charismatic, Faucett piloted the first flight from Lima to Iquitos over the Andes on October 5, 1922, and, with the help of Peruvian financing, started his own airline. In time locals "became familiar with the orange and white aircraft of Faucett Airlines, largely run and operated by Peruvians." Perceived as one of their own, Peruvians held Faucett in high esteem.[19]

In North America powerful U.S. business interests, in alliance with the federal government, challenged Faucett's ambitions in Peru and countered "semigovernmental European air lines in South America." This public-private relationship characterized Pan American Airlines (Pan Am) as the "chosen instrument" and stemmed from the United States' perceived "need for one American foreign airline."[20] Into this mix of personalities, favoritism, intrigue, and politics—and in an extraordinary twist of circumstances—small Huff Daland Dusters proved to be the catalyst in producing, not one, but *three* remarkable twentieth-century aviation enterprises: Pan Am, Pan American–Grace Airways, and Delta Air Lines. And if its influence, though indirect, on Faucett is considered, the number is *four* airlines.

"The relatively underdeveloped state of [Peru's] economy and more important, the pro-American attitude of the Leguía regime" drew Huff Daland Dusters into the fray.[21] Foreign businessmen arriving in Lima were immediately immersed in the political, entrepreneurial, and culture milieu of Leguía's *Oncenio.* Both C. E. Woolman and Harold Harris had authority as vice presidents when representing Huff Daland Dusters in Peru but were never there at the same time. They ensconced in the impressive new Hotel Bolivar, opened in 1924 as part of Leguía's modernization program. The hotel, located on the Plaza San Martin at the center of Lima, was the "meeting point for people of a certain status"[22] As events unfolded, these two extraordinary men were catapulted into long and successful aviation careers—Woolman with Delta Air Lines and Harris, who remained in Peru for several years, with Panagra. Harris rejoined the army during World War II and rose to the rank of brigadier general. Following the war, he served briefly as president of Northwest Airlines.

No one has left a more indelible mark on Delta Air Lines than Woolman. Although the company has encountered turbulence through the years and is now an amalgamation of absorbed airlines, historically, his name is synonymous with Delta's. Woolman's values of thrift, safety, integrity, pride, teamwork, and service set the example for employees and are a legacy of Delta's formative years. His life spanned a time of remarkable inventiveness and opportunity in an industry that did not exist when he was born. What guided Woolman along the path of his life's journey? What was his relationship to the company's origin? When and where does he fit in?[23] Woolman himself provided the answer, dividing his career into two periods. The first, from 1913 to 1925, occurred while he was an agent for the Department of Agriculture at Louisiana State University. The second began when he took a position as chief entomologist with Huff Daland Dusters.[24]

The Woolman family name can be traced to John Woolman (1655–1718), a weaver born in Painswick, Gloucestershire, England, who arrived in New Jersey in 1687.[25] Collett Everman Woolman was born on October 8, 1889, in Bloomington Township, Monroe, Indiana, to Albert Jefferson Woolman (1861–1918) and Doura Campbell (1865–1954). He had two sisters, Xenia May and Rachel Margaret.[26] Rachel was born in Duluth, Minnesota, where their father taught science at Central High School.[27] Albert Woolman earned an A.M. degree from Indiana University in 1893 and became a scientist in ichthyology (the study of fishes) and eventually an assistant professor at the University of Illinois.[28] He studied under Dr. Barton Warren Evermann (absent the second "n," Collett's middle name). Late in life Albert was an agent with the New York Life Insurance Company.[29] The Woolman family apparently placed great value in education, with all the children earning degrees from the University of Illinois: Xenia (A.B. in literature and arts) in 1906; Collett (B.S. in agriculture), 1912; and Rachel (B.S. in household science), 1916.[30]

Collett attended the University of Illinois Academy (1904–8) and the University of Illinois on a scholarship (1908–12). He was a member of the Agricultural Glee Club, Agricultural Dance Committee, and played on the senior football team.[31] During his freshman and again in his sophomore year, the young man sailed to Europe by working as a "chambermaid to over 800 calves."[32]

The reasons for his trips, travel days, and destinations are not evident from surviving materials. Documents do record, however, that on each occasion he returned from Liverpool, England, aboard the White Star liner SS *Cymric*, arriving in Boston on September 17, 1909, and September 1, 1910, respectively. On the first crossing he was accompanied by his classmate Thomas McLean Jasper; on the second, by classmate Orrie Hagar Brown—both earned degrees in 1911. Official entries in the immigration books give their occupations as "cattlemen" and were with a group of "all cattlemen." Famed aviator Claude Grahame-White and AVRO founder Alliott Verdon Roe, participants in the 1910 Harvard-Boston Aero Meet (held September 3–13), were fellow passengers on his second crossing.[33] Woolman recalled: "On the way back, . . . [m]ost of my time was spent in the hold getting his [Grahame-White's] engine in shape for a meet at Boston. I didn't get to the meet 'cause I was due back at school."[34]

After graduation Collett took a job as assistant plantation manager in Pantigo, Beaufort County, North Carolina. In 1913 he went to Allendale, West Baton Rouge Parish, Louisiana, as plantation manager. In 1914 the Smith-Lever Act established the Cooperative Extension Service, and despite his youth, Collett relocated to Monroe as the Ouachita Parish farm agricultural agent.[35] One of the service's objectives was to inform farmers on the best agricultural practices and latest available research. As a college graduate with an agricultural degree, he was exceptionally well qualified.

Woolman's duties required him to travel about the parish, meeting with farmers and planting demonstration plots. He contributed commentary on agricultural matters in a bimonthly column, A Thought for the Progressive Farmer, in the *Monroe News-Star*. His writing was of timely interest, topics including, for example, the quality of cotton seed following a period of wet weather, advice on planting early cotton, how to handle hog cholera, whether to store corn for a better price in the future, and so forth. After a few months on the job, parish officials complimented Woolman on the "splendid work he has done" and recommended him for retention with a pay raise.[36]

In June 1916 Woolman was promoted to district agent for the extension service and moved to Baton Rouge. Taking his leave, a newspaper noted: "Mr. Woolman has done a great work in Ouachita parish as demonstration agent and has won a number of close personal friends who regret to see him leave. Monroe, however, will be within his district and he will visit here every 30 days." Woolman's ties to Monroe and the associations he made with public and business leaders were crucial in the second phase of his life involving Huff Daland Dusters and Delta Air Lines. Prentiss M. Atkins (president of the Monroe Hardware), Oliver (vice president of the Central Savings Bank and Trust), Clarence E. Faulk (editor of the *Monroe News-Star*), and city and parish officials had a favorable impression of him long before they collaborated on starting Delta.[37]

At age twenty-six and coincidental to his promotion to district agent, Woolman took on another responsibility by marrying his college sweetheart, Helen Peters Fairfield, on August 8, 1916. Helen was born in Petersburg, Michigan, on August 17, 1893, to George Day Fairfield (1865–1921) and Mary Adelaide Peters (1866–1942). She had one brother, John Edward Fairchild, born in July 1898 in Illinois. Her father earned an A.B. degree, class of 1888, from Oberlin College in Ohio. And, from 1889 to 1893, he was the U.S. vice consul in Lyons, France, while simultaneously a Faculte des Lettres student. He taught at De Pauw University, the University of Illinois, and Syracuse University. George Fairfield finally joined the faculty of Beloit College in 1907 as associate professor of romance languages.[38]

Helen Fairfield attended Iowa State and Beloit College before earning her A.B. degree, in the class of 1914, at the University of Illinois. Subsequently, she taught home science at East Aurora High School in Aurora, Illinois, and was head of domestic science at the Elgin (Illinois) High School. Helen and Collett were married at the Kappa Gamma sorority house in Champaign, Illinois. About 100 guests and many sorority sisters attended.[39] Afterward, the couple settled at 524 Middle Street in Baton Rouge.[40] Both of their children were born at that residence—Barbara Jane on June 3, 1922, and Martha Ann on July 6, 1924.[41]

In 1918 there was a breakthrough in boll weevil control at the Delta Laboratory. Coad found that the pests drank regularly from raindrops and dew that collected on the plants. When the moisture was mixed with a dusting of calcium arsenate, it created a "knock out drop." This important finding was disseminated in newspapers and through an Agriculture Department pamphlet available for five cents.[42] It is not apparent that Woolman was directly involved with the discovery, although it is reasonable to assume that, in the performance of his duties, he knew of the laboratory's work. He traveled widely from his Baton Rouge headquarters to meet with parish agents and farmers, collectively or individually, to inform them of the latest research. His field diaries and notes from 1916 to 1922 disclose his several visits to Tallulah. Noticeably absent, though, is any mention of experiments, work, or meetings with Coad.[43]

Notwithstanding Coad's research or Woolman's and other agents' efforts to inform planters of the latest practices, Louisiana farmers were not adopting control techniques utilizing calcium arsenate. This was despite "a whole season of talking on the subject," according to Clifton E. Hester of East Carroll Parish, and "several months of demonstration work," according to T. M. Milliken of Morehouse Parish. Better results were attained in neighboring Mississippi. There, applying calcium arsenate, close spacing of plants, sowing an improved seed, and proper draining of fields boosted cotton yields. Consequently, Woolman encouraged Hester and Milliken to take Louisiana farmers on tours across the river to see for themselves. Yet despite the evidence, many stuck with the old ways.

Woolman himself strove to inform planters on the use of calcium arsenate. A well-attended meeting he helped organize in 1924 featured Dr. William Robert Perkins, director of the Louisiana Extension Service, as speaker. Perkins conveyed the benefits of the intelligent use of the poison to control boll weevils.[44] Still, while a solution to that problem was at hand, its adoption remained in doubt. Perhaps this influenced Woolman to take a leave of absence from the extension service in June 1925 in order to test airplane dusting on a 4,000-acre tract near Tallulah.[45] His leave might not have been voluntary but rather an assignment, as he was respected as "one of the leading members of the staff of the Louisiana State University agricultural department." Perhaps it was mere chance, but the timing of Woolman's departure coincided with the move of Huff Daland Dusters from Macon to Monroe.[46]

In 1925 Woolman was thirty-five years old and well established on a career path with the extension service. His experience and expertise were in agriculture; what then accounts for his focus shifting to aviation? Woolman had no background in flying, surely was not aware of the profound significance of his move, and probably had no expectation of spending the rest of his life in the emerging industry. Likely, the key was no one with the dusting company had southern roots. Huff Daland Dusters wanted a person known and respected in the agricultural community—someone to meet with planters and sign contracts. Woolman was the right man in the right place at the right time to apply his intellect, personality, and leadership to an entirely new commercial venture.[47]

Meanwhile, agricultural pests were not endemic just to the United States, and news reached South American planters of the effectiveness of dusting from the air. But the idea to send airplanes, personnel, and supplies south of the equator to take advantage of the opposing seasons did not come from Huff Daland Dusters; it originated with an inquiry by Peruvian planters on how to control infestations on their cotton.[48] Dr. Warren Elmer Hinds, an entomologist with the Experimental Station and Extension Division at Louisiana State University, suggested they use "aeroplane application[s]" of calcium arsenate.[49] Planters saw the advantage of using aircraft to deal with armyworm infestations in the large cotton-exporting regions of coastal Peru and sent a representative to explore the possibility.

Pedro Beltrán, the politically connected owner of a large hacienda, sailed for the United States. He inquired at the Agriculture Department as to what could be done and was directed to the Delta Laboratory in Tallulah. There, Harris recounts, Coad "suggested airplane dusting and there was only one commercial outfit that did that sort of thing. He recommended that Beltrán talk to us."[50] Leguía's pro-American economic policy and Beltrán's assurances convinced Huff Daland Dusters to dispatch a representative to Peru. Traveling to Lima in the fall of 1926, Woolman negotiated a concession and contracted for aerial dusting, although not as a pilot himself. Harris praised him as "a terrific salesman" but cautioned that "he was basically an entomologist; he didn't know anything about aviation."[51]

This assessment begs the question of when Woolman became a pilot. He held Private Pilot Certificate No. 22370, which he renewed with an expiration date of September 30, 1935.[52] Barbara Woolman Preston observed that her father "didn't have many hours and didn't qualify for commercial [flying] or to fly passengers." She "vividly recalls" a "thirty-mile flight which took 45 minutes" with her father from Monroe to Lake Providence "in a Curtiss-Wright Junior plane with two open cockpits and a pusher propeller." The Curtiss was acquired in 1931, delivered from the factory in Saint Louis by Joe Greer to be used as a demonstrator and flight trainer.[53] Its short takeoff distance and slow landing speed made it so easy to fly that it was possible for a student to solo in a day.[54] Perhaps Woolman learned to fly when Delta's scheduled air service was interrupted from 1930 to 1934. According to his son, Greer flew with Woolman frequently, teaching him aerobatics in his fleet biplane "from 1924 to 1934," but the record is inconclusive.[55] Pilots are known to keep careful notes of dates, equipment flown, engine, location, and duration in loose form or in a personal logbook and talk freely of their experiences. That Woolman participated in an air meet in Bastrop, Louisiana, possibly in the Curtiss, on October 8, 1932, is documented, but details are lacking.[56] A logbook is not among the items in the Woolman files.

Years later, in addressing the question of whether Woolman "actually flew," Harris did not know but speculated that he "may have ridden as a passenger with some of the dusting equipment at Tallulah in the experiments carried out by Dr. Coad."[57] Virginia P. Welch, a University of Illinois graduate, recalls Woolman explaining at one of her alumnae meetings in Atlanta that he "got his start as a crop duster."[58] This was not a purposeful misrepresentation by any means, but without clarification, one might conclude that he was a duster pilot, while in fact he was in the business of crop dusting. There is no question Harris flew duster aircraft and therefore was technically a duster pilot but nevertheless acknowledged that he "personally never did any commercial crop dusting."[59]

Notwithstanding Woolman's limited flying background, Harris observed, as a salesman, "that didn't make any difference."[60] Woolman had a congenial personality, understood agricultural issues, and was familiar with cotton pests. He knew the company's policies, had met with planters face to face to negotiate contracts, and, by the time he went to Peru, knew enough about dusting from the air to evaluate conditions. These were reasons enough for Woolman, rather than Harris, who alternatively might have been selected, to make the voyage south. Another, perhaps more compelling reason is that in 1925 George Post had departed Huff Daland to help organize Free Bottom Craft Company.[61] His leaving coincided with the move from Macon to Monroe. Harris had assumed Post's responsibilities and, as general manager, found it prudent to stay behind to supervise the season's dusting activities and make preparations for an expedition to Peru, assuming Woolman's efforts proved successful.

Leaving Monroe, Woolman likely stopped in Bristol, Pennsylvania, for consultations at the home office, then traveled to New York, where he was, using Harris's words, "treated so badly." This likely occurred with the Hayden, Stone group, the investment firm that financed Huff Daland Company and, by extension, its Louisiana duster subsidiary. Although the partner overseeing aviation affairs, Hoyt's involvement at this time is not known. Whatever the problem Woolman encountered, the difficulty seems to have been smoothed over when Huff Daland Company was restructured and recapitalized as Keystone Aircraft and the duster subsidiary, as a separate corporation, retained its own name and management. Referring to this treatment, Harris wrote, "my last information from [Irwin E.] Auerbach [Huff Daland Dusters comptroller], who is up there, seems to indicate that we will have extensive backing from now on and I believe that if that is definitely assured all will be well."[62]

Woolman by then had arrived in Peru. He sailed from New York aboard the Grace Line steamer *Santa Ana.* As the ship made its way out of the harbor on August 5, 1926, Woolman presumably was among the passengers at the rails watching as the Statue of Liberty slowly slipped by. An ocean voyage in those days was a "splendid experience," commented Ellis O. Briggs, at the time a young vice consul assigned to the U.S. Consul General's Office in the port city of Callao, Peru. In his memoirs Briggs observed that transiting the Panama Canal was relaxing and memorable, "with a buffet on deck and a breeze off Gatun Lake, the white cranes on Barro Colorado Island so close you could almost touch them, and the Continental Divide at Culebra." There were few tourists, he noted, and most travelers were "the hewers of wood and the drawers of water—doers, not the time wasters."[63] Perhaps one of those passengers might have been an entomologist, whose voyage would usher in a new age of air transportation. Woolman's mind must have been full of anticipation for the challenges ahead, the prospects for success or failure, and the weight of responsibility resting solely on his shoulders. A lot would depend on his good judgment, as surface mail, the only means of communicating with the United States, was slow, limited by the speed of a steamship.

On Wednesday, August 18, thirteen days out of New York, the *Santa Ana* anchored off Callao, the port serving Lima. Because docking facilities were not completed until the 1930s, passengers boarded launches and debarked on "an inadequate pier called Muelle y Dársena, where customs and baggage handling took place amid scenes of riotous confusion."[64] Woolman remained in Peru for about three months, during which time he was very busy. He retained a Peruvian agent, Pedro Martinto, "an importer of all sorts of things." A newspaper advertisement informed readers that Martinto "had been appointed general representative for the firm, Huff Daland Dusters, Inc., dusters of arsenate by means of airplanes," and recommended "all cotton dealers who wish to make the use of the services of said company for the next crop" to sign contracts.[65]

Woolman met with "various men of interest," including such prominent businessmen as Beltrán, Alexander Howard, Oscar Remos, and "others of similar vision."[66] He offered that Huff Daland Dusters would provide aircraft, personnel, equipment, and supplies "to dust the cotton fields of the Cañete and other valleys" in the coastal areas of Peru.[67] Woolman negotiated a government operating concession, signed contracts, laid the groundwork for dusting operations, and arranged for logistical support. His objectives accomplished, Woolman sailed for the United States and disembarked from the United Fruit Steamship Company's ship *Heredia* in New Orleans on November 22, 1926.[68]

Even before equipment was sent south from Monroe, Manuel A. Rapier, a Peruvian contact "anxious to receive all kinds of publications regarding cotton," informed Woolman of potential competition. In November, he wrote, "I have heard, although without reliable confirmation, that the aviator Faucett is trying to carry out just the same business."[69] Remarkably, just as Huff Daland Dusters had discovered with the White Flying Dusters in Tallulah, competition in the business of aerial applications could quickly develop, even in Peru. Yet this concern proved unwarranted.

More troubling was the response to an op-ed piece of Rapier's that appeared in a November issue of *El Comercio* that highlighted the advantages of crop dusting. With its speed and efficiency, an airplane did the equivalent work of 6,000 laborers, with Huff Daland Dusters providing the equipment and pesticides. Apparently Rapier's enthusiasm was not universally shared, and he castigated his critics with a politically charged rebuttal: "Los espiritus retardarios" (critics) and "los timoratos profesionales" (cautious professionals), Rapier wrote, "do not trust that our national psychology could embody modern ideas and methods."[70] Nevertheless, the arguments against Huff Daland Dusters appeared to be constructive and not politically motivated. Sending equipment and "the most experienced pilots," another op-ed piece argued, was too costly an experiment. Scientifically, it would be better to first use cultural methods, irrigation, fertilization, and seed selection. Only after careful study should modern agriculture methods be adopted generally and not only for cotton.[71] Regardless of the possibility for incipient competition or scientific skepticism, the concession was approved and contracts were signed for the 1927 season. The dispatch of Huff Daland Dusters personnel and equipment was not delayed.

Woolman succinctly summarized the 1927 Peruvian activities in a comprehensive report he prepared for the company's board of directors. Of interest is paragraph two, which confirms that in going to Peru, he had more than one objective. In addition to crop dusting, Woolman scouted for aircraft sales to carry the mail, although at this early stage, any thought of Huff Daland becoming an airline does not seem to have been contemplated.

Survey and Advanced Sales:

In August 1926, Mr. Woolman went to Peru for the purpose of extending winter operations. Costs, flying conditions, and general facilities were investigated and payment plans, banking facilities and a satisfactory contract arranged. He was successful in contracting with the principal planters of Cañete and Chincha valleys in sufficient amount to warrant the sending of personnel of seven, with five dusting airplanes. He also took the first steps toward procuring an introductory patent covering the use of airplanes in all dusting operations in Peru for ten years and secured the promise of the passage of a special law exempting our Company from import duties and fees on all dusting airplanes and insecticides.

Sales Contract for Keystone Aircraft Corporation:

In addition to his work for the duster organization, Mr. Woolman secured advanced information through the family of the President of Peru regarding the LaMerced–Iquitos Air Mail Route and conferred at length with Commander Grow of the United States Naval Mission, who is in charge of the project. Commander Grow became definitely interested in the Keystone equipment for this route, and this led to preliminary negotiations between Commander Grow and the Keystone factory.[72]

While Woolman was away, Harris, in the face of a "terrific drop in the price of cotton," supervised operations in Louisiana while he himself prepared for business in Peru. In a letter addressed to Woolman at the Hotel Bolivar in Lima, Harris summarized Stateside operations for the year. "We have dusted two-thirds more in 1926 than we did in 1925 with one-third less total flying time, even though we had an increase of 142% in the amount of dust used. The acres per hour dusted in 1926 are 132% greater than in 1925, even though we applied 46% more pounds per acre this year." In a handwritten comment below his signature, Harris praised Woolman: "Congratulations on your selling work [in the United States]." In the same letter he informed him, "the planes [for Peru] are practically ready to put into the crates," and he expected "a definite go-ahead from New York . . . any day."[73] In fact, they shipped from New Orleans on the steamship *Garfield,* scheduled to arrive in late December at Cerro Azul, a port serving the Santa Barbara Sugar Mill near the Cañete Valley.[74]

The details are lost to history, but Harris probably sailed from New York. As with Woolman's voyage, Harris must have enjoyed the trip. His photo album provides some personal insight. In Panama he posted pictures from a flight over the canal and locks. At port calls at Talara and Salaverry, Peru, on December 19 and 20, 1926, the passengers viewed primitive street scenes. A picture taken at Callao harbor on December 21 shows a launch, the one presumably used to carry passengers to the dock. The caption of another photo identifies "Mantero [who] met us at the boat in his Sunbeam." Photographs of the Hotel Bolivar and downtown Lima are dated the same day of the ship's arrival. Several pictures in the album are of a "Christmas eve 1926 party at the Army Flying School" in Las Palmas.[75] The entire North American group appears to be present, their invitation likely attributable to Harris's well-known reputation as a military aviator. He was welcomed by brothers-in-arms, although his Huff Daland Dusters mission was nonmilitary.

The final days of 1926 were spent getting ready for the work at hand. "Landing fields were prepared, deposits of calcium arsenate placed, gasoline supplies arranged, entomological surveys made, and many other details attended to, including the necessary banking arrangements."[76] Removing the aircraft from their crates and assembling them appeared to have gone without a hitch. The first crop dusting was "done by pilot [Marvis L.] Alexander, on the Estate of Montalvan in the Cañete Valley" on January 1, 1927.[77]

HAROLD ROSS
HARRIS'S INSIGHT

If you've waited three weeks for a spare part
after you've sent an expensive cable and then it comes wrong
and you have to send a second cable twice as long and
wait another three weeks, well, it's hell.

—HUDSON STRODE, *South by Thunderbird*

The Huff Daland Dusters project in Peru was well planned, well organized, and well executed, its success due in large measure equally to the contributions of Woolman and Harris. Woolman's preliminary survey laid the groundwork for Harris to complete the operation satisfactorily. For a small enterprise to seize an opportunity, send men and equipment so far on a risky venture, and have a profitable outcome was a remarkable achievement. By all indications, the company fulfilled its foreign contractual obligations for 1927. Some additional flying to control the sugar cane borer in the Cañete Valley was similar to experimental work in the United States on sugar cane for Louisiana State University.[1]

Six men accompanied Harris to Peru: an entomologist, J. B. Pope; three pilots, Dan E. Tobin, Henry E. Elliot, and Marvis L. Alexander; and two mechanics, William C. Miles and William E. Beach. Five "Special Small Duster Type" ships—numbers 49, 55, 56, 58, and 60—arrived from Monroe.[2] In a photograph taken in front of the Santa Barbara Sugar Mill, the aircraft are assembled, parked wingtip to wingtip, and appear ready for flight.[3] Each held 600 pounds of dust and was powered by a 200-hp, nine-cylinder, air-cooled Wright Whirl-wind radial engine. A Peruvian English-language newspaper noted that this was the same type of engine installed on the *Josephine Ford,* the Fokker Trimotor that Richard E. Byrd and Floyd Bennett used on their flight over the North Pole.[4] This comment is noteworthy as Lindbergh had not yet made his epochal transatlantic flight in his Whirlwind-powered *Spirit of St. Louis.*

The newspaper article explained the ratio of three pilots (Harris did not do any commercial dusting) to five airplanes ensured reliability, so "no accident can delay the service." In fact, "one bent tail post" was the only damage reported through April 1927. Alexander Howard, director-secretary of the Compania Agricola e Industrial de Cañete, observed, "The steel tube fuselages of these special planes have stood up extremely well in the Peruvian climate, and the Oleo shock absorbing landing gear has proved its worth time after time in operating from rough fields with heavy loads."[5] These specially designed agricultural aircraft were new to South America, but the North American pilots and mechanics did not find the environmental stresses exceptional. The design had already been tested and proved reliable under trying conditions in the United States.

A demonstration flight took place on January 1, 1927, the contractual date specified to begin the service. Flights to dust cotton began in earnest later in the month and were completed by the end of March.[6] Tobin serviced Chincha Valley contracts, while Elliot and Marvis Alexander split the work in the Cañete Valley. Most of the calcium arsenate eradicated the cotton leaf worm, a pest that, when it appeared, could quickly decimate an entire field. Under the circumstances, aerial applications were particularly effective in saving the crop.[7] Howard had high praise for the dusters: "The service proved so efficient that in no case had we to have more than one dusting per field, one of the chief advantages undoubtedly being the rapidness with which the poison was applied before any harm had been done by the worm." The results are documented in a report to the board of directors: "While the Company held contracts for 50,712-acre applications . . . , the efficient control secured in this country, where it never rains, made necessary the use of only 29,652-acre applications," grossing $108,299.45 income.[8] Not surprisingly, Harris "found cotton dusting in Peru a very satisfying experience."[9]

The presence of especially designed commercial aircraft in Peru manifested the country's modernity. "At the personal request of President Leguía," Harris informed, "an exhibition of airplane dusting was given. This exhibition was attended by the President, his Cabinet, high Army and Navy officials, and leading planters of Peru." Leguía "officially welcomed" us.[10] In a photograph of their meeting, Harris's broad shoulders and stocky build contrast sharply with the diminutive figure of the Peruvian president—even while wearing his silk top hat.[11]

The aerial display coincided with the ceremony honoring aviation gradu-ates of the Escuela Militar de Aviacion held on January 29, 1927, at Las Palmas.[12] The Peruvian director of aeronautics, Commandante Juan O'Connor, was likely an acquaintance of Harris. O'Connor graduated from the U.S. Army's flying school at Kelly Field in San Antonio, Texas, where he trained with Lind-bergh and Eugene Stevens, one of the original pilots hired by Harris in 1925.[13] Harris and Marvis Alexander's demonstration simulated the technique used to treat cotton by passing in front of the spectators, while flying low over the ground and dispensing dust. Then, Harris, an "experto piloto," performed some loops and other aerobatics against a cloudless blue sky.[14] He reported "the dusting exhibition so impressed the National Government that they im-mediately requested assistance in combating a serious infestation of caterpil-lars which were defoliating the trees of the beautiful public parks in Lima."[15] The situation was reminiscent of Charles Neillie's problem in the spring of 1921 and his idea to use airplanes to spray treetops in Cleveland. Harris re-called, "Lima wasn't a very high-rise city in those days; I suppose the highest building was the hotel which was about five stories high," making dusting rel-atively easy; "we cut down on the defoliation very much."[16]

Coincidental to Harris's stay, the Army Air Corps Pan American Good Will Flight arrived in Lima. Maj. Herbert A. Dargue led a flight of five Liberty-engine-powered Loening amphibians, each with a crew of two officers, on a mission "to show the possibilities for establishing aerial transportation and communication in Latin America." Landing at Las Palmas airfield, Dargue de-livered a message from Pres. Calvin Coolidge.[17] Unlike the chilly receptions and "unpleasant incidents" they had occurred in Mexico, Guatemala, and Colombia, the crews were warmly received by Peruvian officials and the U.S. ambassador, Miles Poindexter. The welcoming atmosphere was probably not unexpected since the United States supported Leguía in arbitrating the Tacna-

Arica territorial dispute between Chile, Peru, and Bolivia.[18] A formal black-tie banquet at the Hotel Bolivar honored the aircrews.[19]

The army officers of the Good Will Flight were "old Air Corps buddies," and Harris "spent a good deal of time with them discussing the problems they had encountered through Central America, Colombia, Ecuador, and Peru."[20] These conversations gave him a unique insight into the challenges of establishing a commercial air link between North and South America. The army's mission clearly demonstrated that a route was feasible, but whether it was economical remained an open question. Two Loenings returned to the United States, but only one of them completed the entire circuit. In his report Dargue concluded: "The future of airlines in Latin America was bright, but such lines would not at first pay for themselves. It would take time for the populaces to become accustomed to air travel." Perhaps the most important outcome of the flight was its effect on U.S. government policy. In his speech before the Inter-American Aviation Conference in Washington, D.C., William P. MacCracken Jr., assistant secretary of commerce for aeronautics, predicted, "with the co-operation of business and industry, an airline would soon be established over a 'major portion' of the route covered by the Pan American Flight."[21]

Apparently, Harris was thinking along these lines as well. "No meeting, just wandering around," he informally asked "various businessmen" if an air-mail service would be of any benefit to them. From these conversations, he determined a certain amount of business, such as the "movement of funds," was likely, but the problem was whether there would be enough volume to support an airline. Harris was confident airmail "would pay its way in [the] final analysis," but the challenge was with making it turn a profit.[22]

Meanwhile, in the Northern Hemisphere, during the spring planting season, the Mississippi River, swollen from winter runoff and unusually heavy rainfall, crested its banks and caused the infamous 1927 flood. "At 12:30 P.M., Thursday, April 21, [Maj. John] Lee[, the Vicksburg District army engineer] wired General Edgar Jadwin, head of the Corps of Engineers, 'Levee broke at ferry landing Mounds Mississippi eight A.M. Crevasse will overflow entire Mississippi Delta.'" The river broke through protecting levees, and surging into low-lying areas, there was no stopping the flow. President Coolidge appointed Commerce Secretary Herbert Hoover to lead the nation's relief effort. As over-all administrator, Hoover set policy and delegated responsibility for the welfare of thousands of refugees to the Red Cross and local boards. The Red Cross ran 154 tent cities and cared for 325,554 people. African Americans lived mostly in tents, some up to four months, while white refugees generally lived outside the camps. All were fed and clothed by the Red Cross.[23]

Huff Daland Dusters' aircraft at Smoot Field in Monroe were undamaged by the rising water and flew thirty hours while augmenting the Army Air Corps' mission. Engineers initially asked the company for assistance in gauging the extent of the flood, but once the area was fully inundated, its pilots helped the Red Cross search for survivors and fly doctors and medicines to refugee camps. They also flew state officials in charge of the relief effort, since surface modes of transportation were interrupted. Huff Daland Dusters earned "a great deal of good will."[24]

During the emergency, LeRoy Percy's influence and political connections kept Delta financial institutions solvent and money flowing to planters. Relief had to come quickly. As with the boll weevil threat, Percy feared "the [overflowing] river would send blacks flooding north, stripping the Delta of labor." Fortunately, his son, William "Will" Alexander Percy, led a "special flood relief committee. . . . [This,] coupled with his chairmanship of the county Red Cross, gave [Will] near absolute control over the county during the emergency, and over the care of tens of thousands of refugees." He decided to evacuate Black refugees to safer ground, but unfortunately his father, fearing that they would never return, lobbied behind his son's back to have the plan rejected. African Americans were then forced to shelter on the levees, where they lived in poor conditions. When floodwaters finally receded, Black resentment forever ended "the bond between the Percys and the blacks." LeRoy Percy's greatest fear was realized. "One man at a time, one family at a time, in an accelerating flood, blacks left Greenville and the Delta and did not return."[25] As threatening as the boll weevil had seemed to the elder Percy, it could be managed, but the Mississippi River could not. Untamed, it proved his nemesis. The great flood swept away the social and economic order he strove to preserve in the region. This change was too much, and he died two years later in 1929.

Falling prices and drowned fields simultaneously challenged the dusters' North American operation. Only 7,800 acres of applications were performed in the flooded region, compared to 45,000 the previous year. Planters, realizing a negative return on their investment from the sale of cotton in 1926 and losses from the 1927 flood, experienced what amounted to a "financial depression." Consequently, growers were unwilling or unable to commit to advance contracts. Woolman and the company's operating personnel responded aggressively. Huff Daland Dusters expanded its operations west as well as south, treating cantaloupes against powdery mildew in the Imperial Valley of California and dusting truck farms in Mexico.[26] They also offered service to Shreveport and into Texas. But as they materialized, such expansion opportunities were "more or less in the nature of emergency dusting as people were very loath to contract for service except as the Weevil or Leaf Worm put in their appearance." Even then, planters were only inclined to contract when rates were reduced from $4.85 to $3.50 per acre for three applications, including dust.[27]

As if the situation were not bad enough, the possibility of protecting late cotton was proscribed by a second rise of floodwater in June. Then, on July 18 a tornado destroyed the hangar at Smoot Field, severely damaging ship number 61, which had just been refurbished and test flown, further handicapping normal operations. Two other aircraft belonging to the Department of Agriculture, most likely evacuated to Monroe due to flooding at Scott Field in Tallulah, were severely damaged as well. To make up for the government's loss, Huff Daland Dusters sold its Pelican duster to the Delta Laboratory as a replacement, providing some additional revenue to the company.[28]

To help recover from the tornado, the City of Monroe immediately built a workshop and supplied three tent hangars at no cost to Huff Daland. But these were only temporary measures. The limitations of the Smoot Field site gained urgency after Lindbergh's May 1927 flight to Paris. Overnight, communities across the country became air minded, and the Memphis and Shreveport Chambers of Commerce made offers for Huff Daland Dusters to shift its operating headquarters to their respective cities. Shreveport's offer included a hangar and repair building "completely acceptable to you" to be available by January 1, 1928, and the local chamber was willing to cooperate "in the establishment of airmail express lines or commercial passenger lines." Memphis promised "a dandy Municipal Field" with "free rent and sufficient hangars for five full years." R. B. Snowdon, chairman of the Memphis Chamber of Commerce Committee, touted the location "as the center of the poisoning World. An office on Front St. with one man in it will sell more dusting contracts than all your traveling men and expenses put together."[29]

The inducement for the company to remain in Monroe was more convincing. The city and parish jointly bought a 140-acre field five miles east of the city and had plans for the "immediate construction" of a hangar. Theodore F. Terzia, president of the Ouachita Parish Police Jury, anticipated airmail service would begin "at some near future date." He emphasized "the landing field and hangar facility has already been inspected and approved by Lieut. Harris, Messrs. Woolman, Auerbach, Culver, and Dr. Coad . . . as well as numerous air pilots of the Kelly Field." Terzia praised the "splendid type of gentlemen that is and has been associated with" the Huff Daland Dusters organization and hoped the airport would "serve as a permanent home for your industry."[30] The airfield was named after Augustus James Selman, a Monroe aviator who had died in an airplane crash shortly after the armistice in Europe. The company relocated to Selman Field in October.[31]

Due to the depressed agricultural situation in the United States, only two of the five duster aircraft returned from Peru, with a considerable savings in shipping costs.[32] Storage costs for the remaining three were nominal. Furthermore, Lt. Cmdr. Harold B. Grow of the U.S. Naval Mission estimated that overhauling the aircraft in Peru would cost approximately $650, with materials and spares provided, versus $3,500 per plane or machine in the United States. This was "not excessive by any means," Grow wrote to Harris, though what work was actually performed is not known. All personnel, excepting Harris and J. B. Pope, the Huff Daland entomologist, returned to the United States. On his way to the embarkation harbor at Cerro Azul, Alexander had a difficult time on the roads. "After haveing [sic] three flat tires, and abusing our vocabulary with each one, we managed to get here last night at eight o'clock." His note to "Harry [Harris]" covered last-minute details before sailing; he concluded with the pronouncement, "our boat does not arrive until Saturday morning; however, everything is ready to go now."[33]

Pope, stayed in Peru to make a "preliminary survey of those valleys to the north to which operations might be extended, and investigate the entomological problems and possibilities of our operations on cotton, sugar cane, and cocoa in the northern valleys of Peru and southern Ecuador."[34] Harris delayed his departure to arrange advance contracts and to extend the company's customs and tax exemptions. He also followed up with the Leguía government on the sale of Keystone mail planes for the LaMerced–Iquitos Air Mail Route.

By June, Harris had signed commitments to dust 22,330 acres the next season. This was about equal to that for 1927, but there might be an additional 7,000–10,000 acres secured. Since cotton prices fell below the cost of production, contracts were only possible at a reduced price of $31.00 per *fanegada*, down from $43.00. A performance bond and other "protective clauses," previously included in the contracts, now required additional payment.[35] The conditions were spelled out in a comprehensive agreement in both Spanish and English, the Standard Contract for Airplane Dusting Service in Peru, between Huff Daland Dusters and the planter. Clauses stipulated the area of a fanegada to be 30,000 square meters (7.41316 acres). Both parties identified and agreed on the fields to be treated, including the hacienda's name and a "map, sketch, photograph, or written description." The company reserved the right to verify any measurements provided by the planters.[36]

Pedro Martinto, Inc., handled Huff Daland Dusters' business interests on a commission basis from offices and agents in agricultural districts. This was especially important when company representatives were out of the country or otherwise unavailable. The Martinto firm also represented significant North American enterprises such as International Harvester and Babcock & Wilcox, Ltd. It apparently secured additional dusting agreements because, as of November 1, 1927, a total of 3,567 fanegadas (26,443 acres) were under contract for the coming season.[37]

Harris followed up on Woolman's petition for an exemption of customs duties on airplanes, insecticides, parts, and taxes with the Peruvian government. After some delay, the law providing for this passed and was signed by President Leguía. But the tax exemption required an additional signature from the Ministerio de Fermento. By the close of the operating season, it had not yet endorsed the agreement. Huff Daland Dusters anticipated this eventuality, and a stipulation in the standard dusting contract permitted the company to claim an additional fee per fanegada to make up for the difference.[38]

In a cable dated January 27, 1927, and addressed to Huff Daland Dusters in Peru, presumably received by Harris (Woolman had already returned to the United States), Keystone requested "every effort be made to close the contract" with Commander Grow. This was in reference to discussions Woolman had opened on behalf of the corporation to sell mail planes for the proposed LaMerced–Iquitos route. A meeting on March 9 resulted in an agreement in

principle, but arranging the details of the transaction took considerably longer to complete.[39] In this and other matters, Harris represented both Huff Daland's and Keystone's interests. He likely spent most of his time in Lima and
left it to the operating crews to work independently in the field to fulfill the
dusting contracts. Apparently, this was not a problem. *The West Coast Leader*
had high praise for "Messrs. Elliot, Tobin, and Alexander, of the Pilot Staff of
the Company, [who] answer every requirement of knowledge, training and
experience," and the skilled mechanics, who "keep the aeroplanes in perfect
condition."[40]

As a final task, during his return journey to the United States, Harris made
what he called a "cooperative survey trip for the Keystone Aircraft Corporation
and the Huff Daland Dusters, Inc." to Bolivia, Argentina, Uruguay, and Brazil.
He stayed "at each nation's capital long enough to determine whether there
was any interesting crop dusting possibilities and particularly whether or not
local people thought an airline would be a good idea to connect their center
with the other world centers and minimize transportation time required."[41]

During these travels, Harris experienced the undeveloped state of transportation on the continent. "Nearly all internal lines of surface communication reach from their interior regions of agriculture and mineral production
to seaports from which raw materials are shipped abroad. The land routes
which connect one region of concentrated settlement with another, even
within the same country, are poorly developed."[42] How much time he spent
in transit between destinations is not known, but Harris's description of his
route gives an indication of its complexity.

> I traveled by steamer from Callao, the port of Lima, to Mollendo, the point
> where the railroad starts up into the Andes, to Puno on Lake Titicaca. I took
> the train from Mollendo to Lake Titicaca where I got on a small steamer and
> made a night voyage to the Bolivian port, Guaqui, on the lake.[43] I transferred
> to a railroad again and went down the short distance into La Paz, the capital
> of Bolivia. From La Paz, I took the train south on the altiplano, the level plain
> over 12,000 feet above sea level, to Uyuni, Bolivia. At Uyuni the railroad splits,
> the west branch going on to Santiago, Chile, and the east branch going across
> the Argentine to Buenos Aires. From Buenos Aires I took a night boat to Mon-
> tevideo. From Montevideo I took the steamer to Santos in Brazil, the port of

Sao Paulo. From Sao Paulo I took the train to Rio. From Rio, [a] steamer to New York.[44]

Harris departed from Lima on June 15 and spent July, August, and September traveling and contacting embassies, bankers, and businessmen.[45] His timing could not have been better. Lindbergh's flight across the Atlantic in May transfixed people's attention and piqued imaginations in Latin America as well as the rest of the world.[46] No longer was flying something people did for thrills or an activity relegated to the military. Airplanes had a new purpose: Lindbergh proved they could quickly and reliably span great distances and safely cross wide oceans and inhospitable land masses. The idea of carrying mail and passengers in Latin America became achievable. On his travels, Harris, a record-holding pilot himself and aircraft-company representative, benefited from Lindbergh's acclaim when meeting with contacts.[47]

The situation in Argentina captured Harris's interest. "Argentina has a keen air service, both in the Army and Navy. It has excellent, up to date machinery and the Army and Navy stations are very modern and remarkably well equipped." According to historian Dan Hagedorn, "Argentina led all other Latin American nations by far in the advancement of military, naval, and civil aviation at this point." The government invested in equipment, airport construction, and even the "establishment of an indigenous aviation factory." Located approximately 400 miles northwest of Buenos Aires in Cordoba, this was "the first aviation factory established in South America" and influenced Harris's favorable outlook for aviation in the country: "When the Government factory starts production next year I believe the airmen will try for records in long distance flights on a big scale. The only reason they have not done so hitherto is because they do not want to use foreign equipment, but prefer to wait and make the distance records with their own national products."[48]

Harris offered to assist the Department of Agriculture in Buenos Aires with "their terrific locust pests" problem. Negotiations were well advanced and "a program thoroughly worked out" when an opportunity for Huff Daland Dusters to demonstrate its superior capability arose due to a locust outbreak in Cordoba. But the minister of agriculture decided the season was too far advanced for treatment to be helpful. Airplane dusting the previous year, he reasoned, had proved ineffective once the pests had reached the migratory stage.[49]

An unknown type of aircraft had been used then, in Santa Fe Province, "one of the earliest known instances of such work in mainland South America," which, it should be noted, predated Huff Daland Dusters' operation in Peru.[50]

Harris embarked from Buenos Aires by night boat across the Rio de la Plata to Montevideo, Uruguay. Curiously, he chose to go by ship, although air service was available in a trimotor Junkers G-24 floatplane. These flights operated three times a week between March 4, 1926, and October 10, 1927.[51] Of all his travels in South America, this was the only segment he could have flown commercially. Harris must have been aware of the opportunity, as he had studied the operation and determined the German company was "just about making expenses."[52] Possibly, he did not feel the twenty-dollar fare was justified; perhaps the airplane, capable of carrying four passengers, was booked.[53] As a veteran of World War 1, he might have been averse to supporting the German-backed enterprise.[54] Probably, Harris simply had too much baggage for the small plane. Whatever the reason, he chose not to opt for the short flight to Montevideo.

At each major city during his travels, Harris met with businessmen and bankers to gauge the benefits of airmail service between South America's capitals and the United States. He emphasized such an operation "paying for itself in poundage [of] mail carried."[55] Businessmen and bankers did not seem to object to franking of one dollar for an airmail letter between the United States and South America. Harris's proposal to guarantee "a certain amount of business each trip" made the proposition more attractive.[56]

Harris understood that airmail between major commercial centers was the key to the success of air routes. William A. M. Burden, an authority on the development of commercial aviation in Latin America, pointed to late 1927 as the end of the pioneer period on the South American continent. Harris's trip presaged the period of trunk-route development beginning in 1928.[57] With insight from his flying background and the conditions he observed, Harris drew an air-route map "showing how to get started, and describing later expansion" in Latin America, keeping in mind "planes then had only about a 600 mile range."[58] He further outlined a blueprint for development: "I have made a preliminary study of various air mail routes from South America to the United States. While these lines present themselves as a comprehensive whole in their final development there is no reason individual sections may not be initiated and operated independently until such time as the fulfillment of the entire project seems feasible. On the attached map there is roughly indicated the most advantageous routes, taking all things into consideration, and the lines most easily and cheaply installed are numbered in order of their installation."[59]

Geography favored initiating a west-coast route to Latin America. The North and South American continents are offset to each other so that "when a ruler or a piece of string is placed between New York and Buenos Aires, the straightest, shortest route is seen to follow along the Pacific coast of South America to Chile and over the mountains to Argentina."[60] Huff Daland Dusters was uniquely positioned geographically and historically for its role in establishing commercial air transportation in South America. By flying point to point, even when aerial navigation was rudimentary and aircraft lacked range, an airline could directly connect Latin American population centers in competition with slow-moving "mail ships [requiring] twelve days [to travel] from Callao to New York."[61]

The cartoon *Undesirable Citizens* expresses the exasperation of planters.

From *Cotton Journal*, Mar. 25, 1909.

Bert R. Coad in his office at the Delta Laboratory, Tallulah, Louisiana, May 19, 1915.
Photograph courtesy Louisiana Department of Agriculture and Forestry.

Cotton-dusting machines assembled at Scott, Mississippi, in August 1920.

Photograph courtesy Louisiana Department of Agriculture and Forestry.

"View of the first aerial application and aerial crop dusting flight flown by
Army test pilot Lt. John A. Macready on Aug. 3, 1921. The application was made
upwind of a grove of catalpa trees infested by sphinx moth larvae.
The arrow is pointed at the catalpa grove."

George B. Post.
From *Aviation*, Feb. 18, 1924, 161.

Aerial view of different types of dusters—Airplane duster, power duster, four-row mule, two-row mule, saddle gun, and hand gun—at Mansfield, Louisiana, September 21, 1925.

Photograph courtesy Louisiana Department of Agriculture and Forestry.

Pilot Dan Tobin after a flight in a leaky dusting ship, Shirley Field, Louisiana, April 8, 1926. Whether in the air or on the ground, the poison dust was an underappreciated health danger.

Photograph courtesy Louisiana Department of Agriculture and Forestry.

A rare photograph of Thomas Huff and Elliot Daland,
here admiring a model of their Petrel airplane in Ogdensburg, New York.

From *Wings*, December 1977, 57.

Demonstration day, Newellton, Louisiana, April 28, 1925.

Photograph courtesy Louisiana Department of Agriculture and Forestry.

Gov. Henry L. Fuqua conversing with Bert R. Coad at Shirley Field,
Tallulah, Louisiana, July 21, 1925.

Photograph courtesy Louisiana Department of Agriculture and Forestry.

Huff Daland duster aircraft uncrated, assembled, and ready for service in Peru.

Harold R. Harris meeting Peru president Augusto B. Leguiá.

Courtesy Special Collections and Archives, Wright State University Libraries.

Demonstration flight flown by Harold R. Harris and Marvis L. Alexander
at the Jorge Chaves Aviation School, January 1, 1927.

Courtesy Special Collections and Archives, Wright State University Libraries.

Group posing with the Huff Daland large duster model. B. R. Coad, Irwin Auerbach, Earl Potts, Ray Mitchell, and John Payne are third through sixth from *left*. P. Henry Elliot is eighth from *left*.

Photograph courtesy Louisiana Department of Agriculture and Forestry.

Street view of Delta Air Service office with car pumps, Selman Field, Monroe, Louisiana, circa 1929.

Photograph courtesy Robert Poole family.

Delta Air Service terminal and office (viewed from the operations field) and Woolman (standing *right*), Selman Field, Monroe, Louisiana, circa 1929.

Photograph courtesy Robert Poole family.

Delta Air Service personnel with a Travel Air 6000.
Left to right they are: John Howe, pilot; C. E. Woolman, general manager; Douglas Culver, chief of maintenance; Earl Forth, fabric worker and mechanic; Ray Percell, welder and metal worker; J. D. Greer, pilot; Arthur Gary, motor mechanic; Frank Fraser, stock clerk; P. l. Higgins, chief pilot; J. E. Harvey; George Halliday; Henry Curtis, mechanic. Seated on the engine of the second plane is William Wilkerson, mechanic's helper." *Morning Monroe (LA) Post,* October 1929.

Photograph courtesy Delta Airlines Corporate Archives.

'She Will Bring Dallas Closer'

Arrival of the Stinson-A to the Delta fleet.
From *left to right* Oscar Bergstrom, city traffic manager;
Pat L. Higgins, operations manager; C. E. Faulk, president; Laigh Parker,
general traffic manager; and Travis Oliver, Treasurer.

From *Atlanta Georgian,* June 25, 1935.

Atlanta ground personnel outside of the Eastern Airlines hangar used by Delta, 1938. From *left to right:* W. L. "Jack" Bernard, general foreman; Claude P. Lyle, sheet metal; T. J. "Squire" Helms, mechanic; O. B. Deere, foreman, engine overhaul; H. A. "Ham" Moreau, prop shop; and Horace Wrigley (in car), purchasing agent.

Brand-new red fuel truck, circa 1941.
Bob Poole commented, "We were very proud of that fuel truck."

Photograph courtesy Robert Poole family.

Delta aircraft in transition, May 15, 1941.
To the left is a DC-2 (engine and wing), in the background are two DC-3s,
and barely visible on the *right* is the tail of a Lockheed L-10.

Photograph courtesy Robert Poole family.

Employees posing with a Lockheed Electra, March 14, 1939.
According to Gene Christian, this image includes about 80–85 percent of all
Delta employees at this time. *Front row, left to right:* George Hill, Claude P. Lyle,
E. G. "Pete" Jones, A. B. Henny, Carl Nesbit, Wayne Lydon, Vernon Gillette, T. J.
"Squire" Helms, Robert D. Poole, Earl Forth, David Chupp, Dick Bingham, Arthur
Ford, Bill Coats, and Robert White. Middle row, *left to right:* Nipton "Nip" Hill,
Earnest "Sweatpea" Jackson, G. J. (J. D.) Dye, "Skid" Henly, Harold Valentine,
A. D. Clark, O. B. Deere, Bill Stevens, Jack Langford, Jake Morse, Harold Millican,
Sam Everett, J. T. "Tut" Harper, H. A. "Ham" Moreau, Grover Presnell, W. L. "Jack"
Bernard, and Lamar Grover. Back row, *left to right:* Bill Miles, J. D. Crane,
Gene Christian, "Jug" Wilson, Clark French, Ken Ward, Pat L. Higgins,
Helen Callahan, Bob Weeks, Grif Connell, George Cushing, Bob Spalding,
Charlie Payne, Hugo "Dutch" Krantz, "Red" Bounderant, Jack Gross,
Roy White, H. D. Wrigley, and Jim Spratlin.

Photograph courtesy Gene Christian family.

AIRMAIL AND THE
WEST COAST PROJECT

Due to heavy fog at the mouth of the Gulf of Guayaquil
we had to get down close and keep under it. [Dan] Tobin flew a
straight compass course and at times we were 10 to 15 miles out over
the gulf which did not please either [C. E.] Woolman or myself,
but Tobin knew what he was doing evidently.

—ROBERT S. WEBBER to his wife,

July 30, 1928

The problem of financing airway development all but disappeared in the euphoric aftermath of Lindbergh's flight. "Business and government circles, hitherto conservative," author William A. M. Burden writes, "became more sympathetic toward air transport projects."[1] Historian Robert van der Linden's view was less sanguine. He has observed aeronautical investing as irrational, "part of the public feeding frenzy in the stock market."[2] Under the circumstances, Edgar Gott, president of Huff Daland Dusters in Bristol, Pennsylvania, made a pragmatic decision. In a letter dated September 30, 1927, he directed subordinates to submit a report to the board of directors on current and future operations for the company. Gott looked for ideas and opportunities, and who better to ask than the operations staff—Woolman, Harris, and Auerbach, among others. The resulting report, dated October 26, summarized Huff Daland Dusters' operations through September and included an analysis as well as recommendations for a significant "extension of activities."[3] Harris also attached a summary of his survey trip through South America.

Dusting operations were profitable. Performing regular services, Huff Daland earned an average of $298.50 per hour within the United States. The income in Peru was an extraordinary $729.00 per hour. For all flying, including dusting and other activities, the average gross income was somewhat less—$201.00 per hour in the United States and $528.00 in Peru. These figures compared favorably to those for carrying the mail: "The average income for all air mail contracts, as disclosed in the June 30th figures issued by the Department of Commerce, [was] 55¢ per mile, or $55.00 per hour, and for the Western Air Express—the most successful operator of $1.40 per mile or $140 per hour."[4]

While it would seem that agricultural applications were worthwhile and should be expanded, there were systemic problems with Huff Daland Dusters' operations. For one thing, pilot utilization was inefficient. Only 20 percent of pilot days were used for actual dusting. A considerable amount of productivity was lost from inactivity and therefore potentially available for other aerial purposes.

Another problem was the airplanes. Huff Daland operated two designs, a small type, the Petrel 31, a $14,000 airplane powered by a 200-hp Wright Whirlwind J-4, and a large type, the Duster 1, with a 400-hp Liberty engine and costing $20,000 per ship. The small model was useful for fields of all sizes; the large one was designed for fields with long, straight runs. In practice the Duster 1 was "capable of accomplishing less than 15% more dusting than the small duster in a given elapsed time and required more maintenance and additional loading crew."[5] Although the smaller type was more versatile, its cost was nonetheless significantly higher than newer designs available from other manufacturers. Thus, a competitor seeking an edge could choose from these cheaper models. Although half as capable as the Petrel 31, a suitable airplane could be acquired at one-quarter the cost. A single pilot, or a small group of pilots, could get financing and undercut Huff Daland Dusters' prices. So, for the company to be profitable in such a competitive environment, the report recommended replacing its current fleet of crop dusters with "cheap production airplanes and engines."[6]

Pilot retention was another issue. The report warned, "there is the constant danger of present personnel entering this field in competition with this company." With financing, they cautioned, pilots might be tempted to operate independently. In fact, an example (not mentioned in the report) proved the point. Eugene Stevens, an original duster pilot, after having fallen out with Harris over a disputed $60 Model T pickup repair bill, quit and started the Southern Dusting Company. He bought a WACO 9 for "about" $1,600 and modified it and three additional airplanes for dusting purposes.[7] Stevens operated out of Scott Field in Tallulah.

The report recommended that management take steps to diversify Huff Daland Dusters operations: "Chief among these is Air Mail, because of its present rapid expansion and the opportunity to enter this important field at a time when main arterial routes are still to be had." It suggested using the current fleet of dusters as mail planes until new, specially designed Keystone models were obtained for this task. "The Operating Group has come to the conclusion that the Company should bid on air mail contracts, and hereby requests authority to do so."[8] In light of future developments, this recommendation was prescient.

To diversify the company's operations further, the report suggested opening a flying school. Having these new type of aircraft on the ramp would likewise permit "the carrying of passengers on short flights, or on special trips." In addition, the operations staff wanted Keystone's permission to sell its future products, in the meantime asking to serve as agents for other manufacturers. Preliminary negotiations were in progress at this time with the Fairchild Aviation Corporation, organized in November 1927, to market aircraft, engines, cameras, and aviation services in the United States, Latin America, and Europe. Aerial photography in South America to "add another source of income" for Huff Daland Dusters was likely the reason for these discussions.[9]

Even with losses from the Mississippi flood and a drop in worldwide cotton prices, Huff Daland realized an operating profit of $14,274.79 from the 1927 dusting season. Nevertheless, this was "not sufficient to absorb the entire overhead for the non-operating period." To be profitable, the company had to broaden its revenue stream and spread it over the entire year. The report recommended diversification as the underlying strategy to accomplish this.[10] But the salient point of the report (as its authors' subsequent actions suggest) was its argument in favor of scheduled commercial service with a mail subsidy and the potential of passenger revenue.

A copy of this report likely found its way to Hayden, Stone—more specifically the desk of Hoyt—underwriter of Keystone Aviation's financial notes in the 1926 acquisition of Huff Daland Company.[11] Not immediately apparent at the time, Gott's directive to his staff (resulting in the report) signaled the beginning of the end for Huff Daland Dusters. Commercial aviation's future lay with scheduled air service, not crop dusting. Within a year, Hoyt divested the company.

His vision of aviation's future was larger than that contemplated by Huff Daland Duster's operators, and Hoyt became the central figure merging the interests of Keystone, Huff Daland, and Pan American Airways. Pan American's development is essential in understanding his role in commercial aviation, although he was not one of its original founders; neither was Juan Terry Trippe.

Pan American Airways began as the national-security project of U.S. military officers led by Army Air Corps intelligence officer and aviator Maj. Henry H. "Hap" Arnold. They were concerned that the Post Office might award U.S. mail privileges transiting the Panama Canal Zone to SCADTA (Sociedad Colombo Alemana de Transportes Aéreos), a German airline operating in Latin America. Should Postmaster General Harry S. New determine an American line could not perform the service, nothing prevented him from granting a concession to a foreign enterprise.[12] Arnold did not himself pursue the matter and, in an historic twist, chose to stay in the Army Air Corps; he might otherwise have had a stellar commercial-aviation career. Instead, despite putting his military career in jeopardy by testifying on behalf of Brig. Gen. Billy Mitchell at Mitchell's court-martial for insubordination, Arnold rose in rank and commanded the worldwide Army Air Forces during World War II.[13]

Meanwhile, John K. Montgomery, C. Grant Mason Jr., and financier Richard B. Bevier incorporated Pan American Airways in New York State on March 8, 1927. On July 16 the Post Office gave Montgomery—personally—a contract to carry U.S. Mail between Key West and Havana, which he then transferred to Pan American. The postal agreement stipulated that service must begin by October 19 or the right would be forfeited. Trippe and a cohort of aviation industrialists likewise coveted the route and secured from Pres. Gerardo Machado "some form of landing rights in Cuba that the Bevier-Montgomery group did not possess." In early October Trippe merged his Aviation Corporation of America with the Pan American group to secure the mail authority.[14]

Although they had wrestled control from Montgomery and Bevier, Trippe and Hoyt were still obligated to begin service by October 19 or lose the mail contract. As the deadline drew inexorably closer, delivery of the ten-person, high-winged trimotor Fokker FVII Pan American had ordered, was delayed. As it turned out, this did not matter as the landing site, laboriously prepared on a low-lying, swampy Key West island, was unusable from recent heavy rainfall. After a frenetic search, the resourceful Trippe turned up a Fairchild FC-2 float-plane capable of inaugurating the service. He hastily hired a pilot, Cy Caldwell of West Indian Aerial Express, and "in a melodrama rivaling any that might have emerged from the script of a Hollywood scenarist the company met the deadline."[15] At 7:00 A.M., Caldwell showed up at the airplane, loaded seven sacks of mail, and was airborne at 8:04 A.M., as Robert Dailey writes, to save "a tycoon and an Airline."[16] Hoyt, the driving force behind the deal, became chairman of Aviation Corporation of the Americas, the holding company controlling Pan American Airways, its operating subsidiary.[17] Aviation Corporation of the Americas is similar in name, but a separate entity from, Trippe's earlier Aviation Corporation of America.

While the drama of Pan American's founding unfolded, Harris was on his circuitous journey through South America, evaluating the potential for dusting operations, conferring with air-minded people, and mapping air routes. By the time his steamer arrived in New York one afternoon in early October, he understood the state of aviation and its prospects in the Southern Hemisphere. The following morning Harris met with Hoyt, spread his map and figures over the financier's big walnut desk, and "hammered home the facts."[18]

"There it is Mr. Hoyt. The first section we fly is Lima to Talara, with stops in Trujillo, Chiclyao and Piura. It's just along the coast and is practical as your granddad's pants. Then we'll go south to Mollendo, 530 miles. Then from Talara on up through Guayaquil and Buenaventura to the Canal Zone. That will be section three. Then from our base of operations in Peru we'll go down from Mollendo to Valparaiso, 1200 miles or maybe a little more. As soon as we get enough ships and pilots and mechanics, get our bases established and these first sections running smooth, one after the other, we'll put in number five, which goes over the Andes to Mendosa and Buenos Aires."

"Good gosh!" said Mr. Hoyt, "Over the Andes!—Gimmie a telephone!" He asked for one Juan Trippe. While Mr. Trippe was on his way over, Mr. Hoyt was getting an earful of first-hand facts about ports and mileages and traffic, an eyeful of the short practical sections marked on Captain Harris's well-worn map, and a lapful of airplanes and air bases, overhaul shops and greasy mechanics. All of this Mr. Hoyt gracefully unloaded over onto the quiet, soft spoken Mr. Trippe when he arrived. Mr. Hoyt pointed to Captain Harris's wrinkled map and said, "This fellow's two years ahead of us."[19]

The date of this meeting is uncertain, but Harris's plan and route map quite possibly predated, and therefore helped shape, the vision Trippe outlined to his board of directors at a meeting on October 13.

Trippe read a memorandum presenting a blueprint for the airline's development. Starting from Miami, one trunk line extended to Colón, in the Panama Canal Zone, and down the west coast of South America to Valparaiso, Chile. A second line emanating from Miami cut across Cuba to Puerto Rico and Trinidad, a stepping-stone to the east coast of South America. Trippe said they would organize a national corporation in Cuba to seek mail concessions on the island. In Central and South America, franchises and mail contracts would be secured by the purchase of interests in local companies.[20]

To Hoyt and Trippe, crop dusting was now a sideshow compared to the potential of mail and passenger service from the United States to Central and South America. With Harris back in the United States, and in keeping with the tag-team pattern they had established, Huff Daland Dusters sent Woolman back to Peru for the 1928 cotton-growing season. With the emphasis shifting from crop dusting to airlines and airmail, Woolman's instructions now included seeking mail and passenger permits from Peru north to Ecuador and south to Chile.[21]

Discussions with Trippe, Gott, and Harris likely took place in New York before Woolman departed. Congenially, they together attended the Aeronautical Chamber of Commerce of America banquet at the Biltmore Hotel on November 3, 1927. Harris and Woolman were seated at table one, and Gott and Trippe shared company at table three.[22] Woolman, his wife and children accompanying him, sailed sometime in November aboard one of Grace Line's steamships to Lima.[23] That company offered "direct fortnightly passenger service via fast luxurious 'Santa' Steamers modern and spic and span throughout."[24]

Barbara Woolman Preston, then five years old, remembers going through the Panama Canal as well as the small adobe house they occupied in Miraflores, on the coast near Lima. "We were a year in Peru when Daddy was working on the West Coast Air Line of Peru for Pan American."[25] It rained the first time in seven years. "Just a little sprinkle," she recalls, but it was enough for the foot to drop off a little cherub statue on the front porch.[26] Barbara was disappointed in the beach: "It was great big sharp rocks, and you couldn't get to the water really because you'd get thrown against the rocks."[27] Had she ventured into the surf, she might also have recalled the cold water of the Humboldt Current prevalent there.

To compensate for Peru's "extremely high" expenses, Woolman's salary was raised $2.00 per day. He and his family lived among the local population for six months as "residents." He kept careful records, and though they lived "on a reduced scale" (his thrift became legendary in later years), his accounting showed "actual living costs were increased $152.46 per month over a like period in the States." Upon returning to Monroe, Woolman requested reimbursement for the difference from Pan American, claiming he was assured his going to Peru "should not be at a personal financial sacrifice."[28]

Woolman bought two cars while in South America: one, a Buick, cost the equivalent of $1,036.03; the other, a Ford, $588.14.[29] Presumably, Woolman used the Buick for his own purposes and the Ford as needed for general company business. At his request a Victor Orthophonic Victrola was bought in the United States and forwarded to him for his personal use as well as, perhaps, to entertain business guests in his home; it does not appear that Woolman opened an office, although he might have used the office of Martinto, the company's resident agent in Lima. To pay for the phonograph, $95 was charged to his account. Auerbach instructed him to "please enter the amount as an item received on your monthly cash report."[30]

In a memo to Woolman on "Accounting for Peruvian Expedition, 1927–1928," Auerbach asked that all reports be "forwarded to the Monroe office monthly as soon after the first of the month as possible." In order to save on cable fees, he wrote telegraphic communications using the Five-Letter ABC Universal Commercial Telegraphic Code, Sixth Edition. With this practice, messages were composed and deciphered utilizing the various five-letter groupings (and their meanings) found in the guide. Additional codes were created for company requirements. For example, Auerbach instructed Woolman to add "IJIER" for Trippe, "IJEVZ" for Grow, "IJBGE" for airmail, and "IJELP" for Woolman, among others.[31] Sensitive communications were likely sent through the courier service with the U.S. embassy.

Woolman's first order of business was to protect cotton from infestations under existing agreements with planters. Approximately 25,000 acres were under contract for 1928.[32] To augment the three aircraft remaining in Peru at the close of the previous season, two additional aircraft, parts and accessories, tools, and supplies were shipped to Cerro Azul in December 1927.[33] As the contracted season in areas near Lima ended, the company expanded its dusting activities to northern districts.

The previous season before departing Lima, Pope, the entomologist who had accompanied Harris, investigated conditions in the northern valleys of Peru and saw an opportunity to expand the company's services. Martinto was advised to offer a 40-percent reduction in fees to help drum up business. As a result, he found work to rehabilitate degraded cotton-producing areas from infestations in the Piura district, near the border with Ecuador. In Paita Tobin discovered worms "stripping cotton twelve inches high so it looks as if we are going to do some good." He wrote to Woolman, the "results I got on my first days dusting have simply been splendid." Enthusiastically, he further reported, "this dusting business is the rage up here right now."[34]

A Canadian national, Tobin thought his pending application for U.S. citizenship might be in jeopardy by his being out of the country and asked Woolman to intercede on his behalf. Woolman inquired of Ellis O. Briggs, the American vice consul in Lima, what effect this had on Tobin's status. The vice consul was well acquainted with Huff Daland Dusters' personnel, with both Woolman and Harris "frequent callers at the consulate general." Mail was forwarded via the U.S. consulate, and the company's international business involved relations between the American embassy and Peruvian authorities. In fact, Ambassador Poindexter had introduced Woolman to President Leguía, "whose interest was immediate and potent" in establishing mail and passenger service between Peru and Panama.[35] Briggs assured Tobin the five-year residency requirement to become naturalized would not be "broken by his temporary foreign assignments in connection with the field work of Huff Daland Dusters, Inc."[36]

In his dealings Woolman's authority was vested in a power of attorney executed by Huff Daland Dusters' president and certified by Enrique Marriott, the Peruvian consul in Philadelphia. He had broad discretion as the company's "true and lawful representative for it and in its name, place and stead, to negotiate a contract or contracts with the Republic of Peru, or citizens thereof, or persons, firms, associations, or corporations resident, domiciled or qualified therein, for and in connection with the sale of aircraft, spare parts, and aircraft equipment, concessions, for air mail and transport, (both of passengers, express and freight) and airplane dusting, subject to confirmation at the home office of Huff Daland Dusters, Inc."[37] In addition to overseeing dusting operations, Woolman acted as the resident agent for Pan American in seeking for it mail and passenger concessions under the mantle of his Huff Daland authorization.

Initially, Woolman may not have been fully aware of what was taking place diplomatically behind the scenes between the Department of State and the American embassy in Peru. Secretary of State Frank B. Kellogg directed Ambassador Poindexter to aid and support Woolman in any way possible. By January 1928, it was public knowledge that "Washington was definitely giving PAA [Pan American Airways] strong encouragement," helping it plan Central American and Caribbean routes and conduct surveys, although extending those routes to the southern continent was for the moment problematic. Protecting the Panama Canal presented U.S. authorities with a more immediate and strategic concern. And there was another issue in play: "Trippe had to overcome doubts among key colleagues that South America was worth the candle." In this it was the "beachhead" of pro-American elements in Peru that helped Trippe win over the opposition.[38]

The State Department and Trippe took advantage of Huff Daland Dusters' presence in Peru and Grow's position as an American national "entrusted with making a recommendation to Leguía concerning a United States–Peruvian service." Historian Wesley Newton has viewed the dusters' presence as a "stalking horse for PAA's, and Washington's ambitions for the west coast of South America."[39] How much of these diplomatic machinations Woolman knew of is unknown, but his actions were a concern for Matthew E. Hanna, chargé d'affaires ad interim (between ambassadors), in light of competition from foreign enterprises seeking similar privileges.[40] Rudolf Beeck, a longtime German resident of Peru, petitioned the government to establish a commercial aviation company offering weekly service from Lima to Tumbes to the north, Ilo to the south, and Iquitos to the east.[41] The Germans took notice of Peru's naval-aviation route to Iquitos and proposed extending it to originate from Callao, on the coast near Lima. Washington worried Leguía would choose to contract air routes with the Germans rather than with the Americans.[42]

Officially, Grow headed the U.S. naval mission to Peru but held additional sway with the Peruvian government. On January 3 he launched the first domestic Peruvian airline with fourteen "American-built Keystone Pelican (Pronto) aircraft."[43] The Prontos were powered by Wright J-5 220-hp radial engines and could carry 100 kilograms (220.5 pounds) of freight and two passengers. Peru is geographically divided by the formidable Andes Mountains, which stretch north to south along the Pacific coast of the South America. Establishing the combined rail-air service over the mountains to the vast Amazon interior to the east was a major milestone.[44] By air "it took two days for correspondence to reach either Iquitos or Lima, a trip which previously took thirty-two days overland."[45] Grow's achievement, not to mention his "blond and vivacious wife," put him in good standing with the president.[46]

Grow's rapport with President Leguía helped advance the development of a commercial air route to the United States.[47] Leguía assured Chargé d'Affaires Hanna, in a meeting on April 19, that the "persistent reports that the Peruvian Government has signed [a] contract with German aeronautical interests to operate in Peru are not true." The "present intention," the president continued, "is to enter into contracts with both American and German interests and let them compete." Hanna noted that Leguía "added that Woolman is seeking [an] exclusive concession which is not true of the German interests."[48] Events of late April and early May were pivotal for Woolman. He proposed a weekly domestic mail, freight, and passenger service to begin within a year. Reserved for government use would be 120 kilograms (265 pounds) of space, payable at 50 percent of the tariff whether used or not. The rights under the contract were to be transferable, but President Leguía refused the American's request for an exclusive concession.[49]

On April 23, in the first part of a two-part telegram to Washington, Hanna reported that the exclusivity clause had been removed. Woolman, he said encouragingly, "has been told by the Minister of Gobernacion he can consider it [the contract] as good as signed." At the same time, and not so encouragingly, the Peruvian official said an agreement would be signed with the Germans. Woolman, Hanna advised, should have the "decisive advantage in [the] ensuing competition" if he acted quickly and with "energy and determination." Huff Daland Dusters had aircraft and pilots readily available, while the Germans did not.[50] He cautioned, though, that with any delay, the company would "have little or no chance to establish the service." In view of the State Department's role, Hanna suggested that Washington officials might want to advise company managers of its involvement.[51]

In section two of the telegram, Hanna questioned Woolman's competence: "STRICTLY CONFIDENTIAL. Americans who have assisted Woolman in this matter inform me that he had not been skillful in his negotiations, however his relations with the Embassy are very cordial but his ineptitude has made it difficult for the Embassy to cooperate effectively."[52] The Americans he refers to are not named, but given his position, Grow could have been one of them. The State Department forwarded the information and the warning to Postmaster General New, a close associate of Hoyt and Trippe, who likely relayed to them Hanna's concern.[53]

Acting in his capacity as interim ambassador, Hanna dutifully reported the circumstances as he saw them, but Woolman may not have been entirely forthright in his dealings with him and others. Guided to some degree by Trippe (and perhaps Hoyt), he probably did not want to disclose the extent of his authority or his full intentions. Woolman drew on his considerable experience as a salesman in these negotiations. Harris noted that he "never told any lies, but he didn't necessarily tell all the facts."[54]

Seemingly to vindicate Woolman, only two days later, Hanna telegraphed that Leguía had informed Woolman that "his contract will be signed very soon, possibly this week and intimated that [a] competing contract for coast service may not be granted." The German contract would be "to the interior and eastward in which," Hanna advised, "I understand they are interested."[55] Unfortunately, this optimism was premature since the signing did not take place. President Leguía was apparently unaware and surprised by Article 8, the clause reserving 265 pounds of space for the Peruvian government that obligated payment whether used or not. Officials demanded that this requirement be removed. Hanna so informed Washington but added that Woolman has "eliminated it entirely and expects [the] contract to be signed immediately. Subsequently he will have to reach an agreement on tariffs and enter into a contract with the Marconi Company for carrying the mail."[56]

Complicating Woolman's endeavors, the competition between the Americans and the Germans appealed to Peruvian nationalism. Beeck, who represented the German aviation initiative, published a letter in *El Tiempo* on May 5 stating that "his enterprise would be controlled by a Peruvian company which is in the process of formation and would be financed by Peruvian capital."[57] Reportedly, he enlisted one of the president's sons-in-law to help in negotiations. On the other hand, Hanna observed, "Mr. Woolman appears to have had no Peruvian advisor except a rather obscure young attorney."[58] Another rival, Elmer Faucett, the first man to cross the Andes by air, also vied with both Woolman and Beeck for a concession but lacked Washington's political or Wall Street's financial backing. Nevertheless, he contributed to the swirl of aviation intrigue that engulfed Lima at the time.

A key hand in the "poker like rivalry" was dealt in May, when President Leguía put Grow "in charge of all Peruvian aviation, civil, commercial, and military," replacing his own son, "hard-drinking" Juan Leguía, and a German officer. Almost coincidently, on May 28, the Peruvian government awarded Huff Daland Dusters a concession to operate an international air service to the United States, although an agreement still had to be negotiated with the Marconi Company, which held the country's mail concession.[59] During these talks, an Associated Press story declared "Huff Deland Dusters Company has no contract with the United States to carry mail into the United States from Peru."[60] Throughout the negotiations, this right was assumed. Embarrassingly, the story implied, without this authority, the Peru award was effectively permission for Huff Daland Dusters to fly nowhere.

Woolman was not happy. He wrote Harris, "This was great stuff for the opposition and believe me they used it." He also requested of Hanna that "prompt appropriate measures be taken to correct the impression it [the report] has occasioned."[61] Indicative of how tightly American business and political interests were tied, Washington acted quickly. Only two days later, on June 4, Secretary Kellogg telegraphed the embassy in Lima:

Of course there is no truth in the statement that a company holding a contract from Peru could not carry mail into the United States without a contract from the United States Government. It would require a contract to carry the mail on the return trip and . . . the Postmaster General would be glad to negotiate concerning such a contract with any American company capable of rendering the service. The call for this service was issued on Saturday.

You may communicate the above to the appropriate authorities of the Peruvian Government and if necessary issue a statement to the local press correcting the erroneous interpretation of conversation given by the Associated Press.[62]

Probably as a result of the State Department's almost immediate clarification, the Marconi agreement was quickly signed the following day. Huff Daland Dusters could now operate its airline and carry the mail. On receiving the news, Woolman was in the process of typing a letter to Harris. He exclaimed boldly in capital letters:

——WOW——

PHONE JUST RANG AND THE MINISTER STATES THAT THE CONTRACT WITH MAR-CONI HAS BEEN SIGNED, SEALED AND DELIVERED.[63]

That evening Woolman attended a "reception for the new ambassador [Alexander P.] Moore and of course told acting Amb. Hanna and the other officials about the closing of the contract. A shout went up and we all repaired to the punch bowl. It has been a tight fight and they have all been mighty interested in the outcome."[64] By this time, considerable funds had been spent by Huff Daland Dusters for the Pan American project. Gott instructed Auerbach "to set up as an asset the cost of development of the South American Air Mail project" in the company's books.[65] Further, an agreement on June 20 gave Trippe's Aviation Corporation of the Americas the option to buy the Peruvian concessions from Huff Daland.[66]

As Trippe consolidated his route through Central America, Woolman expanded the franchise to Chile and Ecuador. The Department of Commerce learned of an agreement between the Chilean government and a French company to operate an air route to Europe. This knowledge encouraged Commerce officials, who thought a "properly equipped [American] company, agreeing to use Chilean pilots" might get approval from the Chilean postal authorities for an air route to Peru. Woolman's reaction to this advice was tepid. He appointed an agent in Santiago, Francisco Aguilera, as his representative for an exclusive concession "subject to the approval and acceptance of the Company."[67] Woolman was more active to the north.

At Trippe's urging, Gott cabled Woolman on June 21 instructing him to seek a concession in Ecuador.[68] Woolman and Robert S. "Stan" Webber, an American businessman with Ingersoll Rand Company, flew out of Lima on July 14, using a duster piloted by Tobin, bound for Guayaquil with the objective of petitioning Ecuadorian authorities for a mail permit. Woolman carried with him some airmail under authority of the company's recently approved Peruvian west coast mail contract.[69] Writing to his wife, Webber relished the journey as a great adventure. A duster's hopper, however uninviting, could be used to carry passengers.[70] Another passenger, Ellis Briggs, described a previous experience with Harris "in the empty dust hopper of his plane, which afforded a poor view of the country and brought on an attack of sneezing."[71]

The Peruvian portion of the flight was over territory familiar to Tobin, having been up that way to dust cotton in the northern valleys. Crossing the border with Ecuador by air, however, was a new experience for the travelers. Webber wrote:

> Tobin had never been in Guayaquil and it is quite a tribute to his ability as a pilot that we came over Guayaquil through that nasty weather, hitting the town right on the nose. I did not know it until afterward, but Tobin went through his flying course at Kelly Field in the same class with Lindbergh, they graduated together. Anyone graduating from Kelly Field has earned his right to fly they tell me. Well, we made a turn of the town and crossed the river to Duran, made a very nice "zoom" of the field which pleased the natives and landed perfectly, coming up close to the hangars in the midst of a big crowd.[72]

From Guayaquil, Woolman and Webber went by train to Rio Bamba and then by car to Quito, which left them "in a sort of daze trying to absorb so much scenery." They found the Ecuadoran capital a city unspoiled by tourism, "due to the difficulty of getting there." The American minister, Dr. Gerhard Bading, arranged for them to meet the country's president, Isidro Ayora. Webber translated for Woolman, who did not speak Spanish. The president, Webber wrote, "is not the personality that Leguía is, but was very nice." He added, Ayora "is not so pro-American as Leguía."[73] He did not grant Woolman his permit.

Nevertheless, a major milestone occurred on September 13, 1928, when Huff Daland Dusters inaugurated its scheduled passenger service in a Fairchild FC-2.[74] The features of the aircraft are described in detail in an *El Comercio* news report.

> The "Fairchild" airplane is a limousine-type monoplane, with capacity for five persons, including the pilot. It is painted dark green, except for the wings, which are canary yellow. It is driven by a Wright-Whirlwind 220 hp engine. It was specially constructed for this service in the plant of the same name, and is equipped with all the comfort required in a machine which will be used to transport passengers a great distance. It has glass windows on each side of the cabin. It has two great doors, one on each side of the fuselage, in the center of the cabin. It is equipped with a complete restroom. At the front of the cabin, a sliding door gives access to the pilot's compartment, which is roomy, and fully equipped for command. It is shut in by the windshield and the roof of the compartment, which fully protects the pilot from wind and rain, without obstructing his vision. Other technical characteristics of the airplane are those corresponding to the most perfect machines of this type, since this is one of the most modern aircraft.[75]

With Tobin at the controls, the flight departed from Lima at 10:45 A.M. Aboard were A. G. Harrott, temporary postmaster general; Bejamín Romero, editor of *El Comercio;* and some mail. Stops included Chimbote, Trujillo, Pimentel, Paita, and Talara. At each city Harrott established an air postal-service office. The departure was witnessed by a crowd of several hundred, including American officials stationed in Lima, while President Leguía handed over the first sack of mail to be dispatched.[76] William Howell, Panagra's first employee, commented: "The plane took off in a cloud of dust. We spent a week shaking ourselves out." The flight was not without incident. Howell filled in the details for Harris, who had not yet arrived in Peru at the time of the inaugural flight. Tobin, he described, had "a little bit of a gas leak" above the cabin door but stopped it with some soap and a band of tape; Tobin announced, "that's got it." Howell also recounted a tragic incident that reflects a lack of awareness of a spinning propeller's danger and the imperative to complete the flight. When "a speech was being made of welcome . . . I think at Pimentel," an observer "walked into the propeller, since the engine was not shut off. [But, notwithstanding this,] they kept on going with the first flight, to reach Talara before dark."[77] Until such time as through service to the United States became possible, weekly flights connected mail with steamships at ports along the coast, cutting a day off the time for mail to reach Panama or New York.

With the permits originated by Huff Daland Dusters, Trippe and Hoyt merged Pan American Airways with the W. R. Grace Company fifty-fifty to form Peruvian Airways Corporation, a Delaware-based company. The directors included William F. Cogswell, Robert H. Patchin (a Grace vice president), Hoyt, and Trippe. The officers were Trippe as president and Harris as vice president and general manager.[78] The Pan American and Grace partnership exploited the franchise Woolman had won. Trippe confirmed this: "The Peruvian Airways Corporation has purchased from Huff Daland Dusters, Inc., an option covering its air mail concessions and contracts with the Peruvian Government. Mr. Harris is expected to arrive in Peru on or about September 25th. Application will be made to the Peruvian Government for transfer of the above concession and contracts to Peruvian Airways Corporation."[79] On November 26, 1928, the permits were transferred as requested.[80] Once again, this time permanently, Woolman and Harris changed places. Harris stayed in Lima to manage Peruvian Airways, which shortly became Pan American–Grace Airways while Woolman, when he returned to the United States, helped inaugurate a new service in the Mississippi Delta to serve points across the South.

Privately, Woolman, Harris, and Auerbach had previously hatched a plan to buy Huff Daland Dusters assets and start an airline of their own. Hoyt, as they soon found out, was willing to sell.

METAMORPHOSIS

There is nothing in a caterpillar
that tells you it's going to be a butterfly.

—R. BUCKMINSTER FULLER

W hen Peruvian Airways acquired Huff Daland Dusters' route and mail permits, the dusting elements of the company became irrelevant to financier Hoyt and Pan American president Trippe. Along with statesmen at the highest levels of the U.S. and Latin American governments, they focused on building an international enterprise able to leapfrog geographical and political barriers, link continents, and project influence, power, and modernity. Described by Elsbeth Freudenthal as an "imperialistic agent" of U.S. policy, Pan American was the key.[1] For Hoyt and Trippe., connecting destinations south of the equator was a more personally and financially rewarding opportunity and challenge than exterminating agricultural pests or competing with rivals at home.

Domestically, William Boeing, of Boeing Airplane and Transport Corporation, moved to join with Pratt & Whitney's Frederick Rentschler to form United Aircraft and Transport Corporation. Additionally, Clement Keys leveraged his interests in National Air Transport, Transcontinental Air Transport, Curtiss Aeroplane and Motor Company, and Wright Aeronautical Corporation to form North American Aviation, a holding company "more loosely organized than United Aircraft." Another company, the Aviation Corporation of Delaware (AVCO), was "a product of the machinations of some of the greatest financial minds [at one stage involving Hoyt] on Wall Street."[2]

Meanwhile, with roots already set deep in the fertile Mississippi Delta, Woolman, Harris, and Auerbach saw an opportunity on their doorstep, albeit on a smaller scale than Hoyt and Trippe. In a drama involving a betrayal by one of the principals, a new enterprise emerged in Monroe. Carrying the mail was an idea Woolman, Harris, and Auerbach had recommended in their October 1927 report to Huff Daland Dusters president Gott; to proceed, they needed his endorsement. But Hoyt and Trippe redirected Gott's attention to their ambitions in Latin America.[3] As it turned out, this was not without some personal benefit for Woolman and Harris. The Peruvian project ultimately proved a practical exercise in airline development.

The group expanded Huff Daland Dusters' North American operations in other ways. In a memorandum to Harris (a copy was sent to Woolman in Peru), Auerbach outlined a "means of securing the maximum expansion with the minimum of capital investment and risk," offering a "special limited commercial course" of instruction for training pilots. Upon successful completion, the company would sell the newly certificated pilot an airplane and hire him, for all practical purposes, as an independent contractor.[4] As the agent for Travel Air Manufacturing Company, Huff Daland Dusters operated a dual-control trainer for flight instruction.[5] Guy S. Gannaway, an early student, praised the company's instructors: "I don't believe your school can be excelled anywhere and I will always be glad I learned to fly there."[6]

Aerial photography was another service initiated by Huff Daland Dusters as the agent of Fairchild Aerial Services in Louisiana.[7] This activity was not restricted to U.S. territory but extended to South America. During the months of May, June, and September, Henry Elliot flew aerial photographic-mapping missions in northern Peru at Pimentel, Talara, and Casa Grande.[8]

The operating group's dedication and hard work during this period did not go unnoticed by superiors. In July the board of directors gave Woolman, Harris, Auerbach, and Catherine FitzGerald a combined total of 1,000 shares of stock as "a bonus in recognition of past services and to encourage future services." Of that total, Woolman, Harris, and Auerbach received 330 shares each; FitzGerald received the remaining 10. The stock could not be sold and their proxy was assigned to Gott, but if each continued as an employee for five years afterward, these limitations would be removed.[9]

At some point (precisely when is unknown), in what Harris refers to as "our famous statement to the Board," he, Woolman, and Auerbach asked for an option to buy Huff Daland Dusters. The offer "was for a period of one year to purchase all of the capital stock, the outstanding account of the Keystone Aircraft Corp. and all the assets of the Company for the sum of $65,000 payable 25% at the time the option is exercised and 25% annually thereafter."[10] Apparently, this proposition was not taken up by the directors.

On August 24, 1928, Harris went to a scheduled meeting with Trippe at his office in New York and unexpectedly found Gott there as well. He was surprised to discover that at a noon directors meeting that day, Hoyt had told the board he "wanted to close out the dusters to the pilots on any terms . . . for forty thousand dollars, and all notes if necessary." Harris feigned disinterest but later observed to his colleagues that "it looked like a golden opportunity for us to do some good for ourselves."[11] He wired Auerbach in Monroe: "WE ARE BEING APPROACHED TO BUY DUSTERS OUT FOR FORTY THOUSAND NOTES WIRE YOUR IDEAS IMMEDIATELY STOP THEY WOULD LIKE SOME CASH BUT IT IS NOT NECESSARY REGARDS."[12]

Harris considered reducing their earlier offer from $65,000 to "$40,000 payable in about the same way" but cautioned it was probable the directors "will not be interested in the option business as they are seemingly trying to get out at once." Coincidently, Harris was being considered for a job with Pan American, probably the reason for his meeting with Trippe in the first place. "The Panam thing is still hanging fire," he wrote Auerbach, "but it looks as though it was a go since they are talking of me getting Thursday's boat. What a chance."[13] This comment suggests that Woolman and Auerbach knew of Harris's job offer and that, among themselves, they had an open dialogue of ideas and plans on both a personal and professional level.

Auerbach addressed a response to Harris, who was staying at the Commodore Hotel—conveniently located adjacent to the Grand Central train depot—recommending that the group form a new company. His advice displays a shrewd understanding of the financial issues:

BELIEVING BY FAR MOST ADVANTAGEOUS WAY FOR DISPOSING OF DUSTERS IS BY OPERATING GROUP ORGANIZING NEW COMPANIES COMMA INSIST ON LONGEST POSSIBLE OPTION COMMA HAVE NET PURCHASE PRICE AT FIXED FIGURE EXCLUDING AMOUNT CLAIMED DUE FROM ACA [Aviation Corporation of the Americas]

WHICH KEYSTONE CAN MORE EASILY COLLECT STOP ASSURE THAT PURCHASE
AGREEMENT IS FREE OF ALL LEGAL ENTANGLEMENTS WITH OLD STOCKHOLDERS
OR CLAIMS OF KEYSTONE AND PAYMENTS SPREAD OVER THREE YEARS STOP AS-
SIGNMENT OF PERU RIGHTS TO ACA MAY BE LIMITED TO REGULAR TRANSPORT AS
PER YOUR MEMO STOP OUTRIGHT PURCHASE NOT FEASIBLE BECAUSE OUTSTAND-
ING ACCEPTANCES AND PAYROLL REQUIREMENTS NECESSITATE ASSURED CAPITAL
IN CONSIDERABLE AMOUNT IRWIN.[14]

In a detailed memo that may have been actually a note to himself, Harris
reasoned that Hoyt saw Huff Daland Dusters as "more of a liability than an
asset" and was "willing to go out of his way to assist the present operators in
taking the Dusters over to see if they can make something of it." The physical
assets, consisting mostly of airplanes, parts, and other equipment, Harris believed, were worth about $15,000 in their current location and condition. He
thought the company might fetch $40,000 as a going concern. If he, Wool-
man, and Auerbach could get an option for one year, it might be enough time
to reorganize the company to attract investors.[15] They needed the stockholders' money to complete the purchase.

Meanwhile, Auerbach sought investors willing to buy Huff Daland Dusters outright. In a letter to two Monroe aviation enthusiasts, hardware dealer
Atkins, and banker Oliver, he solicited a clean sale of Huff Daland assets, absent liabilities and cash. Oliver was interested but wanted to keep "the local management of Lt. Harris and Mr. Auerbach continuing as heretofore."
Auerbach modified the offer, specifically to include Woolman, and proposed
they buy the assets for $40,000: $20,000 subscribed by the group and $20,000
backed by Oliver and his associates.[16] These overtures were in vain.

Auerbach then divided the assets into two lots. Lot A was for material located in the United States and "the capital stock of Air Operations, Inc., but not
its assets."[17] He, Woolman, and Harris would buy Lot A for $40,000: $20,000
in cash and $20,000 in stock collateral of a new company. Lot B included the
Peruvian assets and was valued at $15,000. Auerbach anticipated traveling to
Lima to consummate the sale of those assets.[18] In essence, this is the deal as
it was finally agreed, but what began as a straightforward plan unexpectedly
turned into a nightmare. Woolman's character and leadership were revealed
in the ensuing crisis, out of which Delta Air Service, Inc. emerged. September

and October were crucial months. Preceding the situation, but relevant to it, was the emergence of Peruvian Airways, a company owned jointly by Aviation Corporation of the Americas and W. R. Grace & Company, the import-export firm run "from a bank like structure in central Lima referred to as 'Casa Grace.'"[19] The advantages were mutual: Grace had ties in "more than half of South America" but "not the aviation side of it." Hoyt arranged the financing to "put the deal across."[20]

Between late August and early September, Harris's future took a dramatic turn when Trippe formally hired him as general manager of Peruvian Airways.[21] Consequently, Gott used the appointment to reconcile Huff Daland Dusters' account for expenses incurred while setting up the Peruvian mail franchise. In a letter addressed to Harris in his new role, Gott recommended that Aviation Corporation of the Americas or affiliated companies (that is, Peruvian Airways) "forthwith exercise the option granted them by our Company under date of June 20, 1928, and make definite arrangements to pay for the concession and its associated expenses."[22] Hoyt, the principal financier behind the separate entities and ultimate arbiter, approved a settlement for $15,000 to cover all costs accrued up to September 1, though not including the purchase of the Fairchild airplane, which would be paid for separately. Thereafter, Huff Daland Dusters would charge Peruvian Airways for salaries and expenses of its personnel and would rent out its airplanes and equipment under specific agreements.[23]

Trippe gave Harris a comprehensive list of instructions. "In taking up your duties and responsibilities as Vice President and General Manager of the Peruvian Airways Corporation," he commanded, "you will follow, in general, the program hereinafter set forth." Twenty-one points followed, beginning with an order to take the Grace Line steamer *Santa Luisa,* scheduled to sail from New York on September 13, or alternatively connect with the *Santa Luisa* at the Canal Zone from New Orleans.[24] On this trip, his second to South America, Harris was accompanied by his expectant wife Grace Clark Harris (their daughter, Alta May, was born in Lima on December 10) and his four-year-old son, Harold Jr. Most likely, Harris first traveled to Louisiana to pick up his wife and young son, then sailed from New Orleans in time to meet the *Santa Luisa* when it transited the Panama Canal.[25] When he arrived in Lima, a few days remained before Woolman departed, allowing them to discuss their plans and bring each other up to date on what was going on locally in Peru as well as corporately in New York. As they said goodbye, Woolman and Harris shook hands aboard the Grace liner *Santa Maria* just before it sailed. Notwithstanding Harris's change in employment (though he still represented Huff Daland Dusters' interests locally), he confirmed his commitment to Woolman and Auerbach, saying, "it's the three of us and now for our wives and babies." In that statement the future of Huff Daland Dusters, Inc. was sealed. Nevertheless, a lot still had to be done if the three were to take over the company.[26] Quite unexpectedly, though, Huff Daland's fate took an unanticipated and dramatic turn.

The stage was set in New York on September 27 while Woolman and Harris were absent. Gott formally tendered an offer to Auerbach, "and/or your associates," an option to buy the company for $15,000 cash and $20,000 in collateral stock notes.[27] Inexplicably, the offer did not specifically mention Harris or Woolman by name. On October 22 Auerbach, claiming to represent Huff Daland Dusters, sent sealed proposals to a list of contacts unilaterally offering to sell the company for $40,000 cash.[28] One of the parties, Jackson B. Ardis, president of Ardis & Company, Inc., a wholesale grocery in Shreveport, answered immediately and turned him down flat, writing, "we find it quite necessary in any line of business to even hope for success to have a perfect understanding of the nature of the business, and yours is all foreign to us."[29]

Woolman returned from South America to discover Auerbach's betrayal. The details are recorded in a typed letter he began to Harris on October 26 but completed later in which he reported of his confronting him. Shockingly, he wrote, "Auerbach seemed shot to pieces." When Woolman asked what the problem was, he responded only that he was "not satisfied with the cooperation" he was getting from him and Harris and would not elaborate further. Auerbach, he continued, "thinks he can put the whole thing over by himself, which he can't, and will dispose of the Peru Co. to his own advantage, which he can't, and is cutting our throats at the first chance he has had."[30]

Woolman acted immediately to protect his and Harris's interests through a series of telegrams. To Harris, he cabled:

AUERBACH DOUBLE CROSSING US ON SALE EQUIPMENT STOP CABLE GOTT TO CANCEL HIS OPTION ON EQUIPMENT MAKING SAME TO US RUSH.

To Gott, he asked:

> WAS OPTION FOR SALE OF EQUIPMENT MADE TO AUERBACH PERSONALLY AND MY-
> SELF (QUESTION) AUERBACH HAS THROWN US OVER COLD AND DEALING FOR HIM-
> SELF STOP REQUEST YOU CANCEL ANY OPTION HE HAS MAKING SAME TO HARRIS
> AND MYSELF STOP.

Gott responded to Woolman:

> UNDERSTANDING WITH HOYT AND OURSELVES WAS THAT YOU AND HARRIS WERE
> INCLUDED STOP OUR REPRESENTATIVE J S WOODBRIDGE ARRIVES MONROE FRIDAY
> MORNING MISSOURI PACIFIC TO ASSIST IN NEGOTIATIONS AND TO ACT FOR US IN
> ALL MATTERS STOP GET IN TOUCH WITH WOODBRIDGE AND BE GUIDED BY HIM
> STOP NO DESIRE TO CHANGE ORIGINAL INTENT STOP QUICKEST AND MOST SATIS-
> FACTORY SALE IS IN OUR ESTIMATION MOST IMPORTANT FACTOR.

Woolman then cabled Harris with the news:

> AUERBACH DISCHARGED STOP WIRE APPROVAL YOU AND I TAKING FIFTY PERCENT
> OWNERSHIP LOCAL COMPANY KEYSTONE FINANCING US TWENTY THOUSAND OUR
> SHARE STOP OUR NOTE TO KEYSTONE BACKED BY OUR STOCK NO OTHER OBLIGA-
> TION STOP THIS ALLOWS PURCHASE PERUVIAN EQUIPMENT FIFTEEN THOUSAND.[31]

When he arrived, John S. Woodbridge assessed the situation. He liked
Woolman; Douglas Culver, the chief of maintenance; and Murrell "Don" Dice,
chief pilot. "These three gentlemen have inspired me with the fullest confi-
dence and I would accept without hesitation as being the strict truth anything
that they would tell me." On the other hand, prospective purchasers, planters, and financiers had soured on Auerbach. "As substantiation of this I would
quote from Mr. Travis Oliver, President of the Central Savings Bank and Trust
Company of this city, an exceedingly airminded individual who impressed me
as a straight shooter, and with whom we are almost compelled to deal if we
dispose of the property locally. Mr. Oliver told both Mr. Fraser and Mr. Woolman that the local people would not have anything to do with the purchase of

this equipment if Mr. Auerbach were in any way connected with it."[32] To make matters worse, as a consequence of Auerbach's offering, a rumor spread that the company was going out of business, and planters became reluctant to sign new contracts.[33] On the surface, the outlook was not bright for the Huff Daland Dusters sale, but Woodbridge was a good judge of character and had the keen eye of a businessman.

Woodbridge appraised the company's equipment and supplies at $43,735, but putting the ships in airworthy condition for the dusting season would cost about an additional $15,000. The aircraft were "strewed all over the floor of the hangar in various stages of apparent decrepitude, with fabric off most of them, and presenting a sorry sight." To get things going, he recommended that Gott advance $20,000 to carry the "organization through until money starts to come in from dusting." The prospects were good. A heavy weevil infestation was predicted, and "responsible planters were crying to be signed up for the next season, right now." Woodbridge asked Gott to give Woolman his approval to "go ahead and sign up his farmer friends, who cannot wait much longer . . . , for whether the Company is owned locally or by Keystone Aircraft, the business ought to be secured at once before it is too late." Woolman, he said, was "inexhaustible in his efforts on behalf of this entire sale business." Then for his consideration, Woodbridge added that the "Monroe group will trade," but "they will probably want to cut the price, too, for they know the equipment, and so does Coad, who is their advisor."[34]

For Harris, the Peruvian operation was similarly in limbo. A new company must be organized by the middle of December, either as a branch of the American firm or as a national corporation, "otherwise the ten-year option for dusting expires."[35] December was critical for another reason: equipment and supplies had to be shipped from the United States in advance. Woolman pressed a potential client, Alfredo Checa in Piura, for his commitment so "that the planes, poison, and men may be sent down from the states in ample time, and so that plans may be made for complete service."[36] Harris underscored the urgency by pleading, "we need airplanes, personnel & supplies here as soon as possible & regardless of what may happen in the U. S. this work here must not be forgotten, as it is a real money maker."[37] He did not know a plan was already being worked out by Woolman, Woodbridge, and Oliver, with the Peruvian business a key component of the deal.

For his part, Woolman found Woodbridge "a hell of a fine fellow and a square shooter" and worked well with him "trying to straighten things out." The resulting plan was for Harris and Woolman to buy Huff Daland Dusters' domestic assets and form a new company, with an option on the Peruvian assets. This was doable, Woodbridge reported to Gott, because Woolman is "firmly convinced that the profit he and Harris make on the Peruvian negotiations will almost be enough to meet their notes on this local sale."[38] Working together "day and night," Woodbridge and Woolman got "the capital raised and expected to close the deal for the purchase locally." Woolman informed Harris: "This gives us (you and I) a $20,000 interest. [Elliot] Daland wired that if we were managing the new organization he would put $5,000 in and has mailed his check."[39]

As an indication of his esteem within the Monroe business community, in a just a few minutes Oliver raised $12,000 of the additional $20,000 necessary to complete the deal and expected the rest as soon as he could communicate with some planters.[40] Woodbridge wired Gott: "INCLUDING DALANDS FIVE THOUSAND NECESSARY TWENTY THOUSAND VIRTUALLY ASSURED LOCALLY NEW ORGANIZATION COMMENCING MONDAY TWELFTH SUGGEST BILL OF SALE AND CHECK TWENTY THOUSAND BE MAILED WOOLMAN AT ONCE STOP CUT OFF DATE CURRENT EXPENSES NOVEMBER TWELFTH."[41]

During the crisis, Woolman did his best to keep Harris in the loop, but events moved at such a rapid pace it was impossible to keep him fully informed in a timely manner. Harris understood this but could not mask his frustration: "Certainly glad to get your letter of December 4th," he wrote, "which was the first real dope I had on the situation in Monroe. I certainly think you are a son of a gun for not keeping me more thoroughly informed but realize that you had a tough time with the reorganization."[42] On the other hand, Woolman was just as uninformed about Peru. "Have been anxious to hear how you are getting along with the formation of the Peruvian Huff Daland company," he wrote, "as the only information I have is the letter I received the latter part of October, which outlined the plan worked out with Calderon."[43] Woolman and Harris resolved these matters equitably in a spirit of cooperation developed over many years. Their relationship is exemplified by the sense of mutual trust and respect evident in their communications. Woolman concisely summarized the domestic agreement for Harris:

To review, when Auerbach went hay wire the option to purchase was granted to us (yourself and myself) contingent upon our forming an American Company and obtaining sale for same for $40,000. Although things were dead and, incidentally, financial conditions in the State have not been at all good, we put over the company with $20,000 raised locally and $20,000 advanced by Huff Daland Dusters to us for stock in the new Company—$10,000 each—which made good our option on the Peruvian Company to purchase same for $15,000.00 as of Nov. 12, 1928, the take-over date of Delta Air Service, Inc. from Huff Daland Dusters, Inc.

The notes which we signed were stock collateral notes and did not bind us personally or our personal assets beyond the stock in our names in the Delta Air Service, which did not jeopardize the security of our families. Under the terms of the option all money received from stock sold in the Peruvian Company [and] of money realized from the Peruvian Company was to first apply against this twenty thousand dollars advanced and against the fifteen thousand dollars owed to Huff Daland Dusters for the Peruvian equipment. It was a very fair and liberal offer and the backing made it possible to put over the American Company which made possible the Peruvian proposition.[44]

Meanwhile, the Peruvian proposition took form. Harris informed Woolman that he was vice president and general manager of a new Peruvian dusting company in which A. Alverez Calderon was president and A. Fernandez Solar, secretary. In accommodation, he wrote: "I have sent Monroe a copy of my letter to [Sidney] Newborg [assistant secretary, Huff Daland Dusters] outlining this matter and presume the entire information is in the Monroe files. If not please let me know." As an afterthought, Harris added in a handwritten addendum, "Where's my radio?"[45] The imperative and his tone suggest this was a transmitter-receiver intended for operational purposes, not a home-entertainment device, and underscored the rapidity of advancing technology.

The crisis displayed Woolman's leadership and character as well as another dimension of his personality. In later years his management style was characterized as that of a compassionate patriarch. An early example of his concern for his employees was evident in a suggestion he made to Harris.

It seems to me Culver has been pretty loyal to the organization and it occurred to me that it might be no more fair if we would assign him from our holdings in Delta Air Service, perhaps a thousand dollars worth of stock on the same basis we are getting ours. Personally, I would be willing to allow half of this amount to go from my holdings, if it is agreeable with you. Think it over and let me know regarding it. I would also suggest that the same arrangement might be applicable to the case of Miss FitzGerald. Personally, I think it is right.

This was agreeable with Harris.[46]

Notwithstanding Woolman's consummation of the sale of Huff Daland Dusters' North American assets honorably on a fifty-fifty basis with Harris, he was a cautious businessman and did not take his financial stake in the Peruvian equipment for granted. Because he and Harris were "operating so far apart and with communications so difficult," Woolman wrote to Gott, "it is only business that I have a statement from you as President showing my fifty percent interest in the Peruvian enterprise and equipment just as I have already arranged for Harris to have in the Delta Air Service, Inc. an equal share with me."[47] In light of the political situation in Peru, his caution was prudent.

The outlook for Huff Daland Dusters' future in Peru was not encouraging. President Leguía used easy credit to bolster his country's economy, but in late 1928 fears of excessive government spending, waste, and corruption caused American banks to restrict further loans.[48] From Woolman's distant perspective, the prospects still looked good. He estimated the Peruvian concession might yield a profit of $10,000 each for himself and Harris at the conclusion of the dusting season. His optimism was unfounded. As the year progressed, the economic circumstances in Peru deteriorated. By December, the financial situation, according to Harris, was "extremely unsatisfactory." He was under pressure by planters who "planned to enter the dusting business themselves in case we would not choose a figure which they considered reasonable." Harris then sold the Peruvian assets for what he could get. He wrote Woolman: "I was able to get exactly $30,000 . . . and have sent you through the National City Bank your portion of it. I trust that this will be a welcome Xmas present to you as it has been for us."[49]

Ultimately, all that remained of Huff Daland Dusters was a dormant corporation. On July 15, 1930, the board of directors recommended the company be dissolved and scheduled a special meeting for that purpose for August 22. The minutes are not available, but presumably at the meeting, the stockholders approved a resolution terminating the company's charter.[50] Thus, the brief seven-year existence of Huff Daland Dusters, Inc. ended, but its role in the development of aviation was substantial. Aerial applications continued to grow and expand into a major mechanized component of the agricultural industry.

Harris remained in Peru as general manager of Panagra, successor to Peruvian Airways. And, significantly, Huff Daland Dusters successor company, Delta Air Service, while maintaining its dusting heritage and guided by Woolman, inaugurated a scheduled-passenger service across the South. Without a mail contract, though, the timing could not have been worse for such a venture.

DELTA AIR SERVICE, INC.

He [Woolman] did not want to fly from Birmingham
to Los Angeles; he wanted to fly where he was flying, and I was
determined to have an operation all the way from Atlanta to Los
Angeles, because I knew from what we had discovered that a short
line could not pay the expense of maintaining a ground force
and the supervisory force that would be necessary.

—POSTMASTER GENERAL WALTER F. BROWN,
testimony to U.S. Senate, 1934

A new corporation, Delta Air Service, Inc., succeeded Huff Daland Dusters. Choosing a name, it appears, was done quickly in a matter of days and perhaps without much deliberation, forced by the rapidity of events following Auerbach's betrayal. A bill of sale dated November 15, 1928, signed and notarized, for some reason does not name the buyer; that space is blank. Possibly there was uncertainty whether to put Woolman and Harris as buyers or wait for the new company's name to be determined. In fact, two days later articles of incorporation were issued for Delta Air Service by Douglas Y. Smith, Travis Oliver, and C. E. Woolman.[1] Catherine FitzGerald chose the name "from her impression of the Mississippi Delta from the cockpit of a duster." It was "a short name," she said, because "I thought people would remember it." It was supposed to be "Delta Air Services" but the plural "s" was mistakenly omitted in the documents.[2]

Delta Air Service was a Louisiana corporation, headquartered in Monroe, and capitalized at $80,000. Its officers were local investors, longtime acquaintances from the Monroe Chamber of Commerce: Smith (10 shares), president;

Woolman (100 shares), first vice president; and Oliver (25 shares), secretary-treasurer.[3] In recognition of his financial interest (held in trust), Harris was temporarily named a second vice president.[4]

Smith invested $1,000 in the enterprise.[5] A cotton planter born in Sterlington, Louisiana, a small community north of Monroe, his father had a large plantation and founded the town. He attended the University of Missouri and graduated from Louisiana State University. Much like the Percys of Mississippi, Smith was more than a planter. He helped his father with many businesses and engaged in politics, serving as a Louisiana state senator and chairman of the state highway commission.[6]

Oliver, "one of Monroe's most promising young businessman," learned early the hazard inherent in aviation, having witnessed a fatal crash during an aerial demonstration in 1911 at the Chicago Aviation Meet. But he also observed aviation's promise in Saint Louis, witnessing Harry Atwood's departure on an endurance flight to Boston. An aviation promoter and member of the Aviation Committee of the Chamber of Commerce, Oliver had convinced Harris to bring Huff Daland Dusters to the city and had supported development of both of Monroe's airports—Smoot and Selman Fields. Held in high esteem by his peers, they had recommended naming the second airfield the Travis Oliver Flying Field before the parish police jury selected Selman Field in memory of a veteran Monroe military aviator.[7]

Delta Air Service's work at first mirrored that of Huff Daland Dusters, treating crops from the air; the airline came later. Although Woolman and Harris were coequal shareholders, the former acted as general manager in Harris's absence. Woolman's letters to him in Peru conveyed a sense of optimism. "It really looks mighty good," he wrote encouragingly in October. The chances of winning a contract to inspect levees for the Mississippi River Commission after the great flood in 1927 were good and his bid "within reason." The company flew survey flights for Standard Oil using a Travel Air acquired from Doug Culver for "$1.00 and other valuable considerations." Woolman concluded on a hopeful note: "We seem to be started well over the hill and going strong. Have 5000 A. [acres] signed in Texas and are starting this week in Texas." Two months later he wrote: "The contract for Mississippi river flying was not let, but new bids were submitted." He lowered Delta's bid to $39.93 per hour by buying factory-rebuilt pontoons instead of new ones. The service would still "make a profit of about nine thousand dollars," he advised Harris, "writing off one entire plane and 20% on the reserve; incidentally, having some income during a time when it will be most welcome."[8] Woolman saved a dollar whenever he could.

In March 1929 Woolman assured Harris: "Delta Air Service is coming along pretty well." Slightly more acreage was contracted for in April than in the previous year. In addition, a new contract for approximately 13,000 acres was signed with the Delta & Pine Land Company, headquartered in Scott, Mississippi, which grew to be one of Delta Air Service's major clients, with billings as high as $11,000 per month.[9] Woolman noted: "The Wharton [Texas] unit shows signs of developing into a two plane unit," and three Travel Airs were sold "under our contract for ten and [we] have a number of good prospects." A new hangar was under construction in Monroe, and he added poignantly, "we are carrying a few passengers [on a charter basis] . . . which is helping our income a little." Woolman hired Pat L. Higgins as an "instructor in our Flying School, which has opened this week. Incidentally, he is a high type of fellow and a good pilot"; Higgins soon became chief of operations. In a rare personal note, Woolman informed Harris that he had "decided to move Mrs. Woolman and the kids to Monroe [from Baton Rouge]. Helen was up here this weekend and picked out a house which we have engaged." On the administrative side, he was "taking over some of Auerbach's duties, and trying to keep the field work going, along with raising capital for operations and so on." Modestly, Woolman told Harris that he was "making a poor substitute for you." When people asked when Harris would be returning, he gave a "'stock' answer of 'not before the season is over in Peru.'"[10] But Harris never returned to Monroe.

Most of the business records for Delta Air Corporation from 1930 to 1940 are missing, leaving an unfortunate void in the company's record of how and when it began passenger service. Possibly the documents were lost when the corporate headquarters relocated to Atlanta in 1941. A more likely scenario is the records remained in storage at Selman Field even afterward and were misplaced or destroyed when the airfield was taken over by the Army Air Forces during World War II.[11] FitzGerald might have shed some light on the missing documents, but fearing a faulty memory as the "oldest living Delta employee," she was reticent to be interviewed about them or that period, perhaps a result of circumstances surrounding her employment. As a young woman in her early twenties, she was asked to leave Ogdensburg and move to Monroe but demurred. Eventually, with her family's blessing, she accepted Huff Daland Dusters' offer of employment to replace an indiscreet secretary who was "telling their business all over town." FitzGerald served as Woolman's secretary for forty years. As a youngster in Monroe, Woolman's daughter, Barbara, remembers FitzGerald as the "loveliest, softest spoken person I had ever known." Barbara believed the reason for her reluctance to tell her story was because "she just wouldn't know what she ought to say and what she ought not to say."[12]

Fortunately, FitzGerald eventually agreed to talk to John N. White of the Delta Marketing Department in the mid-1970s. A slightly edited transcript is available in the corporate archives, but it does not shed any light on the important question of why Delta began passenger service without the benefit of a mail contract.[13] Perhaps "Woolman was not thinking primarily in terms of airmail at the time; his thoughts were centered on creating a passenger carrier."[14] If true, this represented an extraordinary risk. Fundamentally, he and Harris must have understood the importance of a mail contract. This awareness is born out in the 1927 report to Gott (which they helped draft with Alexander Howard) recommending Huff Daland Dusters bid on airmail contracts and from their experience seeking a mail concession in Peru. Without a postal subsidy, Woolman and the directors apparently chose to inaugurate passenger air service in anticipation of subsequently acquiring a mail contract or possibly to stymie Texas Air Transport, then planning a coast-to-coast service from Los Angeles to New York via Dallas and Atlanta.[15]

John S. Fox, son of a wealthy pulp- and paper-mill pioneer and businessman investor from Bastrop, Louisiana, provided Delta with financing and airplanes. At a special meeting in Monroe, the company's directors increased the capitalization of Delta Air Service to $250,000 and approved the purchase of Fox Flying Services in exchange for stock, making Fox the largest shareholder.[16] The deal included a Travel Air monoplane, with five more on order. With this deal, Delta had the financing and equipment necessary to begin operations.[17]

Under the Air Commerce Act of 1926, the Department of Commerce certified aircraft and pilots operating in interstate commerce but did not have an economic role in regulating airlines. Delta was free to choose where to fly, establish fares, and determine its schedule. Its route stretched from Dallas, Texas, to Atlanta, Georgia, with intermediate stops at Shreveport and Monroe, Louisiana; Jackson, Mississippi; and Birmingham, Alabama. The company used a Travel Air S-6000-B, a 300-hp single-engine, high-wing monoplane that carried five passengers and a pilot in an enclosed cabin. It was considered an advanced aircraft for the time, advertised as a luxury: "A Deluxe Monoplane combining Pullman Car comfort in air travel with proven performance and dependability."[18] Delta's startup was not particularly unique. The nation's air-transportation system was growing, albeit randomly and haphazardly. Small airlines like Delta were ubiquitous, even quixotic. For example, the Alimony Express line offered thrice-weekly service between California and Reno, Nevada, to handle the divorce traffic.[19]

The Monroe economy prospered as the "gas and carbon-black capital of America." Hundreds of gas wells fed a pipeline running from Houston to Atlanta.[20] Aerial transportation supplemented its road, rail, and water-borne systems, but there was a challenge for a nonmail carrier. Where were the flying customers? Eugene Stevens, an early pilot, observed that flying was then "new to the American public, as such[,] and not enough people would go and get in one of those crazy things, just to take them from here to yonder. The average guy . . . said heck, the trains are running, the buses are running, and I've got an automobile. Why should I get in one of those contraptions and go somewhere?"[21] Luke Williamson, a Delta line pilot, recalled, the passengers "were mostly men . . . , few women travelers, and no babies."[22]

As progressive as aviation appeared in the late 1920s, Louisianans and Mississippians likely anticipated the completion of the Vicksburg Bridge, spanning the lower Mississippi River, more than the prospect of an airline. For two years they watched as construction proceeded and waited expectantly for its completion. When opened in 1930, highway and rail traffic sped over the river where previously it had floated across on ferries. That it was the only bridge for 850 river miles below Memphis underscored its importance.[23] But the bridge did not encourage people to fly, just the opposite, making the train, bus, or automobile that much more convenient for travel.

As with the emergence of Delta Air Service, the passenger line commenced without public notice, utilizing the Travel Air acquired from Fox. Piloted by John D. Howe, with John Fox, traffic manager, as the sole passenger, a positioning flight departed Monroe on Sunday, June 16, bound for Dallas. At a stop in Shreveport, Fox announced the airline would begin service the following day from Dallas on a flight to Jackson, with stops in Shreveport and Monroe. The lack of publicity, he explained, was because "other interests were understood to contemplate a similar service." Fox retained E. B. Redline of Shreveport Airways to service Delta's transient planes.[24]

A telegram from Dallas in the evening alerted Paul Chambers, president of the Jackson Chamber of Commerce, to expect Delta Air Service's arrival at 1:40 P.M. the next day. This news was unexpected, and Chambers could not be at the airport to greet the arrival. But he did arrange for Walter A. Scott, Jackson's mayor, and other officials to be at the landing field and set in motion plans for a welcoming event that evening.[25]

On Monday, June 17, 1929, Delta's Travel Air, with Howe and Fox on board, lifted off from Dallas. No paying passengers or express were carried. After stops in Shreveport and Monroe, the Vicksburg Bridge (then still under construction) helped as a waypoint for Howe to visually navigate a direct course to Jackson. Howe logged 285 minutes (or 4.75 hours) total for the series of flights.[26] That evening the travelers were enthusiastically feted at the Edwards House, where Fox informed diners, "five new planes are being built and . . . within a very short time the [Delta flight] schedule will take in Birmingham and Atlanta."[27] At first, flights operated eastbound Monday, Wednesday, and Friday; westbound Tuesday, Thursday, and Saturday. Eventually, Delta scheduled roundtrip daily service between Dallas and Atlanta.

Early Tuesday morning, June 18, Delta inaugurated westbound service with a departure from Jackson. Accompanying Howe and Fox were Chambers; A. F. "Gus" Hawkins, commissioner of aeronautics; and L. E. Foster, executive vice president of the Jackson Chamber of Commerce. The black-and-orange Travel Air touched down in Monroe at precisely 11:35 A.M., ten minutes ahead of schedule. Greeting the flight were Mayor Arnold Bernstein; John M. Breard, president of the Ouachita Parish Police Jury; chamber of commerce members; and prominent business leaders. A quick welcoming ceremony and luncheon in the Selman hangar commemorated the event.[28]

Simultaneously, Pat Higgins flew the second eastbound service from Dallas in a new Travel Air, the second aircraft acquired. Again, no passengers were carried.[29] The company's first two airplanes paused together briefly in Monroe and then took off in their separate directions—Howe and passengers to Dallas and Higgins to Jackson.

Returning from Texas with their Mississippi entourage the next day (June 19), Fox and Howe deplaned in Monroe. A replacement pilot took the controls, with the Jackson party and W. C. Walsh, a Dodge Brothers manufacturing representative, on board.[30] Walsh bought a ticket for the seat vacated by Fox, thus having the distinction of becoming the company's first fare-paying passenger.[31] Woolman was "well pleased with the manner in which the general public has reacted to the news of the establishment of the line" and foresaw "much success for the undertaking."[32] Unfortunately, his optimism was misplaced.

Delta's destiny, like other small independent carriers, fell victim to events on a national level that were beyond its control. In Washington, Walter Folger Brown, Pres. Herbert Hoover's postmaster general, adhered to "Teddy" Roosevelt's New Nationalism philosophy that the public interest favored a monopoly in air transportation.[33] Brown consolidated the national air-transportation system from a hodgepodge of existing routes and airlines. According to historian F. Robert van der Linden, he acted in a manner to create an admittedly oligopolistic air-transport system.[34]

Brown convened a meeting of the Interdepartmental Committee of Civil Airways with the intent of rationalizing the process for establishing new airways. In December the committee proposed a southern transcontinental air route between Atlanta and San Diego via Birmingham, Jackson, Shreveport, Dallas, Fort Worth, El Paso, and Los Angeles. Flights were to begin in the summer of 1930 and operate around the clock once beacons were installed by the Department of Commerce.[35]

The proposal for a southern route encouraged Woolman and his associates, who knew their company was losing money by not having a mail contract. In 1929 Delta Air Service had a profit of $20,121.85 from dusting and other operations, but the passenger line compiled $32,603.37 in losses.[36] Stoically, Woolman noted, "we are staying on the passenger line as the route is recognized as a Southern Transcontinental and with the Watres Bill now before Congress we have great hopes of coming in for poundage space for air mail over the run."[37] The Air Mail Act of 1930, the law resulting from the Watres Bill, tied mail rates to the space made available on aircraft (rather than as previously the weight of mail actually carried) to encourage airlines to operate larger passenger-carrying equipment. It also exchanged airmail contracts for long-term route certificates.[38]

The new law authorized Postmaster General Brown to use his broad authority to redraw the nation's aviation map. He called for a conference of airline managers at the Post Office Department in Washington to be held on May 19, 1930. In what became known as the "spoils conference," Brown forced route swaps and mergers to achieve his goal of three transcontinental air routes.[39] Woolman was not among the invitees but, hearing of the meeting, rushed to Washington, "where he put up a gallant but losing fight to secure the mail carrying contract for his line."[40] Brown favored large, well-capitalized companies, and Woolman's appeal regarding Delta's pioneering equity in the route did not sway him. He told Woolman "that it would be far better from the standpoint of the Post Office Department, to have three single organizations crossing the continent rather than a large number of smaller organizations."[41]

AVCO was given the certificate for the Los Angeles–Atlanta southern transcontinental route. Its subsidiary, American Airways, began passenger service in October, using "huge tri-motor transports capable of carrying hundreds of pounds of mail as well as passengers."[42] Not only did AVCO traverse Delta's route but also, in contrast to the small single-engine equipment Delta operated, immediately put larger aircraft in service. Under the circumstances, Delta could not compete. "Our only recourse," stated board member Oliver, "was to discontinue passenger service."[43]

Although Postmaster General Brown disenfranchised smaller independent lines, he was not unsympathetic to their plight and pressured AVCO to buy Delta's assets at a fair price. On July 25 Delta Air Service was sold for $143,000; about "$8.50 per share, which was more than fair market value."[44] At a special meeting of its board of directors in Monroe on October 31, 1930, the sale was approved and the company dissolved.[45] Just as before when the fate of its predecessor company, Huff Daland Dusters, was sealed by Hoyt and Trippe, men with an agenda and better resources sacrificed Delta Air Service in the interest of creating a cohesive national air-transportation system. Despite the primitive nature of air travel at the time, Delta Air Service boasted an exemplary operational record. It suffered no fatalities or serious accidents, with only two minor incidents that required planes to land at emergency fields to entrain passengers onward to their destinations. Nevertheless, praise for its efficient, economic, and safe passenger operation from government and AVCO officials was small consolation.[46]

The agreement between Delta Air Service, Inc. and AVCO transferred physical assets, goodwill, and its name. At a special meeting, shareholders voted to liquidate and dissolve the corporation. In its place Delta Air Corporation was organized and bought back the dusting equipment from AVCO for $12,500.[47] The management team for this new iteration remained essentially the same: Smith, president; Woolman, vice president; Oliver, treasurer; and FitzGerald, secretary, whose appointment as a female member of a board of directors was an historic first for women. The board also included new investors Malcolm S. Biedenharn and Prentiss Atkins.[48] The former was the son of Joseph A. Biedenharn, who made his fortune bottling and distributing Coca Cola. The latter, president of the Monroe Hardware Company and a director and vice president of the Central Savings Bank and Trust, was involved in many enterprises and a member of the Monroe Chamber of Commerce Aviation Committee.[49] "'Whether we will be able to carry out our program will depend largely on the support we receive from the public,' Mr. Woolman said. 'But we have every confidence that the Delta Air Service [he probably used the old name from habit] will continue to operate along the lines for which it was originally established, that of scientific control of those pests which are a menace to agriculture.'"[50]

The years between 1930 and 1934 were unremarkable for Delta except for the fact that the business survived.[51] The company dusted crops, managed the airport, sold oil and gas to transient fliers, and stored and maintained airplanes. For a small town, Monroe uniquely had passenger and mail service as a stopover on the southern transcontinental route of American Airways. Otherwise, with the exception of an occasional transient pilot, once the crop dusters left early in the morning, "there was nothing happening at the airport in the middle of the day." The absence of activity extended into the fall, when dusting operations transitioned to Mexico and Arizona. Money was tight. Barbara Woolman recalled that neither her father "nor FitzGerald drew a salary for a year or two years, something like that."[52]

In South America, where Harris had settled, Faucett Airlines acquired the duster company's assets. Henry Elliot, an experienced pilot, took charge of the operation, with six aircraft and two more on order. He had accompanied Harris on the first expedition to Peru and, more recently, served as a pilot with Peruvian Airways.[53] Harris and Woolman communicated regularly to settle the affairs of Huff Daland Dusters. This warm relationship appears to have created an opportunity for American pilots to travel to Lima to do dusting work for Faucett. Greer and Pete Hansen flew contracts between 1930 and 1932, presumably under an arrangement with Delta Air Corporation, which would have provided additional revenue to the company and employment for the line pilots following the cancelation of passenger service in October.[54]

As if the news of Delta's failure to win the mail contract was not enough for the community to digest, Bert Coad, the head of the USDA's Delta Laboratory in Tallulah, was indicted for defrauding the government. On April 7, 1931, he and F. W. McDuff, his administrative assistant, were indicted by a federal grand jury of the District Court of the United States, Western District of Louisiana, Monroe Division, for conspiracy to defraud the U.S. government by padding the payroll of the Bureau of Entomology. The indictment listed 872 counts for activities between 1925 and 1931. Eugene Stevens, an original duster pilot, remembered: "They were putting in some false vouchers for mule hiring . . . and personnel and what not, out in the fields. . . . [I]t was kind of a general joke down there you know [inflating the payroll]. But finally, it became no general joke. [When] the FBI got into the picture, it ceased to be a joke."[55] Coad quit the laboratory on January 27, 1932, and McDuff resigned a few days later, on February 2.[56] Prentiss Atkins, a Delta director, posted the $10,000 bond for Coad's recognizance, pending an October 5 trial date.[57]

Coad and McDuff claimed they did not intend to defraud the government or obtain funds for their own personal gain or benefit and asked for leniency.[58] On October 6 Coad and McDuff pleaded guilty in U.S. district court to ten misdemeanor counts. Each was sentenced to one year in the Caddo Parish jail in Shreveport for one count and a five-year suspended sentence for the rest, pending good behavior. Thus, they avoided a trial and the possibility of a felony conviction. Following a ten-day grace period to arrange their affairs, the two men were incarcerated on October 16, 1931.[59]

When they were released the following autumn, the community was sympathetic. McDuff opened a filling station in town with a relative.[60] Woolman's compassion for Coad and his family is evidenced by his hiring Coad as an entomologist for the dusting business. It is unclear precisely when and under what conditions this happened, as no personnel record substantiates the date of hire. Given the period of his incarceration, the earliest Coad might have been hired was late 1932.[61] He probably worked for Delta on a seasonal basis, as did other personnel (such as the pilots), since the company had few permanent employees at the time. The point is that Woolman was concerned enough to look after Coad and his family during a difficult time and brought him on board when he could. When the airline renewed passenger service in 1934 and Woolman became occupied with running the airline, Coad managed the dusting operation. They maintained cordial relations for the rest of their lives.[62] Woolman's compassion is perhaps one reason Coad's transgression never tarnished his reputation.

Delta held on until 1934, when it again became caught up in political events beyond its control, which this time led to the resurrection of the airline with authority to carry passengers and mail. The change in policy occurred when Franklin D. Roosevelt, victor in the 1932 presidential election, appointed James A. Farley to replace Brown as postmaster general. There were high expectations for aviation from the New Deal, but "what ensued was neither in line with [Roosevelt's] original plans nor with the optimistic expectations of the air carriers."[63] Sen. Hugo L. Black, the progressive Alabama Democrat who believed that monopolies were inherently bad, held hearings to investigate mail contracts awarded by former postmaster general Brown at the "spoils conference." Woolman's testimony on Delta's treatment buttressed Black's indictment of Brown's seemingly dictatorial actions.[64] The Black Committee's report charged collusion between Brown and the airlines and recommended that Roosevelt cancel the domestic contracts. When the chief of the Army Air Corps, Maj. Gen. Benjamin D. Foulois, assured the president that the army could fly the mail, Roosevelt took Brown's advice and canceled the airline contracts. But the army proved to be inexperienced in the challenges of night and all-weather mail flying, and several of its planes crashed, with resulting pilot fatalities.

Roosevelt was roundly criticized for his handling of the airmail scandal. To extricate himself from the situation, he allowed new temporary contracts to be put out for bid; no prior contractors were permitted to participate. Another condition precluded any officers of companies that had attended the "spoils conference" from being affiliated with a bidding company.[65] The government did not object if a company had simply changed its name. For example, American Airways by now was known as American Airlines and Eastern

Air Transport had become Eastern Airlines. Delta was unaffected as it had reincorporated as Delta Air Corporation and, in any case, had not held a contract. Although Woolman had attended the conference, he was not an invited participant and so was not banned. Nevertheless, to prevent any suggestion of impropriety, he resigned from the board of directors.[66] Politics aside, Robert van der Linden points out that Brown's actions were within the authority granted him by Congress, and the Roosevelt administration subsequently "regulated the industry and its oligopolies in virtually the same manner as the Civil Aeronautics Board later would." The president essentially reinstated Brown's plan: "After the smoke had cleared, the large financially stable firms were once again carrying the bulk of the nation's airmail over a rational route system that followed Brown's original network."[67] One exception authorized small Delta to operate along the route it had pioneered.

In April 1934 the Post Office extended the southern transcontinental route to Charleston, South Carolina, as its eastern anchor. It also was divided into two segments—Charleston to Fort Worth and Fort Worth to Los Angeles— and bid separately. Three airlines submitted competing bids for the eastern section.[68] Of these, Delta's was the lowest at 24.8 cents per mile; Eastern's was 41 cents and American's, 43.5 cents.[69] Following a routine Post Office investigation to determine the corporation's fitness, Delta was awarded the highly valuable mail contract for the eastern portion of this route. A Charleston news article announced: "The Delta Air Corporation of Monroe will start flying the mail over the Charleston–Dallas route 'within fifteen to twenty days,' Travis Oliver, secretary, said today after being notified from Washington that the company's bid had been formally approved by the Post Office Department. Five tri-motor planes of the same type as employed by the American Airways corporation, which formerly carried the mails over the transcontinental route, will be in service."[70]

When American Airways held the southern transcontinental mail contract, it employed Laigh Calhoun Parker as its Jackson, Mississippi, radio operator. He advanced to general district traffic manager but lost his job when Roosevelt canceled the mail contracts. Delta subsequently hired Parker as traffic manager after winning its contract.[71] With the knowledge and experience gained from American, he managed Delta's traffic department through a long career and set a high standard for the carrier's service.

As the company waited for government authorization to begin passenger service, Parker visited stations to instruct personnel on company procedures and ticketing. As a flying businessman, he understood the benefits of air travel as a task multiplier and kept careful track of his miles. From July 1, 1934, to June 30, 1939, Parker estimated that he accumulated 263,575 air miles.[72] No detail was too small for his attention or his concern for passenger comfort and safety. Parker instructed agents to check and remove used "burp" cups on arrival and to ensure three spares were available. He also ordered Wrigley gum and cotton since chewing helped clear pressure-blocked ears and cotton stuffed in them muffled the noise from the engines. He weighed each pilot as part of determining the maximum payload of each aircraft. The company obtained additional scales to weigh passengers, packages, and baggage.[73]

In the remarkably short span of two months, Delta began scheduled service. Passengers were assured of the reliability of its aircraft and the qualifications of its pilots. "The ships to be used in the service are seven and eight passenger Stinson monoplanes, each powered with three 215-horsepower Lycoming motors. All of them equipped with practically all instruments known to modern air navigation, including radio facilities." A new cadre of pilots—Don Dice, Charles H. Dolson, Lee McBride, Andrew Dixon, and others—was hired and trained by Pat Higgins, chief pilot. All held transport-pilot ratings with thousands more hours of flying time than the minimum required and were blind- and instrument-flight qualified.[74] They surveyed their routes from the air to familiarize themselves with land features and regular and emergency airfields.[75] In June James "Joe" Greer flew the inaugural flight from Monroe to Atlanta in a Travel Air 6000-B under the observation of Jack Jaynes, a government inspector.[76] Final authorization was granted by Roy Keely of the Department of Commerce.[77]

Delta initiated scheduled mail service between Atlanta and Dallas on July 4, 1934, with Dice as pilot in command. Monroe journalists touted this "resumption of service . . . , Uncle Sam's Fourth of July gift."[78] Service between Charleston and Atlanta was slightly delayed while the Bureau of Aeronautics determined whether landing fields needed improvement. Mail flights began on July 7 when Dolson, accompanied by Parker, piloted a Stinson Tri-Motor to Charleston carrying nine pouches of mail. Three pouches, mostly first-day covers stamped by the Charleston Chamber of Commerce, were boarded for the return trip. Passenger service on the line began on August 5, flown by George Shealy.[79] With the new government route awards, Delta's "Trans Southern Route" permitted passengers to connect with other airlines at several points on its system, allowing them to fly to Washington, New York, Miami, Memphis, Saint Louis, Chicago, New Orleans, Houston, San Antonio, and points west.[80] Delta and Eastern served Atlanta as a hub, where arriving transient passengers changed airplanes and airlines.

Eastern Air Transport had contemplated a hub-and-spoke model at Atlanta as early as May 1930, when Postmaster General Brown rearranged the aviation map. "It would be a very splendid operation to them, as it would hub out of Atlanta and [service] could be handled both to the north, south, and west, and . . . their chief claim to the route was that they could make it an economical operation."[81] But Brown gave the western route to AVCO. Subsequently, when Delta's Contract Air Mail Route 24 crossed paths with Eastern in Atlanta, Eastern flights from New York to New Orleans and Chicago to Jacksonville were designed to allow mail and passengers to transfer onward to multiple destinations.[82]

Thus, according to Parker, a passenger leaving Monroe at 2:35 P.M. would arrive in Atlanta at 7:30 P.M. The passenger could connect with an Eastern Airlines flight leaving at 8:00 P.M. and arrive in New York City at 5:45 A.M.[83] What was it like? "You bounced around in the hot air thermals at 3,000 to 5,000 feet strapped into a wicker chair with a sickness cup handy," recalled Arthur Ford. "You went blindly through thunderstorms and frequently diverted to alternate airports. [But,] bad as it was, it was still progress. An alternative was black soot [by coal-fired steam train] or flat tires and a journey 4 to 5 times as long."[84] Ford's perspective spanned the most innovative years of air-transport service. Hired by Delta as a stock manager in 1934, he retired as head of the airline's engineering department in the jet age.

9

BRANCHING OUT

ATLANTA MUNICIPAL AIRPORT: The "Hub of Southeastern Aviation"—
where planes arrive every thirty minutes—and serve seven points
of the compass. Large crowds gather twice a day to view the
arrival and departure, within a space of only a few minutes time,
of seven large passenger ships; and this spectacular sight
is known as the famous "Merry-Go-Round."

—POSTCARD CAPTION (ca. 1941)

The award of a valuable mail contract in 1934 and relocation of its headquarters to Atlanta in 1941 boded well for Delta Air Lines. From 1935 until 1941, dependence on airmail decreased from 76 percent to 38 percent of total revenue (dusting included), while the number of passengers increased by an average of 58 percent year over year during the same period.[1] Bolstering its outlook, too, even as World War II loomed, were a viable route structure, modern fleet, sound management, stable work force, and sufficient access to capital. According to Prof. Richard M. McCabe at Graziadio School of Business and Management, these were positive indicators when applied to a new airline's likelihood of success after deregulation in 1978. His methodology for that era is useful in gauging Delta's chances of success leading up to and on the eve of World War II.

"To be successful," McCabe reasoned, "an airline must be effective in four general areas: 1) attracting customers; 2) managing its fleet; 3) managing its people; and 4) managing its finances.[2] As a startup, Delta made strides in all these areas. Routes expanded for both mail and passengers, the fleet modernized, a sound management team and stable work force were assembled, and adequate financing already secured. In McCabe's 1978 analysis, airlines determined their routes and fares in competition with each other. In contrast, contracts with the Post Office Department and certificates of authority from the Civil Aeronautics Board shielded Delta's routes from competition. Route 24 extended from Fort Worth, Texas, to Charleston, South Carolina, with an extension from Augusta to Savannah, Georgia, while Route 54 went from Atlanta to Cincinnati, Ohio, via Knoxville, Tennessee, and Lexington, Kentucky. Their paths intersected at Atlanta, the southeastern crossroads of the air.

Long before Atlanta Municipal Airport became the "Hub of Southeastern Aviation"—indeed, before Atlanta even became a city—topography preordained the site as a crossroads. For hundreds of years, Native Americans, traveling the river valleys and the Peachtree and Etowah Trails, converged here. "Early travelers could journey north up either side of the Appalachian Mountains, as well as, to the south, east, and west, without facing any real obstacles," and in the steam age, "this accessibility led to Atlanta's founding as a rail head."[3] Just as trails, roads, and rail lines converged in Atlanta, so do air routes from all points of the compass.

Asa Griggs Candler Sr., founder of the Coca-Cola Company, chose a relatively flat parcel of land on which to build an automobile racetrack in 1909. The track operated only briefly before becoming a landing place for early aviators in their primitive machines. The landing field grew in size beyond Candler's original 300 acres to accommodate more traffic and larger, more sophisticated airplanes.[4] A driving force for this development came from the city's air-minded mayor, William B. Hartsfield, who "foresaw that Atlanta and aviation would grow together, and steadfastly worked to that end."[5] Atlanta's location, reasonable climate, and entrepreneurial and economic dynamism, combined with Hartsfield's visionary leadership, attracted airlines. Providentially, the city was situated almost at the geographic center of important southern destinations—Richmond, Virginia; Dallas, Texas; and Miami, Florida, are roughly equidistant.[6]

In the 1930s both Delta and Eastern served Atlanta. As noted earlier, Post Office routes fostered cooperation rather than competition between the companies. A network of delegated routes allowed each airline to profit from transporting mail and passengers to their own and the other's destinations. Route certificates under the Civil Aeronautics Board had much the same influence. Delta's passenger numbers grew significantly, from 4,104 in 1935 to 58,208 in 1941, a notable increase applicable to McCabe's first factor of an airline's chance of success, the ability to attract customers.

Managing Delta's fleet—addressing McCabe's second factor—became an issue almost immediately after the company took over the mail from American Airlines in 1934. Monroe officials improved Selman Field to meet the requirements of Department of Commerce "class A" status for night operations on the southern transcontinental route. A rotating beacon pinpointed the airport from the air, boundary lights outlined the landing field perimeter, obstacle lights warned pilots of hazards, bright floodlights illuminated the terminal area, and a powerful Sperry arc light lit the field for takeoffs and landings.[7] But the outdated Stinson-T airplanes Delta acquired from American were not equipped for night operations.

Clarence Faulk, Delta's president, personally helped finance Stinson-A trimotor replacements.[8] "The dignified bespectacled [Faulk] put up nearly half of the $22,000 down payment"[9] These were brand-new, night-capable aircraft, but their fabric and strut-braced wings evidenced obsolescence. Nevertheless, the Stinson-A's speed and comfort demonstrably raised the level of Delta's service. One could relax and smoke or chat in the soundproofed cabin and observe the passing scenery through large windows. "A scientifically designed heating and ventilation system" cleared the cabin air every four minutes. The "wide deeply tufted reclining chairs, insulated in rubber," and corresponding footrests were adjustable. Individual reading lights, ashtrays, attendant call buttons, window curtains, and storage rack enhanced personal comfort. The ultimate luxury was "a large lavatory with running water located in the rear of the cabin."[10]

About this time, Delta began advertising its Trans Southern Route and inaugurated a night schedule on a six-hour flight between Atlanta and Dallas. "The Texan," as the aircraft was dubbed, went westbound as trip no. 3, while another one flew east as trip no. 4.[11] Mrs. Eugene Talmadge, wife of Georgia's governor, christened the first airplane departing from Atlanta "The Georgian." For two weeks, government authorities only permitted mail to be carried by air. Then, on July 19, when airplanes and crews were certified, Woolman announced the immediate inauguration of passenger service.[12] Each of Delta's three Stinson-As met ignominious ends. Shortly after passenger service began, tragedy struck. On the night of August 14, 1935, Delta suffered its first fatalities. An eastbound Stinson-A crashed near Gilmer, Texas, at about 11:45 P.M. The official report blamed an imbalance from the loss of a propeller, causing the left engine of the three-motor airplane to separate from its mount.[13] Andy Dixon, the pilot; his assistant, Herbert Bulkeley; and two passengers perished.[14]

About a year later, Capt. Charles Dolson (who replaced Woolman as president upon his death in 1966 and ultimately rose to the position of chairman of the board) survived a crash in a second Stinson-A while taking off on a test flight.[15] Capt. Thomas "Pre" Ball recalled years later: "The airplane had just been worked on and he was flying it by himself. [A news report has Pullman Norton with Dolson on the flight.] He took off on this test flight and, as far as I can remember now, there was either . . . a bolt or a fitting that sheared at the attach point between the wing structure and the center section. Actually, the wing itself rotated one direction or the other and the airplane rolled. He hit the trees right off of the west end of the runway. Charlie's back was badly hurt. He was in bed most of a year in a body cast." The airplane was "junk."[16]

Capt. George Shealy, with Ball as copilot, flew the remaining Stinson-A to Fort Worth and left it there as a reserve for the western leg of the route. Ball "never saw it again."[17] According to FitzGerald, that airplane was sold; the next day it burned in a fire in Miami.[18] Delta badly needed a reliable modern replacement This turned out to be the Lockheed Electra, which served as the company's main airliner until the interim Douglas DC-2s joined the fleet. Delta was profitable—satisfying McCabe's fourth factor, the ability to manage finances—except in 1935 and again in 1941, when it acquired the necessary, but expensive, Douglas DC-3s.[19]

The Electra, smaller than competing Boeing and Douglas designs, well-suited Delta's operations. In December 1936 the first all-metal, twin-engine Model 10B Electra arrived.[20] It required two pilots—an additional expense—but accommodated ten passengers, so the economics were favorable. Fritz Schwaemmle, one of the newly hired cadre of copilots required to fly the airplane, explained: "You start out initially with a seven-passenger plane [the Stinson-A] and then you get a ten-passenger airplane; that's a 30% increase in the number of seat miles that are available." The Electra was faster, too, "so you're grinding out more seat miles per hour."[21] Copilots backed up the captains and served box lunches to passengers. On the ground they handled manifests, mail, express, and passenger baggage. Norman Stephen Topshe recalled an experience at a stopover with Woolman, Delta's general manager, along as a passenger on the flight. Employees held him in high regard, and Topshe witnessed firsthand the reason why:

> We landed in Jackson, Mississippi, a little before dark. He was one of the last off the airplane and I was behind him. I had my clipboard and I had to walk around to the nose of the Lockheed, get the luggage off, mail off, and [so] on. He walked up to the gas man, Doc Shilling . . . I remember very distinctly, who was dirty and greasy. He walked up to Doc, put his arms around his shoulder, shook hands with him, and said, 'how are things going?' 'Well, things are going fine.' And, I'm hearing all this. 'How are Sally and the kids?' And he said one of the kids was having a little problem. 'And alright, well tell her I asked about her, will you?' Then he went over to the mechanic Mickey Wilson, the same way, put his arm around his shoulder, he said, 'how's your daddy doing.' 'Well,' he said, 'Mr. Woolman, he's doing fine.' 'Has he still got that cast on his leg?' 'Naw," he said, 'we took that off and I took him fishing the other day and we caught a lot of fish.' I'm listening to all this and only when he's finished talking to all these people, then he went into the station. After that I began to realize why he had such a reputation.[22]

Joe Greer Sr. recalls as a young man being introduced to Woolman by his father. "I remember that I knew he was important by the way my father introduced me. Dad said, 'Mister Woolman, this is my son Joe, Joe, this is Mister Woolman.' Dad spoke in a slow and polite tone. Mr. Woolman shook my hand. He was tall and had on a suit and even at five years of age, I felt respect for him. I showed him my 'Oakey-Doakes' [sic] comic book. Mr. Woolman shared my interest in it. He did this for me. This was his nature."[23]

Captain Ball's son, Espy Ball, also recalls the respect his father showed toward Woolman. When he entered his office, Ball stood and always addressed him as "Mr. Woolman." Ball himself rose high in the company's hierarchy, ultimately retiring as vice president of flight operations; tough but fair, pilots respected him—when he retired they gave him a Porsche. On one visit Woolman noticed a well-used pencil stub with a worn eraser in a cup on Ball's desk. As Espy remembers it, the executive said: "I'm glad to see you are using that to the end. It's important to use assets completely."[24] Woolman was very careful with money.

Four factors equally affect a new airline's success in McCabe's analysis, but a stronger one will not offset the weakness of another. Considering this, Delta's future looked good across all factors. But one stands above the others—managing employees. Woolman set the example of how he wanted the airline run, and that engendered employees' loyalty, respect, and work ethic.[25] This is demonstrated in the following stories of individual employees.

Pre Ball's long service with Delta began with the award of Contract Air Mail Route 24. Spanning the era of flight from barnstormers to jumbo jets, his extraordinary career required that he adapt to changing circumstances and technologies. Born in Charleston, South Carolina, in 1906, Ball learned to fly in a Curtiss Jenny with an OX5 engine. It was just bare bones, the instruments basic, and its performance very limited. He earned a transport license and managed the Charleston municipal airport. In 1932 he became a partner in Hawthorne Aviation, the fixed-base operator at the field. Simultaneously, he served as station manager for Eastern Air Transport, later Eastern Airlines. In 1934 Ball assumed another duty as Delta's Charleston station manager. "I had to be there [at the airport] all the time because I had airplane transient pilots who spent the night and wanted to leave early in the morning. So, I had to be up long before dawn every day. I got to the airport before daylight. I stayed there until around 7–8 o'clock every night to pick up the last people who came in as transients who were going to spend the night."[26] Ball was devoted to doing a job well and had a zest for life.[27] In 1936 he drove to Atlanta and applied for a pilot opening.

Flying the southern transcontinental route was memorable. At first, Ball flew the daily eastbound roundtrip from Atlanta to Charleston, with stops in Augusta, Georgia, and Columbia, South Carolina. Stops were short, just long enough to let passengers off and on and to exchange mail bags. "As a matter of fact," Ball remembered, "usually our flight plans were pretty damn good. We would usually get within 5–6 minutes [of scheduled times]." Fueling was done in Atlanta or Charleston.[28] Pilots navigated these trips visually, either by flying close to the ground during the day or by following beacons at night. Routes became familiar. Ball recalled: "We could see cattle. We could see the farms that people had. We could see the smoke on the ground. We were flying at 3–

5–7,000 feet. We could always tell things like that. We could tell which way the wind was blowing. We could see it. We really knew the country. We knew the towns that we flew over. We recognized each little village. We saw the cross-roads. We saw the railroad crossings. All these things were a very familiar part of your day to day life." When radio ranges were installed, electronic navigation permitted all-weather flying, night or day, as well as instrument-guided runway approaches and landings. But this system had a serious handicap in its restrictive straight-line navigation. "With thunderstorms around with all probability," Ball said, "it'd take you through the biggest thunderstorm."[29]

Landing at Monroe, Delta's home office, was special, as Woolman could be counted on to personally greet the crews. "Every time we would land and taxi up," Ball recounted, "if Mr. Woolman was at the airport, he would be out talking to us. We got all of our information about the progress of the airline, its financial situation, what was happening, what was good and what was bad. How he wanted us to operate and all that sort of stuff came on those visits with Mr. Woolman."[30]

An unusual feature in the Electra was a hump in the cabin between the wings—this was the wing spar. Pilots would fly with the cockpit door open, and passengers or flight inspectors often sat on the hump to talk to the crew while in flight. One passenger, Ball remembered, was Howard Hughes, who rode with him two or three times and chatted while so seated.[31] Other well-known passengers who flew on Delta were Amelia Earhart and Eleanor Roosevelt.[32] Delta initially bought four DC-2s from American Airlines to serve until the company could afford new DC-3s. With the purchases of these larger aircraft, Delta marked another milestone by hiring its first cabin attendants, then known as stewardesses.

Early in 1940, Laura Wizark, Delta's chief stewardess, hired registered nurses to staff the newly acquired fourteen-passenger DC-2s. One of the first, Eva Parrish, remembered the training she received: "We had classes in charm, passenger service, airline safety, meteorology, Delta routes and schedules, and ticketing of passengers. Delta sent each of us to Antoine's Beauty Salon at Rich's Department Store in Atlanta for hair styling best suited for the small stewardess caps."[33] Birdie Bomar had the distinction of becoming Delta's first stewardess to take to the air.[34] Inflight safety was and still remains an attendant's key duty, but the reason for hiring nurses as the first stewardesses was not to utilize their medical training in case of emergency, but rather for their mere presence to calm passengers and their nonflying family members' anxieties about flight. Delta's service-oriented cabin service promoted the airline's image of southern hospitality and regional identity. "From the outset," observed one writer, "Delta's flight attendants exuded southernness."[35] Sybil Peacock Harmon recalled her duties onboard Delta aircraft:

> When the flight was called, I would stand by the door. The passenger would come up the steps, give me his or her name and I would check it off my manifest. They would then enter and take a seat anywhere on the plane, we had no seat selection! When all the passengers had boarded, the ramp agent would come up to me and hand me the papers for the pilots. He and I would agree on the number of passengers on board, he would then close the door and we were ready to go!
>
> Before take-off, I would pass chewing gum around to all of the passengers. This was to make them chew and in turn salivate. The swallowing action would relieve pressure on the ear drum as we passed through various altitudes. Even so, there was a lot of trouble with ears in those days. After take-off, we would go around and greet each passenger to put him at ease. For refreshments, I would serve hot coffee or Coca-Cola. We served boxed meals out of Jackson Mississippi on both east and west bound flights. Some of these dinners were not too good and often contained greasy fried chicken, not the best meals if the weather turned rough![36]

Harmon developed an intuition for passenger assistance in rough air:

> There was a lot of motion sickness in those days. The lower altitude where we flew contained the more unstable air and we experienced a lot of bumpy weather. . . . One of my most delicate and difficult jobs was to judge by his color when a passenger was sick enough to get the 'Burp Cup.' This way he would not smell up the airplane if he got sick. Act too soon and you would put ideas into his head, act too late and you had a cleaning job.

Federal regulations forbade consumption of alcohol on flights, and stewardesses had to deal with businessmen determined to imbibe. One "asked for ice water to drink with his 'medicine,'" explaining, "he had had 3 ounces of whiskey prescribed by a doctor as a tonic."[37]

Many of the issues affecting airlines today—transporting pets, for example—first became apparent in the 1930s. The Air Transport Association of America, the aviation trade organization formed in 1936, of which Delta was a member, proposed a rule that member airlines must carry pets. Laigh Parker, general traffic manager, objected emphatically: "We will not accept pets under any circumstances," he declared, for the valid reason the cargo compartments in the Electra were not heated or ventilated.[38] In any case, baggage, mail, and express filled the limited cargo space of the aircraft. Parker asked for an exemption from this mandate, which was granted, but it did not extend to service dogs in the cabin. This led to an incident involving a woman determined to bend the rules with her seeing-eye dog. Her Eastern flight connected with Delta in Atlanta. Unlike Eastern, Delta's policy required the agent to charge an excess-baggage fee for the dog. The passenger asked to speak with an official upon arrival in Monroe, and Parker obliged. In his report he noted: "The woman's vision was apparently impaired in only one eye, as, when I introduced myself to her and offered her my card, she took it out of my hand, looked at me all the time she was talking, and apparently was able to read everything on the card." And to his surprise, the dog was a "medium-sized Bull Terrier curled up behind the rear seat." Parker did not think the intention of the rule was "to accept just any dog accompanying a partially blind person."[39]

Life for a pilot or stewardess (flight attendant), then as today, revolved around their flight schedules. Ball emphasized: "There were fewer copilots originally than there were captains. So, the copilots had to absorb this extra flying, and I used to fly anywhere from 90 to 110–115 hours per month. So, I was flying all the time in the beginning. So, I must have made three or four round trips to Charleston and back each week."[40] Then as now, seniority determined one's bidding priority. The most senior pilot or stewardess selected his or her schedule first, and everyone else followed in order. Seniority is a cornerstone of union organization and was officially adopted by Delta Air Corporation for its pilots, represented by the Air Line Pilots Association (ALPA). Unlike pilot negotiations with other airline managements, Delta's first pilot contract was signed on July 11, 1940, without any acrimony and in record time. Unionization was anathema to southern businessmen, and Captain Dolson later observed: "I don't think Mr. Woolman ever forgave me for getting ALPA started on Delta."[41]

Seniority, according to the contract, "shall be based upon the length of service as an air line pilot with the company."[42] Pay, working conditions, equipment flown, and schedules all follow from this basic precept. Don Dice, formerly with Standard Oil Company, had a seniority date of June 16, 1934, which put him at top of the list.[43] John Howe, who inaugurated Delta's service to Jackson, Mississippi, as the airline's first pilot on June 17, 1929, did not return to the company in 1934 or he would have been most senior.[44]

By 1940, Delta operated reliably as a niche carrier across the southern United States. Three events presaged success leading to the fulfillment of McCabe's four factors. First, the integration into the fleet of the DC-3, the first aircraft capable of operating profitably without having to rely on a mail subsidy, allowed the airline to focus increasingly on carrying passengers. Second, in 1941 Delta began service to Cincinnati to the north and Savannah, Georgia, to the south.[45] Third, that same year Delta moved its headquarters from Monroe to Atlanta. This last decision was not taken lightly by major stockholders, and a tradition of holding board meetings in the "Delta Room" of the Central Savings Bank and Trust in Monroe persisted for many years.

As commercial aviation expanded, municipal authorities competed to attract air service to their communities. Monroe remained a prime destination, but circumstances conspired to remove Delta's headquarters from the city. Monroe officials were challenged by the formidable Mayor Hartsfield and could not match Atlanta's geographic advantage and economic vitality. Hartsfield and airport manager Jack Gray used the Works Progress Administration to lengthen the runways and improve the terminal at Candler Field at no cost to the city. These improvements were underway in 1936, when Delta moved its maintenance and operations divisions to Atlanta. Half of the Eastern hangar became available when that airline moved its maintenance and operations to Florida; four years later Eastern canceled the hangar lease altogether. In 1940 the City of Atlanta and Delta officials executed a long-term lease agreement sharing the cost of a new hangar and office. The new structure was large enough to accommodate Delta's DC-2s and DC-3s as well as providing ample office space for its headquarters.[46] Operationally though, the new DC-2s and DC-3s lacked the runway length to get safely airborne from Candler. And on hot summer days with high ambient temperatures, they required an even longer takeoff run.

Even the smaller Electras had problems at Candler. Ball recalled, "in fact, even in Atlanta, in the summertime, when you've got ten passengers and you have full tanks of gas in the thing, you are right up to your maximum gross weight. . . . [T]hat plane was lucky to get airborne." Famed aviator Eddie Rickenbacker "in no uncertain terms [said] the city must add more hangars and land. 'Atlanta needs a five-thousand-foot runway to be any good as an airport.'" The Civil Aeronautics Authority agreed and admonished airport authorities following two incidents in 1939 in which aircraft went off the end of the runway.

As war clouds loomed, Atlanta was given another leg up on Monroe when Candler Field became an airbase on October 4, 1940, with priority for federal spending.[47] Not until the spring of 1942 was Monroe's Selman Field taken over by the Army Air Corps and expanded to serve as a navigation training school.[48]

Many Delta stockholders were prominent Monroe businessmen and investors in the airline industry. Some, such as the Biedenharn family, would have preferred to keep the company in Monroe. But the move to Atlanta was warranted: it was a hub, Delta's routes intersected there, its maintenance facilities were there, and a new administrative office building at Candler Field would relieve the crowded conditions currently experienced at Selman Field. Delta needed long-term financing, and Atlanta was the place to be.

Delta's likelihood of success was challenged by McCabe's fourth factor, adequate financing, due to uncertainty about accessing capital markets. But a solution came from an investment company that put its faith in the South. Stockbroker Richard W. Courts founded Courts & Company in 1925 to serve southern industry with a regional investment bank. In partnership with his father, Richard W. Courts Sr., the firm provided equity capital to southern corporations. Fundamental to their vision was a faith in the region's business environment and their conviction that the New South would prosper and grow industrially and financially.[49] In 1939 Delta needed financing to expand and to buy modern equipment. Between December 1939 and March 1940, it proffered privately issued stock to Monroe investors and interested parties, including the pilots' group; Ball recalled that he and other pilots "could buy ten shares [of Delta stock] at $10 a share."[50] Courts Jr. happened to be one of the few outsiders to buy shares.

Richard Courts Jr. was unaware that the issue had not been registered by the Securities and Exchange Commission (SEC), which regulated the securities industry. Registration and disclosure of material facts were required to give investors the information necessary to make an informed decision as to the soundness of Delta's offering. Some individual investors subsequently resold their stock to secondary parties, unwittingly placing themselves in the position of brokers. These activities remained undisclosed until 1941, when 60,000 new shares were proffered, with Courts & Company retained to market them. "There was no implication that Delta had knowingly broken the law; its legal advisers in Monroe were simply unfamiliar with the technicalities surrounding the operations of a firm that was all too plainly outgrowing the city that had been its birthplace."[51] With the absence fraudulent intent, prosecution of Delta management was unlikely, but the prospect of government scrutiny must nevertheless have been unsettling. Courts brought the matter to the attention of the SEC, and not finding any evidence of fraud, it applied a remedy to assure full disclosure.[52] The commission mandated that a prospectus be distributed to all stockholders to disclose the facts and offer to repurchase the earlier shares with interest. Fortunately, none of the subscribers demanded their money back.[53]

The 60,000 shares were successfully placed when Courts persuaded R. J. Reynolds, the tobacco heir, to buy a large block of stock.[54] According to *Time* magazine, it was "one of the biggest air-line underwritings ever handled by a single investment banker. Courts & Co. bossed by smart, wise Richard Winn Courts Jr. hung the 'sold out' sign on 60,000 shares of Delta Air Corp. common, priced at $9.50 a share."[55] Justifiably, Courts took particular satisfaction from his company's success in underwriting the sale. The net of $495,000 to Delta boosted its working capital, reduced debt, and brightened the future.[56]

The stock situation can be attributed to a small southern company's managers being unfamiliar with the intricacies of stock dealings.[57] Given the nonpunitive remedy imposed by the SEC, this interpretation is plausible. But a more fundamental structural cause, articulated by SEC commissioner William Douglas, may have been the determining factor. He "believed the principal obstacle to small business finance . . . was the unwillingness of investment banks to make a firm commitment to underwrite the smaller firms' securities."[58] Absent Courts's southern bank initiative, good advice may not have been readily available under any circumstances to Delta's managers. Although the airline broke the rules, the situation was probably not as threatening as some thought. The earlier shares were not widely distributed, and the people who held them were closely associated with the airline.

In such situations, absent indications of fraud or deceit, the SEC offered an interpretative and advisory service. In this regard its *Sixth Annual Report* states, "during the past fiscal year, thousands of requests for such assistance have been responded to by correspondence and in conferences."[59] Under the guidance of Courts, acting as Delta's investment advisor, and without allegations of fraud or deceit, the remedy was a relatively routine matter for the SEC. Regardless, a more dire situation loomed on the horizon.

Leading up to World War II, Delta Air Lines' branches stretched, beyond their roots in the fight against the boll weevil, across the South. In 1941 the company's 385 employees hosted 58,208 revenue passengers and maintained a fleet of nine modern aircraft—four Electras and five DC-3s.[60] On December 7 the airline's and the nation's fates were placed in jeopardy when Japan attacked Pearl Harbor, followed a few days later by Germany's declaration of war on the United States. Following the war's conclusion in 1945, McCabe's methodological four factors would put Delta Air Lines to the test again as it confronted new challenges.

CONCLUSION

The only monotonous thing about
the aviation industry is the constant change.

—COLLETT EVERMAN WOOLMAN

Delta's story is a tangled compendium of time, people, and places, but a common thread leads back to the boll weevil as its origin. This book makes the case that Atlanta's global-powerhouse airline began when an insidious pest upended the agricultural economy of the South, which then led to crop dusting and eventually the airline. With this in mind, a retrospective review of Delta's turning points underscores the boll weevil's seminal position in the company's history.

World War II is a convenient demarcation. At its outbreak, Delta had reached a point of sustainability as a passenger carrier, poised for further growth in the industry. The dusting business continued operating, but as a separate division. During the middle to late 1930s, the company's chances for survival improved with a solid managerial team in place, a fleet of modern aircraft, financial stability, a new north–south route, and headquarters situated in Atlanta. These developments followed the 1934 restart of passenger service following a hiatus of four years. Delta Air Corporation, then headquartered in Monroe, Louisiana, bid for and won Contract Air Mail Route 24, following Pres. Franklin Roosevelt's cancelation of the standing mail contracts in 1930. C. E. Woolman, general manager, reinitiated Delta's pioneering Trans Southern Route soon afterward.

Recommencing passenger service happened as a consequence of Delta Air Service having ceased operations in 1930, when Postmaster General Brown awarded the southern transcontinental airmail contract to American Airways.

Woolman's fledgling air service could not compete against American without a mail subsidy. Delta Air Service was sold and replaced by a new entity, Delta Air Corporation. The same principals (Douglas Y. Smith, president; Woolman, vice president; and Travis Oliver, treasurer) were involved. Between 1930 and 1934, Delta Air Corporation dusted crops and serviced the needs of general aviation at Selman Field in Monroe. While it is important to the Delta story, the corporation is not its point of origin. Delta Air Service was incorporated in 1928 and pioneered its Trans Southern Route passenger service in 1929. The emergence of this scheduled service seems a moment worthy of recognition as Delta's origin, but there is an unavoidable link to its immediate predecessor, Huff Daland Dusters, Inc., a Delaware corporation chartered in 1925.

Huff Daland Dusters was briefly based in Macon, Georgia, with George Post as general manager; Harold Harris, operations manager; and Woolman, entomologist-salesman. In July 1925 it relocated to Monroe, Louisiana, where it took advantage of more-favorable dusting opportunities in the Mississippi Delta region. A significant opportunity arose from Peruvian planters' request for help dealing with pests in South America. In response, Huff Daland Dusters sent aircraft and personnel to Lima, Peru. This set in motion a series of events that led Woolman and Harris to act as agents for New York financiers Richard Hoyt and Juan Trippe, who started Pan American Airways. Hoyt offered to sell the dusting outfit to its operating staff—Woolman, Harris, and the company's comptroller, Erwin E. Auerbach—under favorable terms. The offer collapsed and Huff Daland Dusters shut down when Woolman discovered Auerbach trying to negotiate an independent sale for himself. These circumstances did not lead to Delta's origin, however. Still, Delta Air Service would not have emerged as it did if not for the demise of Huff Daland Dusters.

Furthermore, Huff Daland Dusters originated as a subsidiary of the Huff Daland Company of Ogdensburg, New York, which designed airplanes specifically for dusting. It then began commercial applications with a subsidiary, Huff Daland Dusters, Inc. When the company outgrew its manufacturing plant in Ogdensburg, it moved to Bristol, Pennsylvania. There, Hayden, Stone, & Company, under Richard Hoyt, restructured it as Keystone Aviation Corporation, although the duster subsidiary kept its original name. The emergence of Huff Daland Dusters is not the point of Delta's origin, either, as it devolved from the activities of its parent, Huff Daland Company (later Keystone Aviation).

Commercial aviation and scientific agriculture combined in a new industry: commercial crop dusting ("aerial applications" as it is known today). This convergence took place at the Delta Laboratory in Tallulah, Louisiana, under the direction of Bert R. Coad, where experiments proved the effectiveness of applying calcium arsenate from the air. Dusting tests at Scott Field in Tallulah began in 1922 and continued in 1923, with military aircraft and pilots on loan from Maxwell Field, Alabama. Thomas H. Huff and Elliot Daland, both engineers, supported commercial aviation and designed an aircraft suitable for dusting crops. They manufactured a fleet of dusters and shipped them to the newly organized Huff Daland Dusters company for operations to begin in Macon. Combining agricultural pest control and airplanes in a business venture is an important marker leading up to Delta Air Lines, but this, too, is not its origin. Huff Daland Company's participation in experiments with its duster design would not have occurred without the concomitant discovery of an effective poison.

When the boll weevil threatened southern cotton, the federal government stepped in and established the Delta Laboratory. The search for a practical poison to kill the pest developed concurrently with, but independent of, the airplane. In 1908 William Newell tested a powdered form of lead arsenate on infested cotton. Later, William C. Piver combined lime with arsenic to produce calcium arsenate. Although effective against the boll weevil, ground-based applications were slow and labor intensive. In Ohio an experiment testing C. R. Neillie's idea to spread insecticide by air on catalpa trees proved astonishingly successful, which then prompted Julius A. Truesdell's suggestion to use airplanes on cotton.

Although significant, the development of calcium arsenate and spreading it by air are not determinative of Delta's origin. Advances in agriculture and aviation developed separately. The experiments with aircraft spreading calcium arsenate might seem to be the most-distant point of Delta's origin, but the circumstances of how plane and poison were brought together happened because of the economic devastation and social upheaval wrought by the boll weevil.

Thus, the boll weevil, when it crossed from Mexico into Texas in 1892, completes the tracing of Delta Air Lines to its time and place of origin.

A simple timeline explains the evolution. In 1892 the boll weevil crossed into Texas to begin its destructive migration through the U.S. Cotton Belt. Various methods of control were developed, resulting in the discovery of calcium arsenate. Yet ground-based application methods were time consuming and labor intensive. As the airplane's performance and reliability improved, agriculture and aeronautics merged during the experiments at Tallulah in 1922 and 1923 to poison the boll weevil from the air. Huff Daland Dusters, incorporated in 1925, then began such operations from Macon.

Conditions were not ideal in Georgia, so the company relocated to Monroe, Louisiana. Keystone Aviation, the parent company of Huff Daland Dusters, divested its dusting subsidiary and offered to sell its assets to the managers. The deal collapsed, and Huff Daland Dusters disbanded. Delta Air Service incorporated in 1928 and began carrying passengers in 1929 but could not sustain operations without a mail contract. It ceased operating, and a new company, Delta Air Corporation, emerged in 1930. In 1934 this company bid for and won Contract Air Mail Route 24 from Fort Worth, Texas, to Charleston, South Carolina, adding passenger service along the route soon after. Delta Air Lines has been operating as a passenger carrier continuously ever since.

A particular point in time, person, or place may arguably be more or less important in Delta's timeline. But each has its strengths and shortcomings. To highlight one or another as *the origin* does a disservice to all others, as it would diminish or cancel their roles. Was it Ogdensburg, New York, with Thomas Huff and Elliot Daland in 1920; Tallulah, Louisiana, with B. R. Coad in 1922–23; Macon, Georgia, with George Post and Harold Harris in 1925; or Monroe, Louisiana, with Harold Harris and C. E. Woolman in 1929? All are due their share of credit.

An extra measure can be afforded Collett Everman Woolman. He is justifiably remembered as the patriarch of Delta Air Lines. Up to his death in 1966, Woolman infused his leadership style, conservative business practices, and corporate culture in the company; his life deserves scholarly study. A companion theme would be the evolution of Delta's corporate memory as a managerial and marketing tool through the decades.

Huff Daland Company and its subsidiary, Huff Daland Dusters, deserve more study as well. Both contributed greatly to the development of aviation.

Huff Daland Company developed the first crop duster while Huff Daland Dusters pioneered commercial aviation. Understanding their ties between Wall Street and Pan American and Pan American–Grace Airways will deepen our understanding of those histories.

The roots that tie Delta's origin to the boll weevil stretch forward into the mid-1960s. Even as Delta Air Lines prospered and grew as a passenger carrier in the postwar years, crop dusting continued as a separate division. Only when dusting operations ceased were those ties to the boll weevil permanently severed.

≡ NOTES ≡

ABBREVIATIONS

AFHRA   Air Force Historical Research Agency, Maxwell AFB, AL

DALCA   Delta Air Lines Corporate Archives, Atlanta

LSULSC   Louisiana State University Libraries Special Collections, Baton Rouge

UIUCA   University of Illinois at Urbana-Champaign Archives

WSUSCA   Wright State University Special Collections and Archives, Dayton, OH

INTRODUCTION

1. "General Aviation and Agriculture Use," Alliance for Aviation across America, https://www
.aviationacrossamerica.org/issues/agricultural-use/ (accessed Oct. 23, 2022).

2. "Corporate Stats and Facts," Delta News Hub, https://news.delta.com/corporate-stats-and
-facts (accessed Oct. 18, 2022).

3. W. David Lewis and Wesley Phillips Newton, *Delta: The History of an Airline* (Athens: University of Georgia Press, 1978).

4. Ibid.

1. THE SOUTH, COTTON, AND THE BOLL WEEVIL

1. James C. Cobb, *The Most Southern Place on Earth* (New York: Oxford University Press, 1992), vii–viii, xii.

2. John M. Barry, *Rising Tide: The Great Mississippi Flood of 1927 and How It Changed America* (New York: Simon and Schuster, 1997), 37–39.

3. Cobb, *Most Southern Place on Earth*, 3.

4. Barry, *Rising Tide*, 10–11 (map).

5. Bertram Wyatt-Brown, *The House of Percy: Honor, Melancholy, and Imagination in a Southern Family* (New York: Oxford University Press, 1994), 4, 97.

6. Cobb, *Most Southern Place on Earth*, 92.

7. Wyatt-Brown, *House of Percy*, 4.

8. Lewis Baker, *The Percys of Mississippi: Politics and Literature in the New South* (Baton Rouge: Louisiana State University Press, 1983), 15, 17, 25; Barry, *Rising Tide*, 111.

9. Preface to Mark Twain, *Life on the Mississippi* (New York: Signet Classic, 2001).

10. Cobb, *Most Southern Place on Earth,* 82, 124, 141, 145.

11. James C. Cobb, ed., *The Mississippi Delta and the World: The Memoirs of David L. Cohn* (Baton Rouge: Louisiana State University Press, 1995), 66, 131.

12. James C. Giesen, *Boll Weevil Blues: Cotton, Myth, and Power in the American South* (Chicago: University of Chicago Press, 2011), 56.

13. Gavin Wright, *Old South, New South: Revolutions in the Southern Economy since the Civil War* (Baton Rouge: Louisiana State University Press, 1996), 49.

14. Leon F. Litwack, *Been in the Storm So Long: The Aftermath of Slavery* (New York: Vintage Books, 1979), 308.

15. The southern cotton culture is discussed in Pete Daniel, *Breaking the Land: The Transformation of Cotton, Tobacco, and Rice Cultures since 1880* (Urbana: University of Illinois Press, 1985).

16. Wright, *Old South, New South,* 12, 85–86; Cobb, *Most Southern Place on Earth,* 105. On the Great Migration, see Isabel Wilkerson. *The Warmth of Other Suns: The Epic Story of America's Great Migration* (New York: Vintage Books, 2010).

17. C. R. Parencia, *One Hundred Twenty Years of Research on Cotton Insects in the United States, USDA Agriculture Handbook* 515 (Washington, DC: USDA, Mar. 1978), 6.

18. William A. Dickerson et al., eds., *Boll Weevil Eradication in the United States through 1999* (Memphis: Cotton Foundation, 2001), xxi.

19. Baker, *Percys of Mississippi,* 31.

20. Eldon W. Downs and George F. Lemmer, "Origins of Aerial Crop Dusting," *Agricultural History* 30 (July 1965): 123.

21. Parencia, *One Hundred Twenty Years of Research,* 3, 5.

22. W. D. Hunter and B. R. Coad, *The Boll Weevil Problem, USDA Farmers Bulletin 1329* (Washington, DC: USDA, June 1923), 9.

23. Parencia, *One Hundred Twenty Years of Research,* 7.

24. Baker, *Percys of Mississippi,* 31.

25. T. C. Cleveland and C. R. Parencia, "History of the USDA Cotton Insects Research Laboratory Tallulah, Louisiana, 1909–1973," *Bulletin of the Entomological Society of America* 22, no. 4 (Dec. 1976): 403.

26. Parencia, *One Hundred Twenty Years of Research,* 5; "Weevil Spread Largest in Years," *Atlanta Constitution,* July 10, 1921.

27. P. B. Haney, W. J. Lewis, and W. R. Lambert, *Cotton Production and the Boll Weevil in Georgia: History, Cost of Control, and Benefits of Eradication, University of Georgia Research Bulletin 428* (Nov. 1996), 9.

28. Parencia, *One Hundred Twenty Years of Research,* 8.

29. Lea S. Hitchner, "The Insecticide Industry," in *Insects: The Yearbook of Agriculture, 1952* (Washington, DC: Government Printing Office, 1952), 451.

30. Pete Daniel, *Toxic Drift: Pesticides and Health in the Post–World War II South* (Baton Rouge: Louisiana State University Press, 2005), 8.

31. Hitchner, "Insecticide Industry," 451.

32. Parencia, *One Hundred Twenty Years of Research*, 9.

33. Email message, Ellen Fearday, alumni association records supervisor, to author, Mar. 16, 2000.

34. "Dr. Bert Coad," *Delta Digest*, Apr. 1966, 12.

35. (Title obscured), *Madison Journal (Tallulah, LA)*, May 1, 1926; Eugene "Steve" Stevens, interview by Larry Michaud, Feb. 1984, Casper, WY, tapes and transcript in author's possession.

36. "Bear Lake Club Election," *Madison Journal (Tallulah, LA)*, Apr. 15, 1922.

37. Theodore Roosevelt, "Louisiana Canebrakes," *Scribner's* 43 (Jan. 1908): 55–56.

38. Cleveland and Parencia, "USDA Cotton Insects Research Laboratory," 406; B. R. Coad, *Relation of the Arizona Wild Cotton Weevil to Cotton Planting in the Arid West, Bulletin of the USDA* 233 (Washington, DC: USDA, May 1915), 2.

39. Cleveland and Parencia, "USDA Cotton Insects Research Laboratory," 403.

40. Ibid.

41. Bert R. Coad testimony, Jan. 28, 1924, in U.S. Senate Subcommittee on Appropriations, *Agricultural Appropriations Bill, 1925, Hearings*, 68th Cong., 1st. sess. (Washington, DC: Government Printing Office, 1924), 165.

42. "The Root Saddle Gun," *Madison Journal (Tallulah, LA)*, Apr. 27, 1923.

43. "We find every year that many farmers fail to realize their danger early enough and then start making desperate efforts to poison after the infestation has become very heavy. The[y] scurry around trying to get calcium arsenate and dusting machinery, and nearly always there is considerable delay. Even when they get the poison and machinery, it is extremely difficult to control weevil infestation after it become [*sic*] severe. There are so many weevil stages present in the square and bolls that some of them come out every day and poison must be kept constantly on the plants if any good is to be done by it. This very greatly increases the expense of poisoning. Then, if there is even a short spell of rainy weather, such control that has been gained is lost and the farmer has gone to heavy expense for nothing." "Be Prepared to Poison Boll Weevil at the Right Time," *Madison Journal (Tallulah, LA)*, June 3, 1922.

44. "Seek Way to Halt Boll Weevil Pest," *New York Times*, Sept. 23, 1921.

45. Giesen, *Boll Weevil Blues*, xi.

46. "Seek Way to Halt Boll Weevil Pest," *New York Times*, Sept. 23, 1921.

47. Roy Shoffer, *Pest of Honor: The Story of the World's Most Unusual Monument* (n.p., 1988), 8, 10, 16. For a discussion of crop diversification and its results in Enterprise, Alabama, see Giesen, *Boll Weevil Blues*, 118–27.

48. Hunter and Coad, *Boll Weevil Problem*, 2–4, 16.

49. Haney, Lewis, and Lambert, *Cotton Production and the Boll Weevil in Georgia*, abstract, 6, 8, 12.

50. Doris Davidson, interviews by author, June 2, 9, 2017.

2. DUSTING FROM THE AIR

1. Downs and Lemmer, "Origins of Aerial Crop Dusting," 124.

2. Ibid., 123–24.

3. C. R. Neillie and J. S. Houser, "Fighting Insects with Airplanes: An Account of the Successful Use of the Flying-Machine in Dusting Tall Trees Infested with Leaf-Eating Caterpillars," *National Geographic,* Mar. 1922, 333; J. S. Houser. "The Airplane in Catalpa Sphinx Control," *Monthly Bulletin of the Ohio Agricultural Experimental Station* 7 (July–Aug. 1922): 126–36. Both of these articles incorrectly identify Lt. J. A. Macready as the chief of the flying section. The chief was Harold R. Harris; Macready was his assistant. Harold R. Harris to Mabry I. Anderson, Oct. 15, 1987, folder 1, box 3, Harold R. Harris Papers (MS-214), WSUSCA.

4. Mabry I. Anderson, *Low & Slow: An Insider's History of Agricultural Aviation* (San Francisco: California Farmer, 1986), 7.

5. Neillie and Houser, "Fighting Insects with Airplanes," 336.

6. Ibid., 337, 338.

7. Julius A. Truesdell, "Spraying from Air," *New York Times,* Jan. 8, 1922.

8. Julius A. Truesdell testimony, Feb. 8, 1922, in U.S. House Committee on Agriculture, *Use of Aircraft,* 67th Cong., 2nd sess. (Washington, DC: Government printing Office, 1922): 7. Coad's name in the testimony transcript is misspelled "Cowles," Pete Daniel argues a similar model. In the post–World War II period, ground-based mechanical pickers drove small cotton farmers out of business. Industrial operators using expensive machinery to farm large tracts of land brought an end to the cotton culture. Pete Daniel, *Lost Revolutions: The South in the 1950s* (Chapel Hill: University of North Carolina Press, 2000): 61.

9. Truesdell testimony, 5.

10. L. O. Howard testimony, Feb. 8, 1922, in U.S. House Committee on Agriculture, *Use of Aircraft,* 10.

11. Anderson, *Low & Slow,* 7.

12. Truesdell, "Spraying from Air." This hubris resulted in many aviators' deaths a decade later when the U.S. Army attempted to fly the mail.

13. Downs and Lemmer, "Origins of Aerial Crop Dusting," 129.

14. Bert R. Coad testimony, May 8, 1924, in U.S. Senate *Subcommittee on Appropriations, Agricultural Appropriations, 1925,* 68th Cong., 1st. sess. (Washington, DC: Government Printing Office, 1924), 157.

15. Downs and Lemmer, "Origins of Aerial Crop Dusting," 129.

16. B. R. Coad, E. Johnson, and G. L. McNeil, *Dusting Cotton from Airplanes,* USDA Bulletin *1204* (Washington, DC: USDA, Jan. 1924), 1.

17. Field Diaries, Collett Everman Woolman Papers, 1916–1979, LSULSC.

18. "Personal Report—Officers," Guy L. McNeil, Aug. 1922, call no. 167.4115-8, IRIS no. 912098, AFHRA.

19. "Personal Report—Officers," Charles T. Skow, Aug. 1922, call no. 167.4115-8, IRIS no. 912498, AFHRA; Coad, Johnson, and McNeil, *Dusting Cotton from Airplanes,* 2.

20. Downs and Lemmer, "Origins of Aerial Crop Dusting," 129.

21. Coad, Johnson, and McNeil, *Dusting Cotton from Airplanes,* 2, 7.

22. Ibid., 3–9.

23. Ibid., 9–12.

24. Ibid., 9, 15, 16, 21.

25. George B. Post, "Boll Weevil Control by Airplane," *Georgia State College of Agriculture, Extension Division Bulletin 301* (Nov. 1924): 9.

26. Coad, Johnson, and McNeil, *Dusting Cotton from Airplanes*, 21, 22–25, 31, 37.

27. Ibid., 33, 40.

28. "Army Planes to Fight Louisiana Boll Weevil," *New York Times*, Mar. 14, 1923; "The Fight for Cotton," ibid., June 10, 1923.

29. *Slipstream Monthly*, vol. 27; "Personal Report—Officers," Guy L. McNeil, Apr.–Aug. 1923, call no. 167.4115-8, IRIS no. 912098, AFHRA.

30. "Airplanes and Airships 'Put to Work' Combating Cotton Boll Weevil, Gypsy Moth and Locust" *Aircraft Yearbook, 1924* (New York: Aeronautical Chamber of Commerce, 1924): 76. This article states that Coad learned how to fly to better understand the problem. No other reference or supporting documentation to his being a pilot has been found by the author.

31. Coad, Johnson, and McNeil, *Dusting Cotton from Airplanes*, 39.

32. "Photographs from Air to Fix Cotton Acreage," *New York Times*, Apr. 5, 1923.

33. "Fighting Boll Weevil by Means of Airplanes," *Aviation*, Aug. 20, 1923, 210–12; *Slipstream Monthly*, vol. 25.

34. Brian R. Baker, "Early Dusting Experiments," *American Aviation Historical Society* 114, no. 2 (Summer 1969): 117.

35. Coad testimony, Jan. 28, May 8, 1924, in Senate *Subcommittee on Appropriations, Agricultural Appropriations, 1925*, 157, 162.

36. U.S. Department of Transportation, Office of Environmental Affairs, *A Nation in Motion: Historic American Transportation Sites* (Washington, DC: Government Printing Office, 1976), 113.

37. Downs and Lemmer, "Origins of Aerial Crop Dusting," 131.

38. Post, "Boll Weevil Control by Airplane," 5–7.

39. Ibid., 17.

40. B. R. Coad to Huff Daland Dusters, Inc., July 23, 1924, in Post, "Boll Weevil Control by Airplane," 4–5.

41. "Experiments Completed," *Monroe (LA) News-Star*, Sept. 2, 1922; "Fighting the Boll Weevil in the Famous Mississippi Delta" *Monroe (LA) Journal*, Feb. 2, 1923.

42. Post, "Boll Weevil Control by Airplane," 19–21.

3. A CORPORATE PIONEER IN THE DELTA

1. Writers Program, Works Project Administration, *Who's Who in Aviation: A Directory of Living Men and Women Who Have Contributed to the Growth of Aviation in the United States 1942–1943* (Chicago: Ziff-Davis, 1942), 102, 209; "Who's Who in American Aeronautics," *Aviation*, Apr. 11, 1921, 529; ibid., Apr. 25, 1921, 462.

2. "Airplane Project to Be Decided Monday Night," *Ogdensburg (NY) Journal*, Apr. 26, 1920; "New Airplane Completed at H.-D. Factory," ibid., Nov. 15, 1920.

3. "New Company May Be Formed to Take Over Leyare Plant and Increase the Business," *Ogdensburg (NY) Journal*, Apr. 19, 1920; "Leyare Project Being Considered Now," ibid., Apr. 26, 1920; "New Industry Promises to Be a Valuable Acquisition," ibid., June 2, 1920; untitled item, ibid., May 20, 1920.

4. "Leyare Plant Being Changed for New Work," *Ogdensburg (NY) Journal,* July 3, 1920.

5. "Diocese Left $1M Bequest by Atlantan," *Watertown Daily Times,* June 27, 1988.

6. "Meet Your Leaders: Miss FitzGerald," *Delta Digest,* Nov. 1948, n.p.

7. "Airmen Here after a Trip from Gotham," *Ogdensburg (NY) Journal,* June 30, 1920; "Arrival of Huff-Daland Flier Caused Sensation at the Bay: Carries Her First Passengers," ibid., July 7, 1920; "Plane Flights Planned at the Ogdensburg Fair," ibid., July 22, 1920; "Thrills of Air Riding Delightful," ibid., July 23, 1920.

8. "Who's Who in American Aeronautics," *Aviation,* Aug. ?, 1921, 194.

9. "New Airplane Completed at H-D Plant," *Ogdensburg (NY) Journal,* Nov. 15, 1921.

10. "Make Plane for a Boston Business Man," *Ogdensburg (NY) Journal,* Jan. 20, 1921.

11. "Fine Demonstration of New 3-Seated Airplane," *Ogdensburg (NY) Journal,* Mar. 4, 1922; "New Fliers Being Tried Out," ibid., Mar. 9, 1922; "Plane Climbs 7,000 Feet in 40 Minutes," ibid., June 10, 1922.

12. Alta Mae Stevens, *And Then What Happened? Harold Harris and the Early Development of Aviation* (Bloomington, IN: Author House, 2014), xii.

13. "Brief Biographical Sketch," n.d.; and "Passport," n.d., unmarked folder, box 15, Harold R. Harris Papers (MS-214), WSUSCA.

14. "The H-D Co. to Enlarge Operations," *Ogdensburg (NY) Journal,* Nov. 8, 1922); "New Fliers Being Tried Out," ibid., June 10, 1922; "Big Orders Come to Huff, Daland," *Ogdensburg (NY) Advance,* Nov. 8, 1923; "Huff Daland Is a Very Busy Place," ibid., Dec. 13, 1923.

15. "Lieut. Post Uninjured as Plane Falls," *Ogdensburg (NY) Journal,* Dec. 11, 1923; "First TW-5 H-D Machine Is Shipped," ibid., Dec. 19, 1923. This incident may have given rise to the myth that Post lost power while flying over Tallulah, requiring an emergency landing at the field. Supposedly, the mishap precipitated a chance meeting with Coad and Woolman at the Delta Laboratory, where Post discovered the crop-dusting experiments underway. When he returned to Ogdensburg, the story goes, he encouraged Huff and Daland to design an aircraft to meet the special needs of agricultural flying. The designers were already aware of the activities at Tallulah.

16. C. E. Woolman to Lloyd Stearman, Apr. 19, 1944, copy courtesy Marie Force, DALCA.

17. Post, "Boll Weevil Control by Airplane," 12–15.

18. "Huff Daland Company Get New Contract," *Ogdensburg (NY) Journal,* Apr. 30, 1924; "Test Flights in Midget Airplanes," ibid., July 29, 1924; "Program for Rotary Club on Thursday," ibid., July 30, 1924; "Duster Aero Leaves City for Tallulah," Aug. 4, 1924, ibid.

19. "Winds Hold Up Flight of Duster," *Ogdensburg (NY) Journal,* Feb. 27, 1925; "Huff Daland Duster Plane Given Test," ibid., Mar. 2, 1925; "Airplane Spreads Poison," *New York Times,* Mar. 2, 1925.

20. Oliver I. Snapp, "Airplane Dusting of Peach Orchards," *Journal of Economic Entomology* 19 (June 1926): 453, 459; "Plane Used in Peach Dusting," *Macon (GA) Daily Telegraph,* Nov. 25, 1924; "Dusting Planes to Arrive Soon," ibid., Mar. 5, 1925; "Two Additional Dusters Arrive," ibid., Mar. 19, 1925; "Plan Airplane Dusting of Houston Cotton & Orchards," *Houston (GA) Home Journal,* Mar. 5, 1925.

21. The certificate of incorporation was received and filed by the Delaware Secretary of State's

office on March 2, 1925. Huff Daland Dusters, Inc., Certificate of Incorporation folder 1, box 1, RG01.01, DALCA.

22. "Planes of a New Type to Be Turned Out," *Ogdensburg (NY) Journal*, Jan. 17, 1922; "Huff Daland Co. Buys Plant at Bristol—May Move in Fall," ibid., May 23, 1925; "Huff Daland Plant to Be Closed Soon," ibid., Aug. 27, 1925; "Airplane Company Buys Shipyard," *Bristol (PA) Courier*, May 21, 1925; "Much Interest Shown over Purchase of Shipyard Here," ibid., May 22, 1925; "Announcing the Opening of Huff Daland & Company's New Airplane Factory at Bristol, Pa.," *Aviation*, Oct. 5, 1925, 457. For Huff Daland aircraft designs, see Walter Boyne, "Huff Daland in 3-D," *Wings* 7 (1977): 5–63; and "Ambulance Airplane," *Ogdensburg (NY) Advance*, May 10, 1923.

23. Marylin Bender and Selig Altschul, *The Chosen Instrument: Pan Am, Juan Trippe, the Rise and Fall of an American Entrepreneur* (New York: Simon and Schuster, 1982), 81.

24. "Hoyt, Richard Farnsworth," *The National Cyclopedia of American Biography, vol.* 29 (New York: James T. White, 1941), 160.

25. Ibid.; "Richard F. Hoyt, 46, Financier Is dead," folder 30, box 13, *International Cyclopedia of Aviation Biography Collection* (MS-167), WSUCA.

26. "Tells Plans for Air Races," *New York Times*, Aug. 23, 1926; "Sees Pressing Need for Airport in City," ibid., Sept. 30, 1926.

27. Carl Solberg, *Conquest of the Skies: A History of Commercial Aviation in America* (Boston: Little, Brown, 1979), 120.

28. "Former City Company Has a Big Staff," *Ogdensburg (NY) Journal*, Dec. 30, 1927; "Davis's Big Machine Leaves . . . ," *New York Times*, Apr. 10, 1927; "Airmen Pay Tribute to Crash Victims," ibid., Apr. 27, 1927; "Aviation Leaders Rejoice at Success," ibid., June 27, 1927.

29. Keystone Aircraft Corporation, "Concerning Our Plant and Activities," *Keystone Aircraft Corporation*, n.d., folder 5, box 1, RG01.01, DALCA.

30. "Thomas H. Huff Retires as Head of Airplane Company," *Bristol (PA) Courier*, Nov. 8, 1926.

31. John H. Van Deventer Jr., "The Story of Keystone and Its Latest Contribution to the Advancement of Aviation," *Air Transportation*, Jan. 19, 1929, 56; Keystone Aircraft Corporation, "Who's Who in the Keystone Aircraft Corporation," *Keystone Aircraft Corporation*, n.d., folder 5, box 1, RG01.01, DALCA.

32. "New Office Building for Keystone Plant," *Bristol (PA) Courier*, Oct. 5, 1928.

33. Lorna Carroll, "Excuse His Dust!," *Tampa Bay Times* (St. Petersburg, FL), June 6, 1954.

34. Roger William Riis, "Commercial Crop Dusting, Details of the Operations of the Huff Daland Dusters," *Aviation*, May 25, 1925, 573; *Repartee—Official Newsletter of the Retired Eastern Pilots*, Apr., May, June 1980, 40.

35. A. Scott Berg, *Lindbergh* (New York: G. B. Putnam's Sons, 1989), 84.

36. "Notes for Morrow Committee," Misc. Speeches Given by Harris, folder 13, box 12, Harris Papers, WSUSCA; Dwight W. Morrow to Lieut. Harold R. Harris, Oct. 15, 1925, ibid.

37. "Lieut. Harris to Lead Fight against Boll Weevil," *Ogdensburg (NY) Journal*, Jan. 5, 1925; "Draft Sept. 85" (unpublished manuscript), 1, folder 7, box 3, Harris Papers, WSUSCA.

38. J. J. Brown, "Annual Report of Georgia Department of Agriculture for 1924," *Quarterly Bulletin of the Georgia Department of Agriculture* 99 (First Quarter 1925): 7–8.

39. J. J. Brown, "Biennial Report of Georgia Department of Agriculture for 1925–1926," *Quarterly Bulletin of the Georgia Department of Agriculture* 103 (First Quarter 1927): 56.

40. Post, "Boll Weevil Control by Airplane," 3.

41. Snapp, "Airplane Dusting of Peach Orchards," 450–51; Post, "Boll Weevil Control by Airplane," 3.

42. Riis, "Commercial Crop Dusting," 573; "Open Office of Flying Dusters," *Macon (GA) Daily Telegraph,* Feb. 19, 1925. Camp Wheeler Airfield is the current Herbert Smart Airport.

43. Snapp, "Airplane Dusting of Peach Orchards," 451–52.

44. "Plane Used in Peach Dusting," *Macon (GA) Daily Telegraph,* Nov. 25, 1924; "Dusters Begin Anti-Pest War," ibid., Mar. 24, 1925.

45. *How Huff Daland Airplanes Can Protect Your Crops, Huff Daland Dusters Bulletin 3,* folder 7, box 1, RG01.01, DALCA.

46. Snapp, "Airplane Dusting of Peach Orchards," 453.

47. "Dusting Planes in Pecan Groves," *Macon (GA) Daily Telegraph,* May 11, 1925; "Huff Daland Firm Has Dusted Quarter-Million Peach Trees," ibid., June 7, 1925; Riis, "Commercial Crop Dusting," 573. "Planes Built Here Will Protect Fields of Cotton in South," *Bristol (PA) Courier,* June 11, 1925. "Airplane Cotton Dusting," *Laurinburg (NC) Exchange,* July 8 or 17, 1925; "Airplanes Now Dusting Commercially," *Madison Journal (Tallulah, LA),* June 27, 1925.

48. "Georgia Cotton Dusting Ceases," *Macon (GA) Daily Telegraph,* July 6, 1925.

49. Ibid.; "1985 Biographical Notes," 4, folder 7, box 3, Harris Papers, WSUSCA.

50. J. J. Brown, "Biennial Report of Georgia Department of Agriculture for 1925–1926," *Quarterly Bulletin of the Georgia Department of Agriculture* 103 (First Quarter 1927): 56.

51. Giesen, *Boll Weevil Blues,* 143–44.

52. "Weevil Dusting Concern Considering Monroe for Big Plane Headquarters," *Monroe (LA) News-Star,* July 6, 1925; "Plane Field Selected at South End," ibid., July 14, 1925; "Monroe Is Put on Air Map through Huff Daland Work," ibid., Nov. 16, 1925.

53. "Weevil Dusting Concern Considering Monroe for Big Plane Headquarters," *Monroe (LA) News-Star,* July 6, 1925; "Smoot Field Is Name Selected Honoring Pilot," ibid., Aug. 7, 1926.

4. THE EAGLE AND THE CONDOR

1. "Articles of Incorporation of the 'White Flying Dusters,'" *Madison Journal (Tallulah, LA),* Oct. 24, 1925.

2. Arthur V. Metcalfe, "The Dictatorship of President Leguía of Peru" (MA thesis, University of Southern California, 1934), 67.

3. Peter Flindell Klarén, *Peru: Society and Nationhood in the Andes* (New York: Oxford University Press, 2000), 213, 214, 241.

4. Ibid., 242.

5. Lawrence A. Clayton, *Peru and the United States: The Condor and the Eagle* (Athens: University of Georgia Press, 1999), 74, 104; Thomas E. Skidmore and Peter H. Smith, *Modern Latin America,* 5th ed. (Oxford: Oxford University Press, 2001), 196.

6. Gary Richard Garrett, "The Oncenio of Augusto B. Leguía: Middle Sector Government and Leadership in Peru, 1919–1930" (PhD diss., University of New Mexico, 1973), 125.

7. Skidmore and Smith, *Modern Latin America,* 196.

8. Charles T. Goodsell, *American Corporations and Peruvian Politics* (Cambridge, MA: Harvard University Press, 1974), 40; Klarén, *Peru,* 241.

9. Klarén, *Peru,* 250.

10. "The Modern Traffic System in Lima," photograph album, folder 7, box 14, Harold R. Harris Papers (MS-214), WSUSCA.

11. Metcalfe, "Dictatorship of President Leguía," 71.

12. Klarén, *Peru,* 214.

13. Dan Hagedorn, *Conquistadors of the Sky: A History of Aviation in Latin America* (Gainesville: University Press of Florida, 2008), 130.

14. "World Aeronautics, Peru," *Aircraft Yearbook, 1923* (New York: Aeronautical Chamber of Commerce of America, 1923), 187.

15. Garrett, "Oncenio of Augusto B. Leguía," 150–51.

16. James H. Doolittle, *I Could Never Be So Lucky Again: An Autobiography,* with Carroll V. Glines (New York: Bantam Books, 1991), 114, 117, 122.

17. Wesley Phillips Newton, *The Perilous Sky: U.S. Aviation Diplomacy and Latin America, 1919–1931* (Coral Gables, FL: University of Miami Press, 1978), 83.

18. Herbert H. Moll, *Peruvian Civil Aviation* (Mineola, NY: American Airmail Society, 2000), 33.

19. Clayton, *Peru and the United States,* 131–34.

20. Bender and Altshul, *Chosen Instrument*; Elsbeth E. Freudenthal, *The Aviation Business: From Kitty Hawk to Wall Street* (New York: Vanguard, 1940), 168.

21. Peter Boland Gushue, "Heavenly Influence: Panagra Airways in Peru, 1928–1949" (PhD diss., University of Alabama, 1997), 16.

22. Moll, *Peruvian Civil Aviation,* 33.

23. Woolman did not write a memoir, nor is a comprehensive study of his life available. I use contemporary resources to understand his place in Delta's history.

24. Questionnaire for the University of Illinois Directory completed by C. E. Woolman, Jan. 22, 1926, Collett Everman Woolman Papers, UIUCA.

25. "In 1687 200 acres are deeded to him in Mount Holly, NJ. John and Elizabeth Borton had seven children born in Burlington County, NJ." John Woolman "died February 27, 1718 in Mansfield, Burlington County, Province of New Jersey, (Present USA)." "C. E. Woolman, Founder of Delta Air Lines," Geni, https://www.geni.com/people/Collett-Woolman/6000000023018075017 (accessed Mar. 3, 2017; subscription required).

26. "United States Census, 1900," FamilySearch, https://familysearch.org/ark:/61903/1:1:M93 P-R86 (accessed Mar. 2, 2023; subscription required); "Find a Grave Index," database, *FamilySearch,* https://familysearch.org/ark:/61903/1:1:QK16-4Q5D (accessed Mar. 2, 2023; subscription required); "Daura Campbell Woolman (1865-1954)," *Find a Grave,* http://www.findagrave.com/memorial/1423 54344/daura-woolman (accessed Mar. 2, 2023).

27. Albert Woolman, Duluth city, Ward 03, St. Louis County, "Minnesota State Census, 1895,"

citing line 24, p. 62, State Library and Records Service, St. Paul, MN, and FHL microfilm 565,808, FamilySearch, https://familysearch.org/ark:/61903/1:1:MQD7-RQD (accessed Mar. 2, 2023; subscription required); *Register of Graduates of the Indiana University: Including Advanced and Honorary Degrees 1830–1901* (Bloomington, IN: Published by the University, 1901), 46.

28. *Twenty-First Report of the Board of Trustees of the University of Illinois,* vol. 21 (Springfield, IL: Phillips Bros. State Printers, 1902), xx.

29. "A. J. Woolman Dies, Prominent Scientist Expires at His Home in Urbana," *Pantagraph (Bloomington, IL),* Apr. 17, 1918.

30. Virgil V. Phelps, ed. *University of Illinois Directory* (Bloomington, IL: Pantagraph Printing and Stationary, 1916), 735; *The Semi-Centennial Alumni Record of the University of Illinois* (Chicago: Lakeside, 1918), 267, 480, 654.

31. *Semi-Centennial Alumni Record,* 48; "The *Illio* Class of 1913 University of Illinois," 113, https://libsysdigi.library.illinois.edu/OCA/Books2012-12/illio/illio13univ/illio13univ.pdf (accessed Mar. 1, 2023).

32. Sylvia Beer, "Cupola Chatter . . . Let's Learn from a 'Distinguished Illini,'" *Daily Illini,* Sept. 24, 1964, Woolman Papers, UIUCA. This and other secondary accounts claim that Woolman attended the Reims aviation meet in France held August 22–29, 1909 (the article erroneously gives the year 1910), but no primary source was found to substantiate his attendance.

33. "Massachusetts, Boston Passenger Lists, 1891–1943," FamilySearch, https://familysearch .org/ark:/61903/1:1:23FG-CM9 (accessed Dec. 4, 2014; subscription required); "Massachusetts, Boston Passenger Lists, 1891–1943," FamilySearch, https://familysearch.org/ark:/61903/1:1:23F5-MH7 (accessed Dec. 4, 2014; subscription required); "Massachusetts, Boston Passenger Lists, 1891–1943," database with images, FamilySearch, https://www.familysearch.org/ark:/61903/1:1:23F5-MH7 (accessed Jan. 21, 2022; subscription required), Collett Everman Woolman, 1910, ibid. (accessed Mar. 1, 2023; subscription required); Phelps, *University of Illinois Directory,* 735; *Semi-Centennial Alumni Record,* 480.

34. Harold Rubin, "Boll Weevils Started His Air Line," *Dixie,* Feb. 13, 1955, Woolman Papers, UIUCA.

35. *Semi-Centennial Alumni Record,* 480.

36. A Thought for the Progressive Farmer (column), *Monroe (LA) News-Star,* Mar. 9, 26, Apr. 23, 1914, July 14, 1915; "Old Board Re-Elected," ibid., Jan. 20, 1915; "A Timely Thought for the Progressive Farmer," ibid., July 14, Nov. 24, 1915.

37. "15 Years Ago," *Monroe (LA) News-Star,* June 30, 1931; "Program Arranged for Newspaper Men," ibid., June 3, 1914.

38. "Miss Helen Fairfield Bride of C. E. Woolman" (newspaper clipping), Aug. 9, 1916, Woolman Papers, UIUCA; "United States Census, 1900"; *Beloit College, Annual Reports of Beloit College,* vol. 5, no. 3 (Beloit, WI, 1907), https://books.google.com/books?id=i1lCAQAAMAAJ&newbks=1&new bks_redir=0&hl=en (accessed Jan.17, 2017); "Mrs. Mary Fairfield Dies Here at Age of 75," *Atlanta Constitution,* Jan. 4, 1942.

39. "Illinois Alumni Join Destiny's" (newspaper clipping), Aug. 8, 1916, Woolman Papers, UIUCA; *Semi-Centennial Alumni Record,* 531.

40. Collett Everman Woolman, 1917–1918, "United States World War I Draft Registration Cards, 1917–1918," citing East Baton Rouge Parish, LA, U.S., NARA microfilm publication M1509, and FHL microfilm 1,684,672, FamilySearch, https://familysearch.org/ark:/61903/1:1:KZ88-64K (accessed Jan. 22, 2017; subscription required).

41. Helen Woolman in household of Collett E. Woolman, Monroe, Police Jury Ward 10, Ouachita Parish, LA, "United States Census, 1940," citing ED (enumeration district) 37-18, sheet 63A, line 28, family 320, Sixteenth Census of the United States, 1940, NARA digital publication T627, RG 29, Records of the Bureau of the Census, 1790–2007, roll 1437, FamilySearch, https://familysearch.org/ark:/61903/1:1:VY5S-XSH (accessed Jan. 22, 2017; subscription required). Martha's middle name was Ann. Unidentified newspaper clipping, n.d., Woolman Papers, UIUCA.

42. "Can Poison Boll Weevil, Experts at Tallulah Find," *Monroe (LA) News-Star,* July 12, 1918; B. R. Coad, *Recent Experimental Work on Poisoning Cotton-Boll Weevils, USDA Bulletin 731* (Washington, DC: USDA, July 1918).

43. "Field Diaries 1–3," July 1916–19, Woolman Papers, LSULSC; loose pages of Field Diary, Jan.–Nov. 1922, ibid.

44. "Planters Hold Good Meeting," *Madison Journal (Tallulah, LA),* Mar. 15, 1924.

45. "Woolman Much Enthused, Plane Dusting Plan," *Monroe (LA) News-Star,* June 13, 1925.

46. Harold R. Harris, interview by Dr. Lawrence Clayton, Nov. 5, 1979, Falmouth, MS, folder "Dissertation interviews w/former Panagristas," box 1, RG 245, Peter Gushue Papers, Special Collections and Archives, Ralph Brown Draughon Library, Auburn University, transcript.

47. Ibid.

48. George N. Wolcott, "The Status of Economic Entomology in Peru," *Bulletin of Entomological Research* 20 (Aug. 1965): 225–27.

49. "Dr. Hinds to Study Cotton Pests in Peru," *Madison Journal (Tallulah, LA),* Feb. 6, 1926; Wolcott, "Status of Economic Entomology in Peru," 226.

50. "Panagra," 12, Harris Papers, WSUSCA.

51. Harris interview, 1979.

52. Department of Commerce to Collett E. Woolman, Sept. 29, 1935, Woolman Papers, LSULSC.

53. Barbara Woolman Preston, interview by Delta Air Transport Heritage Museum, Jan. 12, 1993, transcribed Sept. 27, 1999, DALCA; "Mrs. Preston's Dad Gave Delta Start And Spirit," *Atlanta Journal,* June 14, 1979.

54. "Here's [a] Plane for Everyone to Fly Easily," *Monroe (LA) News-Star,* May 26, 1931.

55. Joe Greer Sr. and Joe Greer Jr., "1924–1929 Huff Daland Dusters—Monroe, LA," *James Dorris Greer: Delta's First Pilot Was a Barnstormer,* 2017, https://jamesdorrisgreer.com/ (accessed Jun. 24, 2020).

56. "Bastrop's Aerial Circus Finished," *Monroe (LA) News-Star,* Oct. 9, 1932.

57. Harold R. Harris to Mabry I. Anderson, Oct. 15, 1987, folder 1, box 3, Harris Papers, WSUSCA.

58. Virginia P. Welch, interview by author, Atlanta, GA, July 21, 2009, in author's possession.

59. Harris to Anderson, Oct. 15, 1987.

60. Harris interview, 1979.

61. Draft biography of George Birkbeck Post, Mar. 25, 1930, folder 21, box 22, International Cyclopedia of Aviation Biography Collection (MS-167), WSUSCA. George Post became president of Free Bottom Craft and in 1928 became vice president and a director of the Edo Aircraft Corporation (known for manufacturing airplane floats).

62. Harold R. Harris to Collett E. Woolman, Oct. 6, 1926, "Crop dusting," folder 14, box 1, RG01.01, DALCA.

63. Ellis O. Briggs, *Proud Servant: The Memoirs of a Career Ambassador* (Kent, OH: Kent State University Press, 1998), 20, 29.

64. Scrapbook, Woolman Papers, LSULSC.

65. "Misc. Speeches Given by Harris," folder 12, box 12, Harris Papers, WSUSCA; "Algondoneros," folder 8, box 1, RG01.01, DALCA.

66. "Summary of Huff Daland Duster's Work in Peru to March 31, 1927," *West Coast Leader* (Lima, Peru), Apr. 5, 1927, folder 5, box 15, Harris Papers, WSUSCA.

67. "Panagra," 12, folder 1, box 7, Harris Papers, WSUSCA; *Aircraft Yearbook, 1927* (New York: Aeronautical Chamber of Commerce of America, 1927), 1163.

68. "Louisiana, New Orleans Passenger Lists, 1820–1945," database with images, FamilySearch, https://familysearch.org/ark:/61903/1:1:KZQL-KDP-R9F (accessed Oct. 8, 2015; subscription required); Collett Woolman, 1926, ibid., citing Ship Heredia, affiliate film 114, NARA microfilm publications M259 and T905, and FHL microfilm 2,311,464 (accessed July 16, 2017).

69. Manuel A. Rapier to C. E. Woolman, Nov. 16, 1926, folder 8, box 1, RG01.01, DALCA.

70. Manuel A. Rapier, "El Empleo de Aeroplanos en Nuestra Agricultura" [The use of planes in our agriculture], *El Comercio* (Lima, Peru), Nov. 17, 1926, translation in author's possession (translator unknown).

71. Agró, "El Empleo de Aeroplanos en Nuestra Agricultura" [The Use of Planes in Our Agriculture], *El Comercio* (Lima, Peru), Nov. 18, 1926, translation in author's possession (translated by Jackie Aman, 2009).

72. "Report to the President and Board of Directors of Huff Daland Dusters, Incorporated for 1927," Oct. 26, 1927, 1–2, folder 3, box 15, Harris Papers, WSUSCA.

73. Harold R. Harris to Collett E. Woolman, Oct. 6, 1926, folder 14, box 1, RG01.01, DALCA.

74. "La Desinfección por Aeroplanos" [Disinfection by airplanes], *El Comercio* (Lima, Peru), Dec. 27, 1926; photograph with inscription, "Our planes in front of the Santa Barbara sugar mill," n.d., folder 27, box 2, RG01.03, DALCA.

75. Photograph album, Harris Papers, WSUSCA.

76. "Report to the President and Board of Directors," 2, Harris Papers, WSUSCA.

77. "Summary of Huff Daland Dusters' Work in Peru," Harris Papers, WSUSCA.

5. HAROLD ROSS HARRIS'S INSIGHT

1. "Report to the President and Board of Directors of Huff Daland Dusters, Incorporated for 1927," Oct. 26, 1927, 4, folder 3, box 15, Harris Papers, WSUSCA.

2. "Huff Daland Dusters Go to Peru," *Aviation,* Mar. 21, 1927, 568.

3. Photograph album, Harris Papers, WSUSCA; photograph with inscription, "Our planes in front of the Santa Barbara sugar mill," n.d., folder 27, box 2, RG01.03, DALCA.

4. "Summary of Huff Daland Dusters' Work in Peru to March 31, 1927," *West Coast Leader* (Lima, Peru), Apr. 5, 1927, folder 5, box 15, Harris Papers, WSUSCA.

5. Ibid.

6. Alexander Howard to Harold R. Harris, n.d., in "Report to the President and Board of Directors," 2–3, Harris Papers, WSUSCA.

7. "Summary of Huff Daland Dusters' Work in Peru," Harris Papers, WSUSCA.

8. Howard to Harris, n.d., in "Report to the President and Board of Directors," 3, Harris Papers, WSUSCA.

9. "Panagra," 12, folder 12, box 12, Harris Papers, WSUSCA.

10. "Report to the President and Board of Directors," 2, Harris Papers, WSUSCA. The quotation is attributed to Harris. He is the only person who could speak to this material in the report.

11. Photograph album, Harris Papers, WSUSCA.

12. "La Clausura del Ano en la Escuela de Aviacion 'Jorge Chavez'" [The closing of the year in the aviation school "Jorge Chavez"], *El Comercio* (Lima, Peru), Feb. 2, 1927.

13. Stevens interview, 1984.

14. "Demostracion de los Aeroplanos para Fines Agricolas" [Demonstration of airplanes for agricultural purposes], *El Comercio* (Lima, Peru), Feb. 3, 1927.

15. "Report to the President and Board of Directors," 2, Harris Papers, WSUSCA.

16. Harold R. Harris, interview by Alta May Stevens, Sept. 1, 1980, transcript in author's possession.

17. Maurer Maurer, *Aviation in the U.S. Army, 1919–1939* (Washington, DC: Office of Air Force History, U.S. Air Force, 1987), 255–56.

18. Newton, *Perilous Sky,* 94.

19. "La Llegada de los Aviadores Americanos" [The arrival of American airmen], *Mundial,* Feb. 11, 1927.

20. "Misc. Speeches given by Harris," folder 12, box 12, Harris Papers, WSUSCA.

21. Newton, *Perilous Sky,* 99.

22. "Misc. Speeches given by Harris," Harris Papers, WSUSCA.

23. Barry, *Rising Tide,* 201, 262, 286.

24. "Report to the President and Board of Directors," 10, Harris Papers, WSUSCA.

25. The Delta then became "the land where the blues began." Barry, *Rising Tide,* 206, 302, 304, 334, 416.

26. Shreveport Chamber of Commerce, "Airplane Cotton Dusting for Caddo," *Shreveport,* June 1927, folder 9, box 1, RG01.01, DALCA; "Another Service of the Airplane," *Standard Oil Bulletin,* Aug. 1926, ibid.

27. "Report to the President and Board of Directors," 7, 8, Harris Papers, WSUSCA.

28. Ibid., 10, 12. The Pelican was described as "a convertible five-purpose Navy training plane suitable for all military requirements in its class." Keystone Aircraft Corporation publicity flyer, folder 5, box 1, RG01.01, DALCA.

29. "Report to the President and Board of Directors," 15–17, Harris Papers, WSUSCA.

30. Ibid., 15–18.

31. "Airport Keeps Pace with Needs," *Ouachita Citizen (Monroe, LA),* Mar. 9, 1983.

32. "Report to the President and Board of Directors," 7, Harris Papers, WSUSCA.

33. Lt. Cdr. Harold B. Grow to Harold R. Harris, Apr. 12, 1927, folder 12, box 1, RG01.01, DALCA; Marvis L. Alexander to Harold R. Harris, May 11, 1927, ibid.

34. "Report to the President and Board of Directors," 4, Harris Papers, WSUSCA.

35. Ibid.

36. Standard Contract for Airplane Dusting Service in Peru, folder 6, box 3, RG01.01, DALCA.

37. "Peruvian Contracts—1928," folder 3, box 3, RG01.01, DALCA.

38. Standard Contract for Airplane Dusting Service in Peru, DALCA.

39. "Report to the President and Board of Directors," 6, Harris Papers, WSUSCA. The contract was for the Keystone Pelican (Pronto) aircraft discussed later in chapter 6.

40. "Summary of Huff Daland Dusters' Work in Peru," Harris Papers, WSUSCA.

41. "Report to the President and Board of Directors," 6, Harris Papers, WSUSCA; "Draft Sept 85," folder 7, box 3, ibid.

42. William A. M. Burden, *The Struggle for Airways in Latin America* (New York: Arno, 1977), 8.

43. This "small steamer," the 228-foot-long *Inca,* was built in England and brought to Lake Titicaca in sections for assembly. See Stewart E. McMillin, "The Heart of Aymara Land," *National Geographic,* Feb. 1927, 256.

44. "Draft Sept 85," folder 7, box 3, Harris Papers, WSUSCA.

45. "South America Survey Trip," 1, folder 3, box 15, Harris Papers, WSUSCA.

46. Hagedorn, *Conquistadors of the Sky,* 217.

47. Obituary of Harold Ross Harris, *New York Times,* July 29, 1988.

48. "Argentine Aviation," *Buenos Aires Herald* (Argentina), July 24, 1927, Newspaper and Scrapbook, Harris Papers, WSUSCA; Hagedorn, *Conquistadors of the Sky,* 219.

49. J. E. Varanona to Harold R. Harris, Aug. 1927, folder 3, box 15, Harris Papers, WSUSCA; "South America Survey Trip," 3–4, ibid.

50. Hagedorn, *Conquistadors of the Sky,* 219.

51. Ibid., 218.

52. "South America Survey Trip," 7, Harris Papers, WSUSCA.

53. Hagedorn, *Conquistadors of the Sky,* 211.

54. Obituary of Harold Ross Harris, *New York Times,* July 29, 1988.

55. "Misc. Speeches given by Harris," Harris Papers, WSUSCA.

56. "South America Survey Trip," 14, Harris Papers, WSUSCA.

57. Burden, *Struggle for Airways in Latin America,* 15.

58. Harold R. Harris, "Sixty Years of Aviation History: One Man's Remembrance," lecture, Tenth Annual Northeast Historians Meeting, Windsor Locks, CT, Oct. 12, 1974, IRIS #01042146, AFHRA.

59. "South America Survey Trip," 14, Harris Papers, WSUSCA. The map is not in the files.

60. Bender and Altschul, *Chosen Instrument,* 117.

61. Briggs, *Proud Servant,* 20.

6. AIRMAIL AND THE WEST COAST PROJECT

1. Burden, *Struggle for Airways in Latin America,* 22.

2. F. Robert van der Linden, *Airlines and Air Mail: The Post Office and the Birth of the Commercial Aviation Industry* (Lexington: University Press of Kentucky, 2002), 36.

3. Irwin E. Auerbach to Edgar N. Gott, Oct. 25, 1927, in "Report to the President and Board of Directors of Huff Daland Dusters, Incorporated for 1927," Oct. 26, 1927, folder 3, box 15, Harris Papers, WSUSCA.

4. "Report to the President and Board of Directors," 19, Harris Papers, WSUSCA.

5. Ibid., 19, 20.

6. Ibid., 20.

7. Ibid., 24; Stevens interview, 1984. The repair charge of $33.55 was carried by the company as a bad debt from Stevens. Account 70, Ledger Book, folder 2, box 2, RG01.01, DALCA.

8. "Report to the President and Board of Directors," 21–22, Harris Papers, WSUSCA.

9. Van der Linden, *Airlines and Air Mail,* 23, 52–53; "Report to the President and Board of Directors," 22, 23, Harris Papers, WSUSCA.

10. "Report to the President and Board of Directors," 8–9, 24, Harris Papers, WSUSCA.

11. "Thomas H. Huff Retires as Head of Airplane Co.," *Bristol (PA) Courier,* Nov. 8, 1926.

12. Bender and Altschul, *Chosen Instrument,* 84.

13. Douglas Waller, *A Question of Loyalty: Gen. Billy Mitchell and the Court-Martial That Gripped the Nation* (New York: Harper Collins, 2004), 180.

14. Newton, *Perilous Sky,* 110, 112–13; Robert Daily, *An American Saga: Juan Trippe and His Pan Am Empire* (New York: Random House, 1980), 29, 86.

15. Newton, *Perilous Sky,* 114.

16. Daily, *American Saga,* 35.

17. Newton, *Perilous Sky,* 113.

18. "Daddy of the West Coast Airlines," *South Pacific Mail (Valparaiso, Chile),* Jan. 28, 1937, Scrapbook, Harris Papers, WSUSCA; Harris's travel expenses, June 15–Oct. 15, 1937, "Duster Journal," 19, folder 3, box 2, RG01.01, DALCA.

19. "Daddy of the West Coast Airlines," Harris Papers, WSUSCA.

20. Bender and Altschul, *Chosen Instrument,* 86–87.

21. "Draft, Sept. 85," 12, folder 7, box 3, Harris Papers, WSUSCA.

22. Scrapbook, Woolman Papers, LSULSC.

23. The exact date of their sailing is unknown. An entry in the "Duster Journal" (folder 1, box 2, DL01.01, DALCA) refers to expenditures in Peru for November and December 1927.

24. Advertisement, *New York Times,* Nov. 6, 1927.

25. Preston interview, 1993.

26. Barbara Woolman Preston, interview by Wesley Phillips Newton, Dec. 21, 1977, DALCA, transcript.

27. Preston interview, 1993.

28. "Memorandum to Mr. Woodbridge," Nov. 16, 1928, folder 15, box 1, RG01.01, DALCA.

29. "Duster Journal," 100, folder 1, box 2, RG01.01, DALCA.

30. Irwin E. Auerbach to C. E. Woolman, Jan. 5, 1928, folder 11, box 1, RG01.01, DALCA.

31. "Memorandum to Mr. C. E. Woolman on Accounting for Peruvian Expedition, 1927–1928," folder 11, box 1, RG01.01, DALCA; Irwin A. Auerbach to C. E. Woolman, Jan. 28, 1928, ibid. No examples of coded or decoded messages have been discovered.

32. "Peruvian Contracts—1928," folder 3, box 3, RG01.01, DALCA.

33. "Invoice, Huff Daland Dusters, Inc.," Dec. 17, 1927, folder 7, box 2, RG01.01, DALCA.

34. Huff Daland Dusters, Inc., to Pedro Martinto, Dec 23, 1927, folder 14, box 1, RG01.01, DALCA; Dan E. Tobin to C. E. Woolman, Apr. 3, 6, 1929, ibid.

35. Briggs, *Proud Servant,* 23; Newton, *Perilous Sky,* 139.

36. Ellis O. Briggs to C. E. Woolman, Apr. 17, 1928, folder 14, box 1, RG01.01, DALCA.

37. Power of Attorney, folder 8, box 3, DL01.01, DALCA.

38. Newton, *Perilous Sky,* 140–41, 188–98.

39. Ibid., 140–41.

40. Ambassador Miles Poindexter departed Lima on March 21, 1928. His replacement, Alexander P. Moore, did not take his post until June 11.

41. Rudolf Beeck's letter is dated November 1, 1927. "Proyecto para la Formación de la Compañia National Commercial de Transportes Aereos del Peru" [Project for the formation of the National Commercial Company of Aerial Transports of Peru], folder 16, box 3, RG01.01, DALCA.

42. Matthew E. Hanna to Department of State, Apr. 19, 1928, *Records of the State Department Relating to the Internal Affairs of Peru, 1910–1929, M746,* NARA, reel 29 (hereafter cited as *Internal Affairs of Peru*).

43. Alexander P. Moore to Secretary of State, Dec. 22, 1928, Internal Affairs of Peru; Clayton, *Peru and the United States,* 129.

44. Moll, *Peruvian Civil Aviation,* 21.

45. Ibid., 22.

46. Briggs, *Proud Servant,* 41.

47. Clayton, *Peru and the United States,* 129.

48. Matthew E. Hanna to Department of State, Apr. 19, 1928, Internal Affairs of Peru.

49. Matthew E. Hanna to Department of State, Apr. 21, 23, 1928, Internal Affairs of Peru.

50. Matthew E. Hanna to Department of State, Apr. 23, 1928, sec. 1, Internal Affairs of Peru.

51. Matthew E. Hanna to Department of State, Apr. 23, 1928, sec. 2, Internal Affairs of Peru.

52. Ibid.

53. Secretary of State to Postmaster General Harry S. New, Apr. 24, 1928, Internal Affairs of Peru.

54. Harold R. Harris, interview by Alta May Stevens, Sept. 1, 1980, transcript in author's possession.

55. Matthew E. Hanna to Department of State, Apr. 25, 1928, Internal Affairs of Peru.

56. Matthew E. Hanna to Department of State, May 7, 1928, Internal Affairs of Peru.

57. Ibid.

58. Matthew E. Hanna to Department of State, May 15, 1928, Internal Affairs of Peru.

59. Newton, *Perilous Sky,* 190.

60. Matthew E Hanna to Department of State, June 2, 1928, Internal Affairs of Peru.

61. Harold R. Harris to Robert W. Atkins, June 20, 1928, folder 12, box 1, RG01.01, DALCA; Matthew E Hanna to Department of State, June 2, 1928, Internal Affairs of Peru.

62. Department of State to U.S. Embassy in Peru, June 4, 1928, Internal Affairs of Peru.

63. Harold R. Harris to Robert W. Atkins, June 20, 1928, folder 12, box 1, RG01.01, DALCA.

64. Ibid.

65. "Duster Journal," 110, folder 3, box 2, RG01.01, DALCA.

66. Edgar N. Gott to Harold R. Harris, Aug. 27, 1928, folder 12, box 1, RG01.01, DALCA.

67. Ralph H. Ackerman to C. E. Woolman, June 23, 1928, folder 14, box 1, RG01.01, DALCA; C. E. Woolman to Franciso Aguiera, July 9, 1928, ibid.

68. Edgar N. Gott to Harold R. Harris, Aug. 27, 1928, folder 12, box 1, RG01.01, DALCA.

69. Matthew E Hanna to Department of State, July 17, 1928, Internal Affairs of Peru; "Procedente de Guayaquil Ayer en la Tarde Llego el Aviador Dan E. Tobin" [Aviator Dan E. Tobin arrived from Guayaquil yesterday afternoon], *El Comercio* (Lima, Peru), July 18, 1928.

70. Alexander P. Moore to Secretary of State, Dec. 22, 1928, Internal Affairs of Peru.

71. Briggs, *Proud Servant,* 23.

72. Stan Webber to his wife, July 30, 1928, Woolman Papers, LSULSC.

73. Ibid.

74. Pan American–Grace Airways donated the Fairchild FC-2 to the Smithsonian National Air and Space Museum.

75. "Servicio de Pasajeros y Correo Aéreo al Norte" [Passenger and Air Mail Service to the North], *El Comercio* (Lima, Peru), Sept. 13, 1928, folder 28, box 2, DALCA.

76. Ibid.; Ellis O. Briggs to the Secretary of State, Sept. 17, 1928, Internal Affairs of Peru.

77. "Draft Sept. 85," folder 7, box 3, 14–15, Harris Papers, WSUSCA.

78. J. T. Trippe to S. W. Morgan, Sept. 22, 1928, Internal Affairs of Peru; Bender and Altschul, *Chosen Instrument,* 117.

79. J. T. Trippe to S. W. Morgan, Sept. 22, 1928, Internal Affairs of Peru.

80. Alexander P. Moore to Secretary of State, Dec. 4, 1928, Internal Affairs of Peru.

7. METAMORPHOSIS

1. Freudenthal, *Aviation Business,* 163.

2. Van der Linden, *Airlines and Airmail,* 52.

3. Ibid.

4. Irwin E. Auerbach to Harold R. Harris, Mar. 13, 1928, folder 12, box 1, RG01.01, DALCA; "Memorandum to Harold R. Harris," n.d., ibid.

5. "Huff Daland Company Will Engage in Photography and Sell Airplanes," *Aviation,* Apr. 16, 1928, 982.

6. Guy S. Gannaway to Huff Daland Dusters, Inc., May 8, 1928, folder 5, box 1, RG02.00, DALCA; "Learn to Fly at Delta Air Service School of Aviation," ibid.

7. "Huff Daland Company Will Engage in Photography and Sell Airplanes," 982.

8. "Flying Time Reported by H. Elliot," folder 6, box 2, RG01.01, DALCA.

9. Agreement, July 1928, folder 4, box 2, RG01.01, DALCA.

10. Harold R. Harris to Irwin E. Auerbach, Aug. 25, 1928, folder 10, box 1, DL01.01, DALCA.

11. Ibid.

12. Harold R. Harris to Irwin E. Auerbach, Aug. 24, 1928, folder 12, box 1, RG01.01, DALCA.

13. Harris to Auerbach, Aug. 25, 1928.

14. Telegram, Irwin E. Auerbach to Harold R. Harris, n.d., folder 10, box 1, RG01.01, DALCA.

15. "Memo Regarding Disposal of Huff Daland Dusters," Aug. 28, 1928, folder 12, box 1, RG01.01, DALCA.

16. Irwin E. Auerbach to Travis Oliver, Sept.11, 1928, folder 10, box 1, RG01.01, DALCA.

17. Air Operations was a 1928 corporation chartered in Austin, Texas, by Hy Bird, Q. C. Taylor, and J. H. Gardner with capital stock of $1,000. "Charters," *Austin (TX) American,* Apr. 25, 1928.

18. "Memorandum to Mr. Richard F. Hoyt," Sept. 14, 1928, folder 10, box 1, RG01.01, DALCA.

19. Goodsell, *American Corporations and Peruvian Politics,* 51.

20. "Background Notes on Incidents Leading Up to the Formation and Operation of Pan American–Grace Airways," folder 12, box 12, Harris Papers, WSUSCA.

21. "Memo Regarding Disposal Huff Daland Dusters," Aug. 28, 1928; Harold R. Harris to Edgar N. Gott, Sept. 3, 1928, folder 12, box 1, RG01.01, DALCA.

22. Edgar N. Gott to Harold R. Harris, Aug. 27, 1928, folder 12, box 1, RG01.01, DALCA.

23. Harold R. Harris to Edgar N. Gott, Sept. 3, 1928, folder 12, box 1, RG01.01, DALCA; "Proposed Letter from Pan American Airways of Peru to Huff Daland Dusters Inc.," Sept. 3, 1928, ibid.

24. Juan T. Trippe to Harold R. Harris, Sept. 7, 1928, Harris Papers, WSUSCA.

25. Email message, Alta May Stevens to author, Apr. 8, 2010.

26. Collett E. Woolman to Harold R. Harris, Oct. 26, 1928, folder 15, box 1, RG01.01, DALCA; Telegram, [Harold R. Harris?] to C. E. Woolman, Oct. 4, 1928, ibid.

27. Edgar N. Gott to Irwin E. Auerbach, Sept. 27, 1928, folder 10, box 1, RG01.01, DALCA.

28. Huff Daland Dusters, Inc., to E. J. Bond, Oct. 22, 1928, folder 10, box 1, DALCA. For a copy of Auerbach's offer to sell dated October 22, 1928, see folder 15, box 1, RG01.01, DALCA.

29. Jackson B. Ardiss to Irwin E. Auerbach, Oct. 24, 1928, folder 10, box 1, RG01.01, DALCA; United States Census 1930, FamilySearch, https://www.familysearch.org/search/record/results?q.givenName=jackson%20b&q.surname=ardis&q.residencePlace=louisiana&q.residenceDate.from=1920&q.residenceDate.to=1930&m.defaultFacets=on&m.queryRequireDefault=on&m.facetNestCollectionInCategory=on&count=20&offset=0 (accessed May 23, 2020; subscription required).

30. Collett E. Woolman to Harold R. Harris, Oct. 26 (completed Nov. 15), 1928, folder 15, box 1, RG01.01, DALCA. This letter appears to have been used as notes for a more formal letter "intended for Mr. Harris's edification." See J. S. Woodbridge to Edgar N. Gott, Oct. 30, 1928, ibid.

31. For these four cables, see folder 15, box 1, RG01.01, DALCA.

32. John S. Woodbridge to Edgar N. Gott, Oct. 29, 1928, folder 10, box 1, RG01.01, DALCA. Lt. Kenneth G. Fraser was hired to be Harris's assistant. "Capt. Fraser Off for East on Trip to Many Cities," *Monroe (LA) News-Star,* Oct. 5, 1928.

33. John S. Woodbridge to Edgar N. Gott, Nov. 5, 1928, folder 10, box 1, RG01.01, DALCA.

34. Ibid.

35. Ibid.

36. C. E. Woolman to Alfredo Checa, Oct. 3, 1928, folder 15, box 1, RG01.01, DALCA.

37. Harold R. Harris to Collett E. Woolman, Nov. 15, 1928, folder 15, box 1, RG01.01, DALCA.

38. Woodbridge to Gott, Nov. 5, 1928.

39. Woolman to Harris, Oct. 26 (completed Nov. 15), 1928.

40. Travis Oliver to Edgar N. Gott, Nov. 8, 1928, folder 15, box 1, RG01.01, DALCA.

41. John S. Woodbridge to Keystone Aircraft Corporation, Nov. 8, 1928, folder 15, box 1, RG01.01, DALCA.

42. Harold R. Harris to Collett E. Woolman, Dec. 26, 1928, folder 15, box 1, RG01.01, DALCA.

43. Collett E. Woolman to Harold R. Harris, Dec. 18, 1928, folder 15, box 1, RG01.01, DALCA.

44. Collett E. Woolman to Harold R. Harris, Mar. 27, 1928, folder 15, box 1, RG01.01, DALCA.

45. Harris to Woolman, Dec. 26, 1928.

46. Woolman to Harris, Dec. 18, 1929; Collett E. Woolman to E. N. Gott, Mar. 27, 1929, folder 15, box 1, RG01.01, DALCA.

47. Collett E. Woolman to E. N. Gott, Jan. 7, 1929, folder 15, box 1, RG01.01, DALCA.

48. Klarén, *Peru,* 266.

49. Harold R. Harris to Collett E. Woolman, Dec. 3, 1929, folder 15, box 1, RG01.01, DALCA.

50. "To the Stockholders of Huff Daland Dusters, Inc.," n.d., Woolman Papers, LSULSC.

8. DELTA AIR SERVICE, INC.

1. "Bill of Sale, November 15, 1928," folder 2, box 1, RG01.01, DALCA; "Articles of Incorporation of Delta Air Service, Inc.," folder 1, box 1, RG02.00, ibid.

2. "Miss Fitz's Generosity Aids Nine Catholic Charities," *Georgia Bulletin: The Newspaper of the Catholic Archdiocese of Atlanta,* June 23, 1988; "A Way and a Life," *Delta Digest,* Feb. 1966, 11.

3. "Articles of Incorporation of Delta Air Service, Inc."; "Big-Business Delta Air Lines Still True to Small-Town Louisiana Roots," *Atlanta Journal and Constitution,* Nov. 6, 1983; "Program Arranged for Newspaper Men," *Monroe (LA) News-Star,* June 3, 1914.

4. "Articles of Incorporation of Delta Air Service, Inc."

5. "Charter," *Monroe (LA) News-Star,* Dec. 29, 1928.

6. "D. Y. Smith, Sr. Dies Suddenly at His Home Here," *Monroe (LA) News-Star,* Nov. 13, 1956.

7. "Oliver-Bradford," *Monroe (LA) News-Star,* June 13, 1911; "Local Paragraphs," ibid., Aug. 22, 1911; "South End, Lieut. Harris Approves Site for Big Landing Place," ibid., July 14, 1925; "Citizens Offer Further Suggestions for Naming of Airport in Ouachita," ibid., Oct. 22, 1927.

8. Collett E. Woolman to Harold R. Harris, Oct. 26, 1928, folder 15, box 1, RG01.01, DALCA; Woolman to Harris, Dec. 18, 1928, ibid.

9. Giesen, *Boll Weevil Blues,* 88.

10. Collett E. Woolman to Harold R. Harris, Mar. 27, 1929, folder 15, box 1, RG01.01, DALCA.

11. Email message, Paul Talbott to Marie Force, Aug. 14, 2110. The author did not find the records during his research.

12. Preston interview, 1977. FitzGerald declined to be interviewed by historians W. David Lewis and Wesley Phillips Newton for their book on the airline.

13. Catherine FitzGerald, interview by John N. White, 1976, DAARC, transcript.

14. Lewis and Newton, *Delta,* 22.

15. "Air Passenger Service to Be Started This Morning," *Jackson (MS) Daily Clarion-Ledger,* June 18, 1929.

16. "Delta Air Service Takes Over Fox Co. of Bastrop," *Monroe (LA) News-Star,* June 20, 1929.

17. Lewis and Newton, *Delta,* 23; "Air Passenger Service to be Started This Morning," *Jackson (MS) Daily Clarion-Ledger,* June 18, 1929.

18. "Travel Air, the Limousine of Air Travel" (advertisement), *Aero Digest,* 10 (May 1928): 819.

19. Untitled article, *Greenwood (MS) Commonwealth,* June 15, 1926.

20. Carbon-black is a waste byproduct of gas production. It was used in making paint, ink, and tires. In the treatment of rubber, carbon-black doubled the longevity of tires from 4,000 to 8,000 miles. Ralph A. Graves, "Louisiana, Land of Perpetual Romance," *National Geographic,* Apr. 1930, 447.

21. Stevens interview, 1984.

22. "The Humorous Side of Early Flying," *Delta Digest,* Dec. 1946, 12.

23. "History of the Vicksburg Bridge," n.d., unpublished essay in author's possession.

24. A note in Howe's logbook is confusing: "June 16, 1929. First trip for Delta Air Service passenger, Dallas to Jackson." John Howe logbook, folder 12, box 2, RG02.02, DALCA. According to entries in his logbook, he flew a four-day trip: June 16, Monroe to Dallas; June 17, Dallas to Jackson; June 18, Jackson to Dallas; and June 19, Dallas to Monroe. The use of the word "trip" in today's pilot/flight-attendant jargon refers to the individual's flight duty cycle—three-day *trip;* four-day *trip.* Probably, Howe was referencing his entire journey, not Delta Air Service's. Sources confirm the intent to begin service on June 17, 1929. See "City Now Stop on Air Route," *Shreveport (LA) Times,* June 17, 1927; and "Delta Air Service Starts Passenger Line," *Aviation,* June 29, 1929. A statement in the February 24, 1930, audit of the company states the "initial run was made Monday, June 17, 1929." See folder 7, box, 2 RG02.02, DALCA.

25. "Air Passenger Service to Be Started This Morning," *Jackson (MS) Daily Clarion-Ledger,* June 18, 1929.

26. John Howe logbook; James A. Blackburne, "Remembrances," Aug. 18, 1995, notes from conversation with author, copy in author's possession.

27. "Air Passenger Service to Be Started This Morning," *Jackson (MS) Daily Clarion-Ledger,* June 18, 1929.

28. Ibid.

29. Ibid.

30. The five original pilots were Pat Higgins, Don Dice, John Howe, Elmer Rose, and J. D. Greer. Blackburne, "Remembrances," Aug. 18, 1995, notes from conversation with author, in author's possession.

31. John Howe logbook; "Jackson Air Party Well Pleased with Flight," *Monroe (LA) News-Star,* June 20, 1929.

32. "Jackson Men Participate in Air Line Inauguration," *Monroe (LA) News-Star,* June 18, 1929.

33. The counterpoint was Wilson's Progressive New Freedom philosophy, which held that any monopoly was inherently bad.

34. Van der Linden, *Airlines and Air Mail,* ix, xi.

35. "Plans 2 New Routes for Air Mail to Coast," *New York Times,* Dec. 12, 1929.

36. Cornel & Company, "Audit, Nov. 12, 1928 to Dec. 31, 1929," Feb. 24, 1930, folder 7, box 2, RG02.00, DALCA.

37. Collett E. Woolman to Harold R. Harris, Apr. 22, 1930, folder 1, box 2, RG02.00, DALCA.

38. Nick A. Komons, *Bonfires to Beacons: Federal Civil Aviation Policy under the Air Commerce Act, 1926–1938* (Washington, DC: Department of Transportation, Federal Aviation Administration, 1978; rprt, Washington, DC: Smithsonian Institution Press, 1989), 201.

39. Ibid., 202–3.

40. "Discontinuance of Delta's Air Line Announced," *Monroe (LA) News-Star,* Oct. 20, 1930.

41. U.S. Senate Special Committee on Investigations of Air Mail and Ocean Mail Contracts, *Air Mail and Ocean Mail Contracts,* 73rd Cong., 2nd sess. (Washington, DC: Government Printing Office, 1934), 1597–1611.

42. "New Airmail Lines Here Will Carry Passengers, Taking Over Delta Line," *Jackson (MS) Daily Clarion Ledger,* Oct. 2, 1930.

43. "Discontinuance of Delta's Air Line Announced," *Monroe (LA) News-Star,* Oct. 20, 1930.

44. Van der Linden, *Airlines and Air Mail,* 165.

45. Minutes of Special Meeting, Oct. 31, 1930, folder 7, box 1, RG02.00, DALCA.

46. "Contract Is Obtained by Selman Field," *Monroe (LA) News-Star,* Dec. 19, 1930.

47. A. O. Cushney to C. E. Woolman, Oct. 16, 1930, folder 5, box 2, RG02.00, DALCA; draft of stockholder resolution accepting AVCO proposal of Oct. 16, 1930, ibid.; Special Meeting of the Stockholders of Delta Air Service, Inc., Monroe, LA, Oct. 31, 1939, ibid.; sales contract between Southern Air Fast Express, Inc., and Travis Oliver, Trustee, Nov. 3, 1930, ibid.

48. Lewis and Newton, *Delta,* 32.

49. "J. A. Biedenharn Dies in Clinic Here Today," *Monroe (LA) News-Star,* Oct. 9, 1952; "Officers Named by Central Bank," ibid., Jan. 24, 1935; "C. of C. [Chamber of Commerce] Report Rendered in Its Annual Session," ibid., June 3, 1926.

50. "Contract Is Obtained by Selman Field," *Monroe (LA) News-Star,* Dec. 19, 1930.

51. Lewis and Newton, *Delta,* 30.

52. Preston interview, 1977; "Local Aviation Progress Shown In News Story," *Monroe (LA) News-Star,* Jan. 11, 1933; "Planes Are to Leave Here for Old Mexico," Sept. 13, 1932, *Monroe (LA) News-Star;* "Fall Dusting to Be Initiated by Delta Planes," ibid., Sept. 29, 1932.

53. "Faucett to Expand Activities," *Aviation,* Feb. 1, 1930.

54. Joe Greer Sr. and Joe Greer Jr., "1926–1932 Huff Daland Dusters—Peru," *James Dorris Greer: Delta's First Pilot Was a Barnstormer,* 2017, https://jamesdorrisgreer.com/ (accessed Apr. 29, 2019).

55. Stevens interview, 1984.

56. Cleveland and Parencia, "USDA Cotton Insects Research Laboratory," 406–7.

57. U.S. v. B. R. Coad and F. W. McDuff, District Court of the U.S., Monroe, Docket 6040 (1931), Shreveport accession 021-54A0589, location A0902111, National Archives–Southwest Region, Fort Worth, TX.

58. "Coad and McDuff Are Given One Year in Prison," *Madison Journal (Tallulah, LA),* Oct. 9, 1931.

59. U.S. v. B. R. Coad and F. W. McDuff.

60. Stevens interview, 1984.

61. Lewis and Newton, *Delta,* 37; U.S. v. B. R. Coad and F. W. McDuff. In later years, when the company was on a more secure financial footing, a system was set up to recognize employees for their years of service, but Coad's awards are inconsistent. According to the company magazine, *Delta Digest,* in 1948 he was given a fifteen-year service pin, meaning he was hired in 1933. Then, he was awarded a twenty-year pin in 1956, placing his hire date in 1936. His twenty-five-year pin was presented in 1957 and thirty-year award in 1962, pointing to 1932 as the hire year.

62. "Dr. Bert Coad," *Delta Digest,* Apr. 1966, 12.

63. Komons, *Bonfires to Beacons,* 226.

64. U.S. Senate Special Committee on Investigations, *Air Mail and Ocean Mail Contracts,* 1597–1611.

65. Komons, *Bonfires to Beacons,* 263.

66. Email message, Marie Force to author, June 27, 2005.

67. Van der Linden, *Airlines and Air Mail,* xi, 286.

68. "Route from Here to California by Airline Planned," *Charleston (SC) News and Courier,* Apr. 5, 1934; "Charleston Given Chance to Be Air Center of Future," ibid., May 6, 1934.

69. "Three Bids Made on Local Air Line," *Charleston (SC) News and Courier,* May 26, 1934.

70. "Local Air Route Will Start Soon," *Charleston (SC) News and Courier,* June 10, 1934.

71. "Meet Your leaders; Laigh Parker," *Delta Digest,* Nov. 1949, n.p.; "Delta Mourns Death of Laigh C. Parker; Delta Executive Headed Traffic and Sales for 25 Years," ibid., Jan. 1960, 16.

72. "Air Miles Flown by Laigh C. Parker," folder 11, box 3, RG06.03, DALCA.

73. Traffic Manager to Mr. Woolman, Mr. Higgins, July 14, 1934, folder 9, Box 2, RG04.01, DALCA; General Manager, Monroe, to General Traffic Manager—On the Line, July 25, 1934, ibid.

74. "Delta Air Opens New Passenger Service Monday," *Monroe (LA) News-Star,* Aug. 5, 1934.

75. "Pilots Prepare for Mail Trips," *Monroe (LA) News-Star,* June 20, 1934.

76. Jack B. Jaynes, *Eagles Must Fly: A History of Aviation from Open Cockpits to Jets,* ed. Charles H. Young (Dallas: Taylor, 1982), 193.

77. "Pilots Prepare for Mail Trips," *Monroe (LA) News-Star,* June 20, 1934.

78. Resumption of Air Mail Here July 4th Gift," *Monroe (LA) News-Star,* July 4, 1934.

79. "New Mail Route Opens Tomorrow," July 6, 1934, *Charleston (SC) News and Courier*; "Air Mail Route to West Opened," ibid., July 8, 1934; "Dallas Air Line to Take People," ibid., Aug. 5, 1934.

80. "Schedules and Fares," July 1, 1935, Delta Subject File 1940–1949, Mississippi Department of Archives and History, Jackson.

81. U.S. Senate Special Committee on Investigations, *Air Mail and Ocean Mail Contracts,* 1597–1611.

82. "Charleston Given Chance to Be Air Center of Future," *Charleston (SC) News and Courier,* May 6, 1934.

83. "Delta Air Opens New Passenger Service Monday," *Monroe (LA) News-Star,* Aug. 5, 1934.

84. Arthur Ford, interview by author, Sandy Springs, GA, Sept. 5, 1996; "Obituaries, Ford," *Atlanta Journal and Constitution,* Oct. 4, 2001; Delta/Eastern Joint Schedule, Delta Timetable Collection, DALCA.

9. BRANCHING OUT

1. "Annual Report Delta Air Corporation," 1941, https://dlg.usg.edu/record/delta_dal-ar_dal-ar -1941 (accessed Mar. 2, 2023).

2. Richard M. McCabe, "Airline Industry Key Success Factors: The ability for Airlines to Succeed Today Is Measured According to Several Key Factors." *Graziadio Business Review* 9, no. 4 (2006): 4, https://gbr.pepperdine.edu/2010/08/airline-industry-key-success-factors/ (accessed June 10, 2022).

3. Betsy Braden and Paul Hagan, *A Dream Takes Flight: Hartsfield Atlanta International Airport and Aviation in Atlanta* (Athens: University of Georgia Press, 1989), 1, 4.

4. Ibid., 4. The banked curves of the old racetrack have long since disappeared, but the ground where they once stood is occupied today by the Delta Corporate Campus on the north side of Hartsfield-Jackson Atlanta International Airport.

5. James J. Hoogerwerf, "Mighty Hartsfield," *Southern Aviator* 6 (Mar. 1995): 20–24.

6. From Atlanta to Richmond is 474 nautical miles; from Atlanta to Dallas, 633 nautical miles; and from Atlanta to Miami, 517 nautical miles.

7. "Improvement of Airport Here Is Asked by Board," *Monroe (LA) News-Star,* Feb. 22, 1935; "Night Schedule to Be Launched Here by Delta," ibid., Mar. 20, 1935; "Flying by Night Begun as Lights at Airport Glow," *Charleston (SC) News and Courier,* Dec. 12, 1931.

8. "Night Schedule to Be Launched Here by Delta," *Monroe (LA) News-Star,* Mar. 20, 1935.

9. Lewis and Newton, *Delta,* 52.

10. Delta Subject File, 1940–1949, Mississippi Department of Archives and History, Jackson.

11. Ibid.

12. "Governor's Wife Will Christen Mail Plane," *Monroe (LA) News-Star,* July 1, 1935; "Air Service Here Gets Permission," ibid., July 15, 1935.

13. "Scheduled Air-Line Accident Reports," *Air Commerce Bulletin,* June 15, 1936, 92.

14. Lewis and Newton, *Delta,* 53. In one report, Bulkeley is identified as a "courier." Either as an assistant or a courier, he was not officially a copilot.

15. "Delta Chief Executive Dolson Replaces C. E. Woolman," *Atlanta Journal,* Sept. 15, 1966; Lewis and Newton, *Delta,* 54.

16. Thomas P. Ball, interview by author, Sept. 6, 1995, Atlanta, in author's possession; "Pilot Slightly Hurt in Plane Crash Here," *Atlanta Constitution,* Aug. 28, 1936.

17. Thomas Ball interview, Sept. 6, 1995. Pullman Norton was flying with Dolson as a copilot or assistant and was unhurt. "Test Pilot Dolson Hurt as Crash Wrecks Plane at Candler Field," *Atlanta Journal,* Aug. 27, 1936; "Pilot Slightly Hurt in Plane Crash Here," *Atlanta Constitution,* Aug. 28, 1936. Dolson logged one minute for the flight. Bonnie Peet (daughter of Charles Dolson), interview by author, July 23, 2004, Roswell, GA.

18. FitzGerald interview, 1976.

19. "Annual Report Delta Air Corporation" 1941.

20. Lewis and Newton, *Delta,* 54.

21. Fritz Schwaemmle, interview by Delta Air Transport Heritage Museum, Dec. 7, 1973, DALCA.

22. Norman Stephen Topshe, interview by author, Oct. 28, 1995, Atlanta.

23. Joe Greer Sr. and Joe Greer Jr., "Delta's First Passenger Flight—June 1934," *James Dorris Greer: Delta's First Pilot Was a Barnstormer,* 2017, https://jamesdorrisgreer.com/ (accessed Jun. 24, 2020).

24. Espy Ball, telephone interview by author, June 29, 2022.

25. John E. Ellington, telephone interview by author, June 29, 2022.

26. Thomas P. Ball, interview by author, Oct. 3, 1994, Atlanta.

27. Espy Ball telephone interview, 2022.

28. Thomas Ball interview, 1995.

29. Thomas Ball interview, 1994.

30. Ibid.

31. Thomas Ball interview, 1995.

32. Lynn D. Field, ed. *From Travel Air to Tristar: The First Fifty Years of Delta Air Lines, 1929–1979* (Miami: Halsey, [1979?]), 11; Lewis and Newton, *Delta,* 62.

33. Eva Parrish Fitch, "Personal Profile of Eva Mae Parrish Fitch," copy in author's possession.

34. Lewis and Newton, *Delta,* 72.

35. Helen E. McLaughlin, *Footsteps in the Sky: An Informal Review of U.S. Airlines In-Flight Service, 1920–Present* (Denver: State of the Art, 1994), 4; Drew Whittelegg, "From Smiles to Miles: Delta Air Lines Flight Attendants and Southern Hospitality," *Southern Cultures* 11, no. 4 (Winter 2005): 8.

36. Sybil Peacock Harman, "Delta's First Stewardesses," copy in author's possession.

37. Ibid.; J. S. Heggie Jr., Station Manager—Atlanta, to Superintendent of Stations—Atlanta, June 10, 1941, Folder 10, Box 4, RG04.01, DALCA.

38. Laigh C. Parker to M. F. Redfern, Oct. 29, 1939, Folder 8, Box 1, RG16.03, DALCA.

39. Laigh C. Parker to M. F. Redfern, Apr. 26, 1940, Folder 1, Box 1, RG16.03, DALCA.

40. Thomas Ball interview, 1994.

41. "ALPA Celebrates 50 Years at Delta," *Widget* (June 1991): 1, 4.

42. Delta Pilot Contract, Aug. 1, 1940, 11, copy in author's possession.

43. "Airport News," *Madison Journal (Tallulah, LA),* Mar. 23, 1929.

44. Charles M. Taylor, speech presenting Brig. Gen. John D. Howe for induction into the Arkansas Aviation Hall of Fame, Nov. 9, 1984, copy in author's possession. Howe had a successful career flying for the U.S. Army Air Corps, later the U.S. Air Force.

45. Lewis and Newton, *Delta,* 77.

46. Braden and Hagan, *Dream Takes Flight,* 93, 95; "City to Spend $50,000 on New Hangar," *Atlanta Constitution,* Nov. 5, 1940. This structure is now the oldest surviving building on the airfield and houses the Delta Flight Museum.

47. Thomas Ball interview, 1995; Braden and Hagan, *Dream Takes Flight,* 93, 99, 104.

48. "Airport Keeps Pace with Needs," *Ouachita Citizen (Monroe, LA),* Mar. 9, 1983.

49. *Courts & Co. Celebrating 35th Anniversary, 1925–1960* (Atlanta, 1960), 5.

50. Thomas Ball interview, 1995.

51. Lewis and Newton, *Delta,* 78.

52. "The Laws That Govern the Securities Industry," U.S. Securities and Exchange Commission [SEC], http://www.sec.gov/about/laws.shtml (accessed July 1, 2010). The author's search for an SEC case was assisted by Tim Dodge and Harmon Straiton at the Ralph Brown Draughon Library, Auburn University, but did not reveal any involving Delta under the circumstances outlined.

53. Lewis and Newton, *Delta,* 80.

54. Ibid.

55. "Aviation: Dust and Passengers," *Time,* June 23, 1941.

56. "Annual Report Delta Air Corporation," 1941.

57. Lewis and Newton, *Delta,* 78.

58. Joel Seligman, *The Transformation of Wall Street: A History of the Securities and Exchange Commission and Modern Corporate Finance* (Boston: Houghton Mifflin, 1982), 202.

59. U.S. *Securities and Exchange Commission, Sixth Annual Report of the Security and Exchange Commission for the Fiscal Year Ending June 30, 1940* (Washington, DC: Government Printing Office, 1941), 137.

60. "Annual Report Delta Air Corporation," 1941.

≡ BIBLIOGRAPHY ≡

PRIMARY SOURCES

Archives

Air Force Historical Research Agency, Maxwell AFB, Alabama

Delta Air Lines Corporate Archives, Atlanta, Georgia

Louisiana State University Libraries Special Collections, Baton Rouge

       Collett Everman Woolman Papers, 1916–1979

Mississippi Department of Archives and History, Jackson

National Archives–Southwest Region, Fort Worth, Texas

       U.S. v. B. R. Coad and F. W. McDuff, District Court of the U.S., Monroe, Docket 6040 (1931)

National Archives and Records Service, Washington, DC

       Records of the Department of State Relating to the Internal Affairs of Peru, 1910–1929, M746, microfilm

Ogdensburg Library Archives, Ogdensburg, New York

Special Collections and Archives, Ralph Brown Draughon Library, Auburn University, Auburn, Alabama

       RG 245, Peter Gushue Papers

University of Illinois at Urbana-Champaign Archives

       Collett Everman Woolman Papers

Wright State University Special Collections and Archives, Dayton, Ohio

       Harold R. Harris Papers (MS-214)

       International Cyclopedia of Aviation Biography Collection (MS-167)

Internet Sources

FamilySearch. https://familysearch.org

Find a Grave. http://www.findagrave.com

Geni. https://www.geni.com/people

Greer, Joe, Sr., and Joe Greer Jr. James Dorris Greer: Delta's First Pilot Was a Barnstormer.
    2017. https://jamesdorrisgreer.com/

U.S. Securities and Exchange Commission. http://www.sec.gov/about/laws.shtml

University of Illinois Library. http://libsysdigi.library.illinois.edu

Interviews

Ball, Espy. Telephone interview by author, June 29, 2022. Notes in author's possession.

Ball, Thomas P. Interview by author, October 3, 1994, College Park, GA. Author's
    possession.

———. Interview by author, July 6, 1995, College Park, GA. Author's possession.

Davidson, Doris. Interview by author, June 2, 9, 2017, Alpine, AL. Author's possession.

FitzGerald, Catherine. Interview by John N. White, 1976. Delta Air Lines Corporate
    Archives, Atlanta, GA.

Ford, Arthur. Interview by author, September 5, 1996, Sandy Springs, GA. Author's
    possession.

Harris, Harold R. Interview by Dr. Lawrence Clayton, November 5, 1979, Falmouth,
    MS. Folder "Dissertation interviews w/former Panagristas," box 1, RG 245, Peter
    Gushue Papers, Special Collections and Archives, Ralph Brown Draughon Library,
    Auburn University. Transcript.

Peet, Bonnie (daughter of Charles Dolson). Interview by author, July 23, 2004. Author's
    possession.

Preston, Barbara Woolman. Interview by Wesley Phillips Newton, December 21, 1977.
    Delta Air Lines Corporate Archives, Atlanta, GA.

———. Interview by Delta Air Transport Heritage Museum, January 12, 1993. Delta Air
    Lines Corporate Archives, Atlanta, GA.

Schwaemmle, Fritz. Interview by Delta Air Transport Heritage Museum, December 7,
    1973. Delta Air Lines Corporate Archives, Atlanta, GA.

Stevens, Eugene. Interview by Larry Michaud, February 1984, Casper, WY. Author's
    possession.

Topshe, Norman Stephen. Interview by author, October 28, 1995, Sandy Springs, GA.
    Author's possession.

Newspapers and Magazines

Aero Digest

Aircraft Yearbook

Atlanta Constitution

BIBLIOGRAPHY

Atlanta Journal

Atlanta Journal and Constitution

Austin (TX) American

Aviation

Birmingham (AL) Age-Herald

Bristol (PA) Courier

Buenos Aires Herald (Argentina)

Charleston (SC) News and Courier

El Comercio (Lima, Peru)

Delta Digest

Georgia Bulletin: The Newspaper of the Catholic Archdiocese of Atlanta

Greenwood (MS) Commonwealth

Houston (GA) Home Journal

Jackson *(MS) Daily Clarion-Ledger*

Laurinburg (NC) Exchange

Macon (GA) Daily Telegraph

Madison Journal (Tallulah, LA)

Monroe (LA) News-Star

Mundial (Lima, Peru)

New York Times

Ogdensburg (NY) Advance

Ogdensburg (NY) Journal

Ouachita Citizen (Monroe, LA)

Repartee—Official Newsletter of the Retired Eastern Pilots

Shreveport *(LA) Times*

Slipstream Monthly

Southern Aviator

Tampa Bay Times (Saint Petersburg, FL)

Watertown (NY) Daily Times

West Coast Leader (Lima, Peru)

Widget (Delta Air Lines Pilot Association newsletter)

Published Primary Sources

Aircraft Yearbook, 1923. New York: Aeronautical Chamber of Commerce of America, 1923.

Aircraft Yearbook, 1927. New York: Aeronautical Chamber of Commerce of America, 1927.

"Airplanes and Airships 'Put to Work' Combating Cotton Boll Weevil, Gypsy Moth, and Locust." *Aircraft Yearbook, 1924.* New York: Aeronautical Chamber of Commerce, 1924.

BIBLIOGRAPHY

Coad, B. R. Recent Experimental Work on Poisoning Cotton-Boll Weevils. *USDA Bulletin 731.* Washington, DC: USDA, July 1918.

———. Relation of the Arizona Wild Cotton Weevil to Cotton Planting in the Arid West. *USDA Bulletin 233.* Washington, DC: USDA, May 1915.

Coad, B. R., E. Johnson, and G. L. McNeil. *Dusting Cotton from Airplanes. USDA Bulletin 1204.* Washington DC: USDA, January 1924.

Brown, J. J. "Annual Report of Georgia Department of Agriculture for 1924." *Quarterly Bulletin of the Georgia Department of Agriculture* 99 (First Quarter 1925).

———. "Biannual Report of Georgia Department of Agriculture for 1925–1926." *Quarterly Bulletin of the Georgia Department of Agriculture* 103 (First Quarter 1927).

Graves, Ralph A. "Louisiana, Land of Perpetual Romance." *National Geographic,* April 1930, 393–482.

Houser, J. S. "The Airplane in Catalpa Sphinx Control." *Monthly Bulletin of the Ohio Agricultural Experimental Station* 7 (July–Aug. 1922): 126–36.

"Hoyt, Richard Farnsworth." *The National Cyclopedia of American Biography.* Vol. 29. New York: James T. White, 1941.

Hunter, W. D., and B. R. Coad. *The Boll-Weevil Problem.* USDA *Farmers' Bulletin* 1329. Washington, DC: USDA, June 1923.

McCabe, Richard M. "Airline Industry Key Success Factors: The Ability for Airlines to Succeed Today Is Measured According to Several Key Factors." *Graziadio Business Review* 9, no. 4 (2006): 1–12.

McMillin, Stewart E. "The Heart of Aymara Land." *National Geographic,* February 1927, 213–56.

Neillie, C. R., and J. S. Houser. "Fighting Insects with Airplanes: An Account of the Successful Use of the Flying-Machine in Dusting Tall Trees Infested with Leaf-Eating Caterpillars." *National Geographic,* March 1922, 333–38.

Phelps, Virgil V., ed. *University of Illinois Directory.* Bloomington, IL: Pantagraph Printing and Stationary, 1916.

Post, George B. "Boll Weevil Control by Airplane." *Georgia State College of Agriculture, Extension Division Bulletin* 301 (November 1924): 1–22.

Register of Graduates of the Indiana University: Including Advanced and Honorary Degrees 1830–1901. Bloomington, IN: Published by the university, 1901.

Roosevelt, Theodore. "Louisiana Canebrakes." *Scribner's,* January 1908, 47–60.

The Semi-Centennial Alumni Record of the University of Illinois. Chicago: Lakeside, 1918.

Shoffer, Roy. *Pest of Honor: The Story of the World's Most Unusual Monument.* N.p., 1988.

Snapp, Oliver I. "Airplane Dusting of Peach Orchards." *Journal of Economic Entomology* 19 (June 1926): 450–59.

Solberg, Carl. *Conquest of the Skies: A History of Commercial Aviation in America.* Boston: Little, Brown, 1979.

BIBLIOGRAPHY

Twenty-First Report of the Board of Trustees of the University of Illinois. Vol. 21. Springfield, IL: Phillips Bros. State Printers, 1902.

U.S. Department of Transportation, Office of Environmental Affairs. *A Nation in Motion: Historic American Transportation Sites.* Washington, DC: Government Printing Office, 1976.

U.S. House Committee on Agriculture. *Use of Aircraft.* 67th Cong., 2nd sess. Washington, DC: Government Printing Office, 1922.

U.S. Securities and Exchange Commission. *Sixth Annual Report of the Security and Exchange Commission for the Fiscal Year Ending June 30, 1940.* Washington, DC: Government Printing Office, 1941.

U.S. Senate Special Committee on Investigation of Air Mail and Ocean Mail Contracts. *Air Mail and Ocean Mail Contracts.* 73rd Cong., 2nd sess., January 11, 1934.

U.S. Senate Subcommittee on Appropriations. *Agricultural Appropriations, 1925.* 68th Cong., 1st. sess., January 28, May 8, 1924.

Van Deventer, John H., Jr. "The Story of Keystone and Its Latest Contribution to the Advancement of Aviation." *Air Transportation,* January 19, 1929, 54–55.

SECONDARY SOURCES

Anderson, Mabry I. *Low & Slow: An Insider's History of Agricultural Aviation.* San Francisco: California Farmer, 1986.

Baker, Brian R. "Early Dusting Experiments." *American Aviation Historical Society* 14 (Summer 1969): 115–24.

Baker, Lewis. *The Percys of Mississippi: Politics and Literature in the New South.* Baton Rouge: Louisiana State University Press, 1983.

Barry, John M. *Rising Tide: The Great Mississippi Flood of 1927 and How It Changed America.* New York: Simon and Schuster, 1997.

Bender, Marylin, and Selig Altschul. *The Chosen Instrument: Pan Am, Juan Trippe, the Rise and Fall of an American Entrepreneur.* New York: Simon and Schuster, 1982.

Berg, A. Scott. *Lindbergh.* New York: G. B. Putnam's Sons, 1989.

Boyne, Walter. "Huff Daland in 3D." *Wings* 7 (December 1977): 55–63.

Braden, Betsy, and Paul Hagan. *A Dream Takes Flight: Hartsfield Atlanta International Airport and Aviation in Atlanta.* Athens: University of Georgia Press, 1989.

Briggs, Ellis O. *Proud Servant: The Memoirs of a Career Ambassador.* Kent, OH: Kent State University Press, 1998.

Burden, William A. M. *The Struggle for Airways in Latin America.* New York: Arno, 1977.

Clayton, Lawrence A. *Peru and the United States: The Condor and the Eagle.* Athens: University of Georgia Press, 1999.

Cleveland, T. C., and C. R. Parencia. "History of the USDA Cotton Insects Research Laboratory Tallulah, Louisiana, 1909–1973." *Bulletin of the Entomological Society of America 22, no. 4* (December 1976): 403–7.

Cobb, James C., ed. *The Mississippi Delta and the World: The Memoirs of David L Cohn.* Baton Rouge: Louisiana State University Press, 1995.

———. *The Most Southern Place on Earth.* New York: Oxford University Press, 1992.

Daily, Robert. *An American Saga: Juan Trippe and His Pan Am Empire.* New York: Random House, 1980.

Daniel, Pete. *Breaking the Land: The Transformation of Cotton, Tobacco, and Rice Cultures since 1880.* Urbana: University of Illinois Press, 1985.

———. *Lost Revolutions: The South in the 1950s.* Chapel Hill: University of North Carolina Press, 2000.

———. *Toxic Drift: Pesticides and Health in the Post–World War II South.* Baton Rouge: Louisiana State University Press, 2005.

Davies, R. E. G. *Airlines of Latin America since 1919.* McLean, VA: Paladwr, 1997.

———. *Delta: An Airline and Its Aircraft.* Miami: Paladwr, 1990.

Dickerson, William A., Anthony L. Brasher, James T. Brumly, Frank R. Carter, William J. Grenfensette, and Aubrey Harris, eds. *Boll Weevil Eradication in the United States through 1999.* Memphis: Cotton Foundation, 2001.

Doolittle, General James H. *I Could Never Be So Lucky Again: An Autobiography.* With Carroll V. Glines. New York: Bantam Books, 1991.

Downs, Eldon W., and George F. Lemmer. "Origins of Aerial Crop Dusting." *Agricultural History Society* 30 (1965): 123–35.

Field, Lynn D., ed. *From Travel Air to TriStar: The First Fifty Years of Delta Air Lines, 1929–1979.* Miami: Halsey, [1979?].

Freudenthal, Elsbeth E. *The Aviation Business: From Kitty Hawk to Wall Street.* New York: Vanguard, 1940.

Giesen, James C. *Boll Weevil Blue: Cotton, Myth, and Power in the American South.* Chicago: University of Chicago Press, 2011.

Goodsell, Charles T. *American Corporations and Peruvian Politics.* Cambridge, MA: Harvard University Press, 1974.

Hagedorn, Dan. *Conquistadors of the Sky: A History of Aviation in Latin America.* Gainesville: University Press of Florida, 2008.

Haney, P. B., W. J. Lewis, and W. R. Lambert. Cotton Production and the Boll Weevil in Georgia: History, Cost of Control, and Benefits of Eradication. *University of Georgia Research Bulletin* 428 (November 1996).

Heppenheimer, T. A. *Turbulent Skies: The History of Commercial Aviation.* New York: John Wiley and Sons, 1995.

Hitchner, Lea S. "The Insecticide Industry." In *Insects: The Yearbook of Agriculture, 1952,* 450–54. *Washington, DC: Government Printing Office,* 1952.

Janes, Jack B. *Eagles Must Fly: A History of Aviation from Open Cockpits to Jets.* Edited by Charles H. Young. Dallas: Taylor, 1982.

Klarén, Peter Flindell. *Peru: Society and Nationhood in the Andes.* New York: Oxford University Press, 2000.

Komons, Nick A. *Bonfires to Beacons: Federal Civil Aviation Policy under the Air Commerce Act, 1926–1938.* Washington, DC: Department of Transportation, Federal Aviation Administration, 1978; reprint, Washington: Smithsonian Institution Press, 1989.

Lewis, W. David, and Wesley Phillips Newton. *Delta: The History of an Airline.* Athens: University of Georgia Press, 1979.

Litwack, Leon F. *Been in the Storm So Long: The Aftermath of Slavery.* New York: Vintage Books, 1979.

Maurer, Maurer. *Aviation in the U.S. Army, 1919–1939.* Washington, DC: Office of Air Force History, U.S. Air Force, 1987.

McLaughlin, Helen E. *Footsteps in the Sky: An Informal Review of U.S. Airlines In-Flight Service, 1920–Present.* Denver: State of the Art, 1994.

Moll, Herbert H. *Peruvian Civil Aviation.* Mineola, NY: American Airmail Society, 2000.

Newton, Wesley Phillips. *The Perilous Sky: U.S. Aviation Diplomacy and Latin America, 1919–1931.* Coral Gables, FL: University of Miami Press, 1978.

Parencia, C. R. One Hundred Twenty Years of Research on Cotton Insects in the United States. *USDA Agriculture Handbook* 515. Washington DC: USDA, March 1978.

Seligman, Joel. *The Transformation of Wall Street: A History of the Securities and Exchange Commission and Modern Corporate Finance.* Boston: Houghton Mifflin, 1982.

Skidmore, Thomas E., and Peter H. Smith. *Modern Latin America.* 5th ed. Oxford: Oxford University Press, 2001.

Stevens, Alta Mae. *And Then What Happened?: Harold Harris and the Early Development of Aviation.* Bloomington, IN: Author House, 2001.

Twain, Mark. *Life on the Mississippi.* New York: Signet Classic, 2001.

Van der Linden, F. Robert. *Airlines and Air Mail: The Post Office and the Birth of the Commercial Aviation Industry.* Lexington: University Press of Kentucky, 2002.

———. *The Boeing 247: The First Modern Airliner.* Seattle: University of Washington Press, 1991.

Waller, Douglas. *A Question of Loyalty: Gen. Billy Mitchell and the Court-Martial That Gripped the Nation.* New York: Harper Collins, 2004.

Whittelegg, Drew. "From Smiles to Miles: Delta Air Lines Flight Attendants and Southern Hospitality." *Southern Cultures* 11, no. 4 (Winter 2005): 7–27.

Wilkerson, Isabel. *The Warmth of Other Suns: The Epic Story of America's Great Migration.* New York: Vintage Books, 2010.

Wolcott, George N. "The Status of Economic Entomology in Peru." *Bulletin of Entomological Research* 20 (August 1965): 225–31.

Wright, Gavin. *Old South, New South: Revolutions in the Southern Economy since the Civil War.* Baton Rouge: Louisiana State University Press, 1996.

Writers Program, Works Progress Administration. *Who's Who in Aviation: A Directory of Living Men and Women Who Have Contributed to the Growth of Aviation in the United States 1942–1943.* Chicago: Ziff-Davis, 1942.

Wyatt-Brown, Bertram. *The House of Percy: Honor, Melancholy, and Imagination in a Southern Family.* New York: Oxford University Press, 1994.

Theses and Dissertations

Garrett, Gary Richard. "The Oncenio of Augusto B. Leguía: Middle Sector Government and Leadership in Peru, 1919–1930." PhD diss., University of New Mexico, 1973.

Gushue, Peter Boland. "Heavenly Influence: Panagra Airways in Peru, 1928–1949." PhD diss., University of Alabama, 1997.

Metcalfe, Arthur V. "The Dictatorship of President Leguía of Peru." MA thesis, University of Southern California, 1934.

INDEX

INDEX

INDEX

Leyare, Joseph, 27

Lindbergh, Charles, 32–33, 54–55, 58, 62, 83, 96

Lyle, Claude P., *80, 82*

MacCracken, William P., 56

Macready, Lt. John A., 17–18, *68*

Martinto, Pedro, 49–50, 60, 89–90

McConnell, William (Sgt.), 30

McCook Field (Dayton, OH), 17, 23, 28–30, 32

McDuff, F. W., 120–21

Mississippi Delta; the Delta, 2, 6–15, 16, 19, 24, 38, 56, 98, 100, 111, 139

Moll, Herbert H., x

Moore, Alexander P., 95

Moreau, H. A. "Ham," *80, 82*

Neillie, Charles Robert, 16–17, 55, 140

Newellton, LA, 35, *72*

New South, the, 135

New, Harry S., 86, 93

Newton, Wesley Phillips, 2, 91

Oliver, Travis, 3, 36–37, 45, *79*, 102, 105–7, 111–12, 118–19, 122, 139

Panama Canal, 4, 38, 49, 86, 88–91, 103

Pan American Airways (PAA; Pan Am), 3–4, 31, 42, 86–87, 89–91, 98, 99, 101, 139, 142

Pan American Good Will Flight, 4, 55–56

Pan American–Grace Airways (Panagra), 3–4, 42, 97–98, 110, 142

Parrish (Fitch), Eva, 131

Parker, Laigh Calhoun, *79*, 122–24, 133

Patrick, Mason (Major Gen.), 20, 33

Percy family, 3, 7–9, 37, 112

Percy, LeRoy, 7–10, 13, 57

Percy, William (Will) Alexander, 57

Peruvian Airways Corporation, 4, 98, 99, 103, 110, 119

Piver, William C., 11, 140

Poindexter, Miles, 55, 90–91

Poole, Robert, *81, 82*

Pope, J. B., 53, 59, 90

Post, George Birkbeck, 21–25, 27–30, 33, 48, *69*, 139, 141

Potts, Earl, 33, *77*

Preston (Woolman), Barbara, 47, 89

Rickenbacker, Eddie, 135

Roosevelt, Franklin, 5, 121–22, 138

Roosevelt, Theodore, 8, 12, 117

Schwaemmle, Fritz, 128

Selman, Augustus James, 59

Selman Field (Monroe, LA), 36, 59, *77, 78*, 112–13, 116, 127, 135, 139

Shealy, George, 124, 128

Smith, Douglas Y., 111–12, 119, 139

Smoot Field (Monroe, LA), 36–37, 57–58, 112

Southern culture, effect of boll weevil, 2, 6–15, 16

Southern Field Crop Insect Investigations Laboratory, 3, 10. *See also* Delta Laboratory

Standard Oil Company, 112, 134

Stevens (Harris), Alta Mae, 29

Stevens, Eugene, 33, 55, 85, 115, 120

Stinson airplanes, *79*, 123, 127–28

Terzia, Theodore F., 37, 59

Thrush aircraft, 1–2

Tobin, Dan E., 33, 53–54, 61, *70*, 83, 90, 96–98

Topshe, Norman, 129

Travel Air aircraft, 1, *78*, 100, 112–116, 123

Trippe, Juan Terry, 4, 86–98, 95–96, 118, 139

Truesdell, Julius A., 18, 24, 140

U.S. Army, 18–22, 26, 28–29, 32–33, 43, 55–57, 62, 86, 113, 121, 135; Army Air Forces, 86, 113; Army Air Service, 17, 19–21, 29, 33

van der Linden, Robert F., 83, 117, 122

Vicksburg Bridge, 115–16

INDEX